HOUSE HOLD

House Hold

A Memoir of Place

Ann Peters

The University of Wisconsin Press

The University of Wisconsin Press
1930 Monroe Street, 3rd Floor
Madison, Wisconsin 53711-2059
uwpress.wisc.edu

3 Henrietta Street
London WC2E 8LU, England
eurospanbookstore.com

Copyright © 2014
The Board of Regents of the University of Wisconsin System
All rights reserved. No part of this publication may be reproduced, stored in a retrieval system, or transmitted, in any format or by any means, digital, electronic, mechanical, photocopying, recording, or otherwise, or conveyed via the Internet or a website without written permission of the University of Wisconsin Press, except in the case of brief quotations embedded in critical articles and reviews.

Printed in the United States of America

Library of Congress Cataloging-in-Publication Data

Peters, Ann (Professor of English), author.
House hold: a memoir of place / Ann Peters.
    pages   cm
Includes bibliographical references and index.
ISBN 978-0-299-29620-9 (cloth: alk. paper)
ISBN 978-0-299-29623-0 (e-book)
  1. Peters, Ann (Professor of English)
  2. Fond du Lac (Wis.)—Biography.
  3. New York (N.Y.)—Biography. I. Title.
PS3616.E8375Z46   2014
813′.6—dc23
[B]
2013011470

For my mother
Mary Wehner

Contents

List of Illustrations — ix

Part One: The House

1. The House on the Ledge — 3
2. The Architect — 31
3. The Second House — 53
4. The Holy Land — 70
5. Leaving — 98

Part Two: The Apartment

6. Reid Terrace — 113
7. Manhattan — 136
8. Lafayette — 163
9. Brownstone — 179

Part Three: The Return

10. Lake City — 205
11. Ancestors — 219
12. Jefferson — 234

Acknowledgments — 255
Notes — 257
Bibliography — 265
Index — 271

Illustrations

My parents, before they were married	9
My father on the farm	23
My parents, the house on the ledge	46
Robbys restaurant	61
The house bordering woods	73
Lester	116
Kathryn	129
Willa Cather's bedroom	150
Maeve Brennan	166
The Graham Home	183
Lake City	212
Edmund Wilson's house	226
Old brooding coop, Jefferson	237
Ann Hanson	247

The House

1

THE HOUSE ON THE LEDGE

Usually, when I return to the house, it's been lifted, as if by some fabled tornado, to an alien locale. The key will not fit the lock. At the door, dogs rattle their chains, strangers stare before snapping shut the blinds, and in place of our field, there are new buildings casting shadows on streets whose names are indecipherable. Streets end in cul-de-sacs with no escape.

In another dream, the house is on fire and seen from a great distance. Someone nearby must be warned, a man who looks enough like a faded Laurence Olivier for me to marvel afterward at how deeply the film *Rebecca* has lodged in my consciousness. I even see the Hitchcock ending—a red glow at the tree line, a body outlined in flames—but instead of moors, I move through Wisconsin farm country; instead of turrets burning, there is a low-lying house made of wood set back in a stand of hickory and ash.

Lately, though, when I dream about the house, I find the rooms just as I left them. My hand knows where it will land on a light switch or the knob of a door. I step over pets, long dead, now sighing in their sleep. When I wake up, I turn to my husband and report, "Last night I dreamt I went to Manderley again." He looks at me the way people look when obliged to listen to someone else's dreams, and I turn away, squinting to make out the figure at the edge of sleep, a white blur who, like the moon swift behind clouds, like Alfred Hitchcock in a crowd, shows himself and then disappears.

Most of the time the shadowy person in these dreams is my father. Always, the house is the one he designed and built in 1971 on a stretch of farm country twenty miles north of the town of Fond du Lac in eastern Wisconsin.

The house is still there, but if you pass it driving north on Highway 151 from Madison on your way to Green Bay, you might miss it. During the day, except for a glint of reflected light, it vanishes behind trees, and at night, it seems to offer only form, no walls, just a golden rectangle like a tent you come upon unexpectedly in the dark.

The house has become what my father intended: unassertive, another shade of the landscape, no more remarkable than a field of corn, no more jarring than the colors on the old silo down the road, a faint and barely readable advertisement for Chief Oshkosh beer. In the minds of those neighbors who once marveled or flinched at the sight of a fresh gap in the woods, I doubt it now registers any interest. There are only five people left who might dream about it: my mother, who never talks about it; my brother and sister and I, who do; and Gracie, the present owner, a concert promoter from Chicago. She bought the house from my parents in 1988 but, since her husband's death, comes only a few weekends a year to air the bedding and dispose of mice in the basement traps.

Built against a ridge of tree-covered limestone, fronted by a wall of glass, the house looks out on descending expanses—a hill sloping down, a field, a highway, a farm, another field, and then the lake. Inside, the proportions worked to make the space feel vast, but when I see it now, I am surprised by its modesty. We had multilevels and lots of glass, but no flagged mudroom or staircase with any kind of sweep. The house wasn't really seventies in ethos either, or at least not what I think of when I'm driving Catskills back roads—no oddly cut windows in the shape of diamonds or portholes, no wind chimes made of colored glass. They would have hated that. My dad designed an A-frame for the grade school principal in the woods near us, but that was as far as he went. And there were too many odd corners for it to fit neatly, cleanly, inside the modernist box. My father liked to say it was a glorified enlarged split-level with most of the walls taken out.

Out of accidents, last-minute epiphanies, came whimsical additions. Made of unfinished wood, remnants from his construction company, the walls were so rough to the touch that skidding around a corner, you'd find splinters in your fingernails. Above a closet, he'd discover wasted space; why not take down a wall and build a loft? They ran out of wood after building the beams and the ceilings, so had to make do with a combination of tile and carpeting for the floors, shades of brown that looked like sand and dirt.

Behind the house was rock, a geological formation called the Niagara Escarpment. We locals called it the ledge. It begins at Niagara Falls, and I used to believe that if I put my ear to rock, I could hear far off the din of falling water, a honeymooner's cry. From Niagara, the ledge curves up through Ontario and forms the northern cliffs of Lake Michigan, disappears beneath water, rises as the thumb of Wisconsin in Door County, and then, where we are, follows the eastern shores of Lake Winnebago. It ends at the Illinois border, a barely discernible bump.

In parts of Canada, the ledge is mountain-sized. Behind our house it isn't very high, maybe one hundred feet, but it loomed in the local mythology. Native Americans used it as a lookout, and in the caves behind our house my brother found arrowheads and once the skull of what we thought was an antelope but must have belonged to a dairy cow who had strayed and fallen off the cliff. Down the road, roped off by a chain-link fence, were burial mounds in the shape of bear, raised tufts that made me think of inverted snow angels and made me want to lie down. My father, attuned to legends—and hungry for a view—chose to build the house backed so close that it would seem nothing more than an outcropping. At the ledge's top, almost an extension of the house, chunks of moss-covered rock, the size of a bed or a car or sometimes a room, formed protruding platforms with caves underneath where you could hide. My parents' bedroom was at the front of the house, with a balcony that looked out through two red oaks to the field, but the children's rooms were in the rear, against the ledge—mine in the farthest corner, so that it seemed half-buried. Even though our rooms were on the second floor, they were dark and smelled like a cave—packed dirt, cold stone. The only natural light was filtered through trees. In summer, moths the size of a child's palm rubbed ecstatically against the screens. The trees tapped at the glass, took root beneath the bed.

The three bedrooms were in a line—mine, then my sister's, then my brother's—small cells, each exactly alike: one single bed, a built-in bookshelf above it, a built-in desk against the one window, a folding chair, a closet with sliding wooden doors. The rooms were designed this way—prim, monastic, and impossible to rearrange—because in college my dad had been inspired by the simplicity of dormitory rooms. They made him think. They made him want to work. At night, I lay there imagining my room from above, one section of a floor plan: the angled line for a door and an X across the closet, the neat rectangle for a bed, and on it, a little square for the pillow. I drew in the circle for my head.

From the children's bedrooms at the back of the house, we started our day in enforced austerity—the first thing we saw when we woke up was that solid little desk, a work ethic that wouldn't budge—but from there, the house loosened up. I'd leave my room and walk down a narrow hallway open to the ceiling two stories above. There were few walls dividing the two main levels of the house, just slats of wood, ideal for dangling legs. The railings couldn't have been regulation safety height, at least not by the standards of today, and were worthless when it came to protecting children from a fall. Once, a little girl, the daughter of one of my dad's clients, crawled under a railing and fell, hit the stairs two and a half stories below, slicing off the tip of her nose.

My siblings and I knew the house too intimately to ever take a false step. We climbed the beams, leapt from the bridges, curled in the lofts above our parents' heads, cats reclining in the sun. The rafters opened up in sound. The owners after us were musicians and told us the space had near perfect acoustics; they set up practice spaces in the three back bedrooms—mine was for the sax—and from the stereo in the living room blew Stan Getz from room to room.

In the walk from the bedrooms out to the rest of the house, we moved out of darkness to light, solitude to communion, constriction to expanse. Once you reached the end of the hallway from the bedrooms, you stood on a kind of promontory, an extended deck, an L that included the kitchen at the back, and looked down over the main living room, which was open thirty feet to the ceiling. The skylights were designed to catch the morning sun over the top of the ledge. Six stairs down and you were in that light, looking down again through the glass of the living room windows to woods, lawn, field, farm, and lake. There were no curtains.

Before 1971 we lived in town in a series of houses also built by my father, ranch homes and pseudocolonials with wood paneling and breakfast nooks. I remember only one of them: white with black shutters facing a strip of sidewalk that ended at the edge of a weedy field. It was the sixties, but my parents seemed for the first years of their marriage a fifties couple who, like other young-marrieds in their neighborhood, lived rich in the shiny gadgets of midcentury: the electric carving knife, the camera recording small-town sophistication in grainy Super 8. If you watch the only surviving reel from those days, you can see my parents hosting the company office party. My father, in coat and tie, slaps his employees' backs, mans the cocktail shaker; my mother, gloved to the elbows, presides, like Jackie Kennedy at a White House ball.

With the purchase of twenty-three acres north of town and the building of our house, everything changed. My parents traded in one American fantasy for another. The sleekness of the Frigidaire given up for unfinished wood and homegrown tomatoes perched on the sill. If in the fifties the romance of American retreat was mostly realized in the watered-down pastoralism of suburbia, for my parents in the early seventies it took another guise: "real country," what our neighbors called "acreage," with neighbors few and far between. In photos we are almost unrecognizable: my mother, sporting John Lennon glasses, my father, muttonchop sideburns. We kids were stripped of our dresses and sport jackets and bedecked in Wrangler and macramé. My mother set up a loom. She read Virginia Woolf and Margaret Mead and collected a new circle of friends, one who blew glass, another who taught her how to play the guitar on a sheepskin rug next to the fire.

My father, who admired Buckminster Fuller, built a geodesic dome on the slope in front of the house. We used it as a jungle gym. They bought cross-country skis, with different colored wax applied according to the temperature, and took a subscription to *Whole Earth Catalog* so they could study the principles of organic gardening. At the edge of the woods, they planted apple trees and a massive vegetable garden with rows of strawberries, each measured by my father, one foot in front of the other and a hand holding onto a string. In the mornings, we were woken to the sound of the Peterson bird recordings, the trills and squawks of North America heard so clearly birds seemed to have nested in our ears. After each call, a man with a British accent enunciated: Indigo Bunting, Rose-breasted Grosbeak, Great Horned Owl.

Wanting us to quiet the mind, my father's mind especially, my mother hired a woman to come out and teach us all transcendental meditation. Because I was too young to sit still, I meditated while making my bed. I was not supposed to tell anyone my secret mantra, but I did, and it turned out to be the same as everyone else's in the family: "ing." Intended to wipe the mind clean of associations, the mantra was for me an unfortunate choice, since acquiring it coincided with a phase of my education that involved the learning of verb forms—gerunds and participles leaping and chattering as I folded down the sheets.

It would be easy to attribute my parents' transformation to mere faddishness, but the relief was too palpable for me not to believe in the sincerity of the escape. Building the house and moving to the country was more than a whim; it was a form of renunciation. No more drinks in the backyard, feet cooling in the kids' plastic swimming pool. No more gossip in the breakfast

My parents, just before they were married, in the backyard of my mother's house in town. (author's collection)

nook. For my mother, the move was also, I think, a way for her to participate late in some version of a counterculture. However tame and respectable this countering might have appeared to others, it was real enough to her. Married and settled when others her age were howling their dissent, she had missed out. Embracing the back-to-the-land fantasy, she found a way to make up for the loss.

By turning their backs on the small town, my parents also reversed the American trajectory of progress admired by their parents' generation: flee the farm, move to town. This was the story of my father's early years, the first fourteen of which were spent on one mile-long stretch of road. The road (and fields adjoining it) delimited his existence: on one end, the farm of his maternal grandparents; on the other end, the farm belonging to his paternal ones; and in the middle, his own place, a few paces from the one-room school where until the eighth grade his teacher tried unsuccessfully to beat left-handedness and dreaminess out of him with a stick. There was no electricity, only cows to milk on bitter mornings, rocks to pick in the field. In the only photograph of my father at play (and almost the only photograph taken of him as a child), he is alone, a fishing pole in hand, dirty overalls rolled to the knee. Behind him a flat treeless field and beyond that a square farmhouse with no front porch to propose rest or soften the severity of windows and door. The photo is in black and white but in color the scene would have looked just as gray.

My father didn't talk about any of this much, except for a story he repeated about my grandmother hysterical over a dime spent by her mild-mannered husband on a beer, an event so shriekingly traumatic that in that moment my father vowed, like Scarlett O'Hara in the turnip field, that he'd never go hungry again. He escaped in 1946 on a milk truck to the high school and until 1971 it didn't seem he ever looked back.

In the nineteenth century the romantic ideal of unspoiled American wilderness—and the conservation movement inspired by it—mostly originated in the cities and towns, in the private libraries of a Wordsworth-reading upper class. The back-to-the-land impulse in the 1970s was not much different: it came from college campuses, from a generation disenchanted by city and suburb. My parents read Scott and Helen Nearing's *The Good Life*, a memoir and manual on back-to-the-land simplicity. Inside I remember a photograph of a gaunt man in flannel tapping a maple tree, a woman looking up adoringly—at the tree or the man, I wasn't sure. In another, a group of shaggy college students sit with notebooks on their laps, cross-legged at the feet of their gnarled prophets who, from a stone wall they'd built by hand, preached routine and a restorative diet of apples and Karl Marx.

In those days, my parents had a friend, a young college student who'd come over for dinner and talk about farming in the reverential tones of the born-again. My mother remembers Howie arriving in a sweat to tell us about the delights of his first day picking rocks—an account of Tolstoyan camaraderie and the midday sun affirming and hot on his neck. She also remembers my father's annoyance. I can picture his response—a rustling followed by a violent shake of the newspaper; or, more likely, instant head-bobbing sleep. My dad had picked rocks every day of every spring of his childhood. He didn't see the rapture in it.

My mother responded to country life differently. She had grown up in town, and town gave her advantages. Social skills, which my father would have to copy and practice like dance steps, or the verb forms of a foreign tongue came to her naturally. A more ebullient personality gave her words. Though she'd moved only twenty miles or so from where she'd grown up, country life was a lark; her response to it took the form of a constant and animated tribute. From the car she'd point out the shape of a hill, dogwood in a ditch. From the kitchen window, we'd hear her call—Come, quick! Kids! Come! Look. Come. Quick!—and we would come quick, our eyes following where she directed them, past a tree to where a woodpecker arched for a strike. We liked this about my mother—the stream of proclamations, the gift for seeing through the forest to the tree, liked it even when her looking interrupted our own.

My dad liked it too, but because he saw nature through the filter of his own history, he didn't say much, just lowered his newspaper to grunt affirmation, or followed her—and where she looked—with his eyes. His parents had not modeled exaltation, and even if they had, I doubt he would have been inclined to put words to his feelings on a walk around the property. We knew he felt the beauty of the ledge—he had designed a house to honor it—but he wouldn't rhapsodize over it. The taciturn farmer was still too much in his blood, and farmers, faced with a hill to plow every day, will be less inclined to praise the allure of its curves.

Still, even if he couldn't fully yield to the romance of rural life celebrated by my mother and her friends, he did harbor his own fantasies about what he was doing moving to the country. Homesickness, the longing for a familiar landscape, was part of it, and homesickness, of course, has as much to do with what one wanted and didn't get as it does with the facts of the past. I've always thought that by purchasing farmland and building a house on it, he imagined he could revise his childhood: line the shelves with books that converted memories bereft of beauty into poetry; transform the gloomy interiors of his own history into a house flooded with light. Our house, stained the same color as the trees in the woods, dug to conform to the limestone rock, was meant to be art in harmony with a remembered landscape. Modern, with shelves and shelves to hold the books missing from the gray farmhouse where he was born, it was my father's most beautiful house, unmatched by anything he did before or after.

There are people who define their lives by the places where they live. I am—and there's no mistaking it—one of them. We fixate on rooms and their arrangements; on the book report, we cannot see the difference between setting and plot, between the landscape and the characters in it; we hold houses close. I had a friend once who couldn't walk past Grace Church in Greenwich Village without seeing the word *eglise* next to a picture in her high school French textbook. For me, the house my dad built is the line drawing beside the word *house* in the dictionary. However happy I've been in the places I've lived since leaving Wisconsin at eighteen, I've also been a little ill at ease, as if the last twenty-five years have been one long slumber party, and I, stiff on the rollaway, must keep one eye open for morning—listen for a rescuing honk in the driveway from the car that will take me home. On the evening of 9/11, when others were immobilized at the television or frantically dialing their mobile phones, my sister and I comforted ourselves by recounting every detail we could remember of the house. We sat on my couch in Brooklyn, beer bottles sweating in our grip, and walked through each room, looked out every window, until finally, in our minds, we separately and silently closed our bedroom doors.

My sister and I used to say that the house raised us more than our parents did. This is untrue and probably unfair. What we partly meant is that the house offered us what my parents could not. They had too much energy, too much charm, and we were immobilized in our veneration. They moved across the stage; we clapped. The house, we said, gave us what we missed in them. A consistent presence, a lap. You moved; it did not. In saying this, of course, we begrudged them their due, since what we also meant is that from the design, as much or more than from their words (my mom's rapid fire, my father's more a clearing of the throat), we succumbed to the shape of their personalities. On their behalf, the house admonished and praised. It told us what to wait for and what to lament.

The first training was in aesthetics. From early on I believed, although I was not told, that our house was a primer; alerted to its good taste I could understand what good taste was not. At the actual slumber parties of my childhood, I did not like the smell of the pillows or the taste of the eggs or the shells of soap coyly arranged on the bathroom vanity. I learned to compare—and to pass judgment. When my parents were first drawing up the floor plans, they had to draw me aside, then five years old, to explain that they were sorry to disappoint me but in my new room there would be no lime green carpeting, no canopy over a bed fitted with Snow White sheets. Occupancy brought the lesson home; after a year or two, I could visit my friend Tess's bedroom, observe her Barbies entangled in the tall grasses of seventies shag, and feel nothing, hardly a twinge.

We moved to that house when I was five. Just as I was coming into consciousness, my parents, like many of their generation, were coming to an awareness of the natural world and the need to conserve it. I picked up on this early, although I had the haziest notion of what it all meant. I knew to wince at yard art and to disdain artificially clipped hedges and nonnative trees. I was righteous over hillsides strewn with disemboweled cars and shook my head when sighting snowmobile tracks in the woods. But because I was young, I couldn't help translating what I heard into prim dichotomies. Nature was clean, man messy. Or, reversely, nature was gracefully unkempt, man too intent on tidying up. When I heard the Hamm's beer commercial on television ("From the land of sky blue waters, waters"), I hummed along, but I remember uneasiness when a friend of mine turned on the Hamm's beer sign that hung in her basement. Illuminated, it revealed a river panorama with moving waterfall and a curl of campfire smoke pulsing red and blue; it also cast a cold light on the glass case just above, where my friend's dad stored his deer-killing guns. I was surprised to discover that for many people guns and campfires go together; to me, a gun was something from one of those coloring book puzzles, the shiny object you circled next to the pictures of trees and flowers to show it didn't belong.

From the layout of rooms, I learned how the self can change size; how at night, in the bedroom, I grew to fit space, pulsing and ungainly, like Alice in the book on the shelf behind my head, Alice squeezed inside a rabbit hole. Later, getting a glass of water and making my way out into the night, I shrank again—an insect against the window screen, a star on the other side of the glass. From the view and the progress to it—down and out, from small room to larger ones, from woods to lawn, field to lake—I internalized a conviction that would fail me later in life, a belief in a narrative of daily drama. Every day, a simple walk—from sleep to breakfast cereal, from the black morning at the front door to the early sun reflected in the school bus windows—could, in the parlance of the time, blow your mind. We lived as if seated in a makeshift camp chair, perched—back against rock, feet pointed to water. From the view, my sister, brother, and I absorbed the lesson of the horizontal line; we looked out every day on a Rothko painting, the colors changing with the seasons while the lines stayed the same. You felt you could be remade, like reading Genesis before getting bored by the genealogies, or like hearing Karen Carpenter singing, "I'm on top of the world, looking down on creation," which was for a long time the only song I knew by heart.

But along with all these quasi-mystical transformative offerings, there were the contradictions particular to my parents and particular to the time. The house was, on the one hand, a product of postwar optimism—a split-level, however glorified, founded on split-level values. With it my parents fulfilled a dream of improving their lot, renouncing the memory—their own, their parents—of Depression-era bleakness. From it I learned some of the important lessons of the middle class: about privacy (what it means to be hidden and to have enough room) and about privilege (what it means to look down).

The house was a dock from which to embark, a cave tendering withdrawal. At the time my father and mother believed, without question, in the power of self-transformation, the value of the forward march, and we felt this optimism—even, I think, registered it in the visual cues. Gazing west, out on field, farm, lake, we saw an American landscape charged with American myth. Squint and you saw wheel ruts in prairie grass. Underlying all that boom-time certitude, though, were currents of nostalgia you couldn't ignore. As much as it asked us to start fresh, it told us to hold fast to the memory of a pristine history, an American pastoral without the ruts. Go back, it said. To the earth. To a simpler time. Believe in progress while mourning what it will destroy.

It's hard to know if I could help my own inclinations—all those dreams of ruins—having been raised in a place and a time where a sense of loss, like the bookshelves or kitchen cabinets, came already built in. The house set me up. Wistfulness was in the air. You could listen to it from the speakers screwed to the beams of the living room ceiling. When we were little, my parents would leave, and we'd lift from the turntable the Modern Jazz Quartet (my mother) or Rachmaninoff (my father) and replace them with records of theirs that made sense, played so often that we could predict the skips: Cat Stevens foreseeing apocalypse in the sprawl of modern America ("where do the children play?"); Joni Mitchell telling us how they paved paradise to put up a parking lot; and our favorite, Simon and Garfunkel harmonizing over the memory of that man my father loved: "So long, Frank Lloyd Wright." We sang along: "Architects may come and architects may go and never change your point of view."

We could read these divided impulses—forward and back—on the spines of the books lining the living room shelf. Next to *The Collected Poetry of Robert Frost*, brown cover, was *Future Shock*, the 1970 bestseller by Alvin Toffler, in psychedelic pink. On one of my parents' bedside tables sat a fat biography of Ray Kroc, the founder of McDonald's, and on the other, the Nearings' *The Good Life*. In the bathroom where my mother thought we were likely to be free of interruption lived permanently a copy of Henry David Thoreau's *Walden* beneath Norman Vincent Peale's *The Power of Positive Thinking* and a bowl of potpourri.

In the placement of our house and in the arrangement of the rock gardens at the edge of the woods, I recognized my father's love of the circle and of the precipice. He liked to hold council. He liked a gathering place and the girdling embrace of other people: a conference table, a fire ring, a clearing in the woods. But he was also drawn to the lone figure on the cliff, the solitary thinker staring out over water or a field of grass.

Nearly every summer we traveled on a pilgrimage, north to Ellison Bay in Door County where we'd spend a day at Jens Jensen's Clearing. Jensen was a Danish landscape designer who, like his contemporary Frederick Law Olmsted, had rejected the principles of the European formal garden. He believed in "planting in the vernacular," featuring native plants and stone for his designs. While working in Chicago for the West Park Commission, Jensen had designed the first American Garden in 1888, an effort—at least so the story goes—that came about after a garden of exotic flowers died and he went out into the surrounding woods and prairies to collect and transplant native wildflowers. Jensen would work with most of the Prairie School architects, including Frank

Lloyd Wright, and after years designing public gardens for the City of Chicago and private ones for millionaires like Edsel Ford in Detroit, he settled at the end of his life in northern Wisconsin on 129 acres in Ellison Bay. There he built the Clearing, a retreat and school for conservationists and landscape designers, an arrangement of stone cottages, sunken wildflower gardens, and clearings in the woods ringed by stones.

Those vacations to the Clearing were, for me, a journey into a Hans Christian Andersen fairy tale. The crossing of a border. In just a couple of hours' drive, we left behind a region inhabited mainly by German Catholics to Door County on the peninsula, an area that at least then in the seventies still seemed a reproduction of Scandinavia. On our way, we always stopped at the same tourist pull-off, a Swedish restaurant that featured a sod-covered roof where goats grazed and shook their bells. In the shop next to the restaurant, I thought I could smell and touch the North: Norwegian wood, wool mittens knitted in the pattern of a snowflake, cabinets with rosemaling designs painted on secret drawers that opened with a key.

This stop was a children's fantasy of the North, an illustration in a picture book and always the prelude to something more serious, what for my parents was the real enchantment. When we arrived at the Clearing, approached like so many Jensen properties through a curved road in the woods, my parents were giddy. They loved everything about the place, the paths and the blue of Lake Michigan glimpsed through white birches, the stone schoolhouse, and cabins with climbing vines, a haze of flowering dogwood and hollyhocks tall at the door.

At the Clearing, there were two places my parents loved best. One was a circle of stones where students could gather called the Council Ring. Sometimes we stayed for an hour, my father moving from stone to stone, trying out each view, sitting, standing, pacing. As he moved, we moved. It was a game of musical chairs, a rotating communal dance. From reading Jensen, my father borrowed an adage—"a clearing in the woods and a clearing of the mind." When I think of it now, our house was built to expand outward onto a long view but it was also designed to enclose. The front lawn was a nestling, a circle of trees and through it a vista.

The Clearing also inspired my parents to construct rock gardens next to the house to mimic the limestone slabs of the ledge and the wildflower gardens (violets, bloodroot, trillium) nearby in the woods. At the end of a path below the ledge, they had cut away brush and saplings to reveal another circle of light, a glade in front of two box elders that had grown together into the shape of a wishbone. We called it the Wishing Tree. In front, my brother and I made a stone ring, and sometimes we camped there in a tent, always waking in the middle of the night to walk the path back to the house and sleep in our own beds.

The other destination at the Clearing was a little one-room cabin called the Cliff House, a retreat for students and sometimes for Jensen himself. The cabin hung precariously close to the falling away of the bluff, and because the door and windows faced the cliff side, you had to bravely sidle around it to look inside. The cabin was locked but once my father found a way in—I don't remember how. From the outside, my mother, brother, sister, and I looked in the window: a simple room, a little table and a Hudson Bay blanket tucked tight to a single bed. Looking in now, from the distance of memory, I see my father's love of a little room (those inspiring dorm rooms) and of the rock formations jutting from the top of the ledge. I remember envy—I wanted to be inside there myself—and I remember thinking he looked as if he wouldn't mind if we left him there, a man alone and balanced on the edge of a cliff.

My mother always liked to tell people the house on the ledge was a California house. She would say this proudly and a little apologetically when taking people on a walk through the house. The tour was the obligatory start to any social occasion, and it wasn't until years later that I understood that not all mothers did this. I thought the guided tour a form of good manners, a universal custom approved by Emily Post. Only after moving into my first apartment with more than one room did I discover my error in the uncomprehending looks of my party guests as I led them into the bedroom to uncork the wine.

At the time, I thought all the talk about California had something to do with complaints about heating bills, Wisconsin winters, but later, a friend visited and said my father must have been influenced by the architects of Sea Ranch, a planned community in Sonoma County. I went to the library to look at Sea Ranch houses in a book and saw what my friend was getting at. Conceived in the sixties by the landscape architect Lawrence Halprin and a handful of architects—Charles Moore, Joseph Esherick, and Donlyn Lyndon—the five-thousand-acre development along the Pacific coast was meant to preserve the natural beauty of the landscape: houses were timber-framed with unpainted siding; exteriors were simple, meant to weather in the wind and sun. Most came with multilevel decks. The insides had crossing beams and interior bridges. From all sides slid shafts of dusty light.

I found it hard to look at those photographs for long—one kind of grief is just feeling sorry for what the dead miss out on. Some of the Sea Ranch properties are rented as vacation homes, and I thought of how on my father's seventieth birthday not long before he died we spent a week at a place only a few miles down the coast. It wasn't a happy vacation: the rental came with all the features he'd tried to avoid when building his own home, rooms airless and cramped, the windows draped in noise-proof velvet— you couldn't hear the surf—and his grown children sullen like teenagers. All the time, Sea Ranch, with its windswept boards and lofts with ladders, was there, just down the road.

But if the Northern California aesthetic of the sixties and seventies was an inspiration, it must have happened through cultural osmosis; I don't remember any mention of Moore or Esherick or Sea Ranch. Had my dad been forced to name his inspiration he would have chosen Frank Lloyd Wright. My father liked to take us to Taliesen, Wright's home in southwestern Wisconsin, which was just a few hours' drive from our house. Taliesen was mecca. I can still smell the rooms—ancient wood smoke, lemon-scented wood—and can still see the spots of mildew on the Japanese screens. Outside, the bridge extended like a long pier into a lake of prairie grass—if you weren't careful you might forget and take a dive. We'd stay all day, then wait in an empty parking lot as the sun went down while inside my father paced, upturning rope barricades and alarming the tour guides as he'd make his way to the doors marked Private, Keep Out. I can see him there, exhaling air through his teeth—a manic tic, something he did when charged, excited, and when about to blow his top. And I can see him pacing out the dimensions of a wall, going slow but wanting to run, swinging one foot to align in front of the other, like a man at the side of the road trying to convince the police he is sober when he's not.

Our front door, the only glimpse of color, was painted Wright's favorite Cherokee red; the house fit snugly against the rock ledge at the back, harmonizing with the landscape of eastern Wisconsin the way Taliesen merged with Wisconsin's western hills; and there was that essential piece in any good Prairie School house, an enormous hearth to draw the eye and, we were told, bring the family together. Even as a child, I knew that Wright's buildings aged into a need for constant repair. So did my father's. Always more enthralled by the process than the enduring fact, he could be indifferent to tight-as-a-drum standards of architecture. He let things go. The skylights, angled to catch the slide of the moon, leaked and were streaked with condensation. The roof over our bedrooms couldn't withstand the ice, and every winter beads of water gathered at the ceiling, ran down the walls. My room took the greatest hit, and I was perpetually rescuing books from the onslaught. Even now, I can open a box, turn the decomposing pages of a book, *Little House on the Prairie* or Judy Blume's *Are You There God? It's Me, Margaret*, and catch a whiff of mildew and childhood rage.

What Wright did with heights—the levels of the ceiling changing to pull you in, draw you out—my dad accomplished with changing width: a narrow hallway opening up to three stories of uninterrupted space. In a Frank Lloyd Wright house, you feel the architect's control: he often designed down to the place settings on the table and famously commanded his clients not to rearrange the furniture. In our house, you sensed instead that the space led the architect, that he gave in to it, revising as he went along.

After my father died, my sister and brother and I divided his collection of books. We each took home boxes, and I inherited a copy of Frank Lloyd Wright's autobiography. Shaped like a box, like a block of wood wrapped in heavy white paper, it was a gift too beautiful to open, meant for the coffee table and impossible to read in bed. But my dad had marked it up as he marked most books—the marginal scrawl illegible, the underlines a faint quavering that trails off, a sign of him drifting into sleep. I hadn't read Wright's autobiography before, and at first I was disappointed, mostly by the prose, which is overwrought and self-important, thick with clichés. Brendan Gill, in his biography, calls the autobiography an "extended apologia—a fabrication that takes the form of a bittersweet romance, with Frank Lloyd Wright as hero." Casting Wright as a brilliant self-mythologizer—the title of Gill's book is *Many Masks*—Gill is especially hard on Wright's retelling of childhood and plays fact-checker here more than anywhere else. Was Wright's father really such an ogre, his mother such a saint? Did the etchings of cathedrals that hung over Frank's cradle and the blocks he played with as a child really exist, or were they lies drawn in retrospect by mother and son for the creation of an architectural destiny?

To me the facts (or lack of them) don't matter. The contradictions, the gift for self-mythology, are revealing, even familiar, especially when applied to Wright's account of his boyhood in Spring Green. Most of this section, "Family," celebrates hard work, simple food, a mother's devotion, and the influence of his maternal uncles who worked the family farm. The word *stalwart* shows up more times than I cared to count. Here, Wright recounts a litany of misery: sore arms, boiled dinners, and early morning stumblings to the outhouse in the dark. Three times he tried to run away from the valley, but in the end, he learns his lesson: pain is recast as vital education. From hoeing and plowing, from the "honest Bucksaw" and "persuasive hammer," he learned the family gospel of hard work.

Wright's retelling of his boyhood on the farm proffers the image of the architect as a man of the earth, "muscles hard," who later will climb the scaffolds of his great buildings the way as a boy he climbed Wisconsin rock. But Wright also hints at a deficiency in the philosophy of his Spring Green relatives. The Lloyd-Jones family, his mother's relatives, had given short shrift to the call of beauty. For pages, Wright praises the landscape—"white birches gleaming," "milkweed blossoming"—a landscape his pioneer grandfather hardly noticed, so enamored was he with the Bible and the stumps he needed to clear from the fields.

Wisconsin teaches Wright to see. It gives him style, a vocation. Wright's famous signature crest, the flame-red art deco square stamped on all his drawings, came from the emotion of seeing a red lily "afloat" on Wisconsin meadow grass. Even the hills instruct him in how to situate a house. Taliesen, he always said, was built "not on the hill but of the hill," a phrase my father quoted so often to describe our place on the ledge I thought he came up with it himself.

At the gift shop counter at the Guggenheim Museum I see men of a certain generation loading their shopping baskets with Wright memorabilia—the paperweights, the stationery, the silk scarves they'll give their wives for Christmas, ribbons of stained glass to wear around the neck. They remind me of my father, and I stare. At other times, though, they don't remind me of him at all. The truth is he didn't belong to the cult entirely, hardly noting Wright as a personality, ignoring the egomania, the many wives and murderous servants, ignoring even the facts about Wright's carelessness—with money, with his own children—characteristics that, according to a spate of documentaries I've watched recently, too many architects seem to share.

No, if my father considered Wright as a man, it was as a worker, head bent under the desk lamp, or as a fellow Wisconsinite.

My father on the family farm. (author's collection)

Wright mattered because he was an idea: another native son made good. Taliesen stands on family land, the first settled by Wright's Welsh grandfather, the same land Wright knew from having worked it with his uncles as a child. In building Taliesen, Wright sought to merge the farmer and the architect, the old self and the new one. Taliesen would be a work of art and a working farm, with cows and gardens planted to feed the family. In building it and in living there, Wright could return to his agrarian boyhood and the values extolled by his uncles while drawing on the aesthetic principles he found so lacking in them. Like Wright, my father had refashioned his geographical history. Our property was ten miles from the farms of my father's early years. By building a house on familiar ground, he had rewritten his childhood, turning the asceticism of a rural Wisconsin boyhood into a pastoral idyll, a forward-thinking utopia, and a return.

For a few years later in his life, my father became a passionate genealogist. It was something we did together; he liked the digging, I liked the stories unearthed. This wasn't an easy partnership: he conducted his search the old-fashioned way, calling random numbers from phone books and knocking on doors. At the kitchen tables of distant relations in New Hampshire or Maine or Northern Ireland, I drank cold coffee and kept up a strained smile, watching while across the linoleum he and a stranger traced the family tree.

Even then I realized that the curiosity about his ancestry was a kind of orphan fantasy, a way to reconstruct his childhood, to improve it and to find someone back there he could identify with and revere. He found Emerson and Ben Franklin. He found a witch hung in Salem and Anne Boleyn. None of us at the time quite believed in these forebears, but it turns out he was right about all of them except for Boleyn, the link an error in the Church of Latter Day Saints genealogical database, easily overlooked by those aspiring Americans with a too keen desire for a coat of arms.

In my father's case, royal blood wasn't the aim. He didn't seem at all embarrassed by his family and liked to repeat the stories of his more humble ancestors; the three-hundred-pound grandmother eating lard straight from the bucket was his favorite. But there was enough of the American striver in him to long for a bit of shine, culture, glamour, someone to reflect his own longings, someone to explain how he had landed in the lap of Clem and Reinhold Peters on Artesian Road in the early morning of an autumn day in 1932.

Often by the end of those trips, he showed less interest in the people across the table from him and more in the old maps of village plots or the deeds of farms he had me crank from the antiquated copy machines in the local libraries of Pittsfield, Litchfield, Westfield, any of the New England towns on the route of a family's advance west. It was as if he were searching for a spot of earth to claim, some marker of an ancestral home. Once we even found an early settler's farm still in operation, an apple orchard and a stone farmhouse owned by descendants, two Yankees leery behind the cracked door. They showed us a gnarled apple tree planted by distant Puritan kin and told us how over the years other family history buffs had come knocking for the same reason. This seemed to surprise my father, as if somehow he had forgotten all those multiplying tendrils—marriages and births shooting off into infinity—as if he believed that the apple farm would remember him and had waited for him alone.

Everywhere we went on those genealogical drives, he moved oblivious to the march of time, hardly noticing as he measured out the perimeter of a land parcel in Ipswich, Massachusetts, that he was crossing suburban lawns, skirting pool toys and barbecues, that there was nothing from his ancestor Ezekiel and his wife, Remembrance—no house, no pastures, no pewter ladles or feather beds—left to parcel out. In Connecticut we studied a map of the house of another settler, a man who had fought the Pequod Indians in King Philip's War, and found ourselves under a highway ramp, a barbed wire fence on all sides. Visible through the wire, the high towers of insurance offices. I tried to look past the knotted off- and on-ramps, past the garbage blown against the fence, and back to my own imaginings of the place: Over there, the village green, a pack of dirty men leaning on their hoes. Or beyond them, the Indian captive Mary Rowlandson chewing on a bit of bear gristle and kneeling at the fire. Or, farther back, a wigwam at river's edge. Then, just trees and a bird taking flight.

It never worked. The present was deafening, a roar on the exit ramp overhead. The past was gone, and we were orphans at the side of the road.

After a while, my father turned away from distant relatives out east and concentrated on a sentimental origin closer in time and closer to home. Where he turned was not to the farm where he'd grown up but to the "big house," the farm belonging to his maternal grandfather, Charles Keys. As a child he and all his cousins converged there every Sunday for the family dinner. A four-hundred-acre showplace—or that's what people always said—the Keys farm came with red barns, stone silos, and an Arts and Crafts house set on the hill. Charles farmed the land and raised thoroughbred horses. For a few years at the turn of the century, he was sheriff in the county, and the story is he built his house with help from the inmates of the jail. Outside were gardens of foxglove and phlox, and inside a library with french doors. Behind those doors, my father remembered Charles in his Stickley recliner reading up on the newest agricultural advances. The house had three sun porches and over fifty windows. My grandmother complained of the long hours it took to clean them when she was a girl.

My father was proud of this grandfather, and usually he had more to say about the big house than he did about his days at home with his own parents. He saw his grandfather as a visionary—the son of the first farmer to introduce alfalfa to the state, he told us. Here was someone who explained his own yearnings, someone he could identify with and revere. It's hard, though, to know how much to believe. Charles Keys died when my dad was twelve; there wasn't enough time to be disabused of his fantasies. I also have trouble reconciling the image of this forward-thinking enlightened man with the daughter he raised: my grandmother Clem, so entrenched in her views and spartan in her habits, seemed to be still emerging from the depths of the nineteenth century. But if Charles Keys was a myth, he was a useful one, as useful to my dad as those ever-stalwart uncles were to Frank Lloyd Wright. Wright sought a salt-of-the-earth ethos in his portrayal of his mother's family; my father was after something else: the farmer as businessman, the farmer in the Jeffersonian sense. Sitting in his own chair (a battered Eames) and reading from the *Whole Earth Catalog* about the newest techniques for building a compost bin, he could think back to that man who after Sunday dinner retreated behind glass doors, an armchair and a book open at the lap. These memories of his grandfather also gave my father a vision of an ancestral home, one with rows of windows that invited you to look out, look ahead, that were more than just panes of glass calling to be washed.

◇

Our place was not a farm, but my dad sometimes forgot this fact and ran it like one. He could not plant a row of strawberries because he didn't know how; he planted an acre. He could not while away a Saturday morning, since the idea of "weekend" was foreign to him. Never in my memory did he throw a ball to his son; rarely did he get down on the floor with his daughters. What he knew of companionship between parent and child compelled him to rouse us from Saturday sleep and send us to the garden to weed. He applied the work ethic he acquired growing up to all he did later on. At four in the morning, the hour when he'd once risen with the cows, the briefcase snapped open and from it spilled straight edges, airline tickets, old hotel keys, a change of clean underwear, and finally, from under all this, an enormous rubber-banded profit and loss statement. In the dim light, from behind his eyeglasses—usually broken, sometimes taped with masking tape to the bridge of his nose—he peered at the columns of numbers the way a man might squint at a row of corn in desperate need of rain.

Even his language referred back to the rhythms of the farm. Like many businessmen he spoke in a patois of mixed American metaphor. We were team players back from the trenches, three strikes and we were out. When my parents divorced, we were soccer balls being kicked around the combat zone. More instinctual than the sports or war metaphors, though, were the agricultural ones: "a hard row to hoe," "chickens roosting," "higher up the cherry tree, sweeter are the berries." To describe a decision that had to be made fast, he'd talk of having "one leg over a barbed wire fence." The return in the seventies to the country took him, or he believed it did at least, from metaphor back to the source, back to the pure manure-scented earth.

But the truth is that the facts never quite matched the fantasy. He didn't really want to go back—not all the way. In his biography of Frank Lloyd Wright, Brendan Gill writes of how in building Taliesen, the architect was creating myth more than mining the facts of his past. "Wright put on and discarded many masks, but that of the dedicated manual laborer would be sure to rank among the least plausible." Of farming (and he kept this out of his autobiography entirely), Wright once told an apprentice, "it's all pulling tits and shoveling shit." He was, Gill explains, "inspired to sing of pastoral joys because the labor required to create them was being carried out by others"; the apprentices at Taliesen, who came thinking they would learn to be architects, did the field work. Mostly Wright liked to drive the tractor around, or from the sweeping veranda up above watch his apprentices in the field, like peasants in a painting, like those lilies he loved, dots of color on meadow grass.

In my father's case, my mother, my siblings, and I were the apprentices and no good at it. The garden that began in a fury of enthusiasm, Dad zealous behind the rototiller, business loafers coated in mud, would almost always be a jungle of weeds by mid-July. More than once the sight of it made my mother cry. When my dad met people and they asked him what he did, he'd reach out his hand for a shake and use the same hearty refrain: "Architect by education, builder by trade." (Someone once told me Mies van der Rohe said the same thing.) But if "builder" was intended to emphasize the homely unassuming side of his character—a fair enough representation most of the time—it didn't always match his interests or his daily activities. I don't recall him using the persuasive hammer much. After my brother asked for a tree house in the woods, my father spent days designing a space out of *Swiss Family Robinson*. Over his shoulder we peered at fantastic sketches of overhanging decks, bridges, ladders from floor to floor. But he never got around to constructing them. My mother, faced with my brother's disappointment, walked out into the woods to nail two boards to the branch of a tree.

Growing up, we were taught to revere and observe the natural world—to tromp with Thoreau through the woods—but we also knew to regard land as property, to respect the marked boundary.

On a walk in the woods, I hardly registered the flash of an orange No Trespassing sign nailed to the bark of a tree. When I came upon a barbed fence, I might bend back the wires to take passage underneath, but I was never insulted; I never wanted a fence brought down. Thoreau, in his essay "Walking," admonishes the surveyor for attending to the stone wall and not the open meadow, for looking for an "old post hole in the midst of paradise." We were just kids. To us, the remains of a pasture fence were no less remarkable, no less moss encrusted and inviting, than the ice-age glacial ledge rock we played on every day. Thoreau's philosophy didn't always square. My father's avidity for trespass, his indifference to ceremony and the opinions of his neighbors, made him Thoreau's kind of man, but in other ways, he carried all the tools of the trade Thoreau derided: the straight edge and surveyor's string, a stake in the ground. On a walk with my dad, you'd set out following the tracks of some wild animal and find that at the end you'd come upon a perfect spot to sink a septic tank. He walked as much to measure an acre as to roam mythic paradise. I accepted this unblinkingly. As much as I believed in the fantasy of an untouched landscape, I understood the impulse to populate it, knew the exhilaration that comes after a box of Lincoln Logs gets tipped onto a field of vacant floor.

For a few months every year, we saw reminders of this message just looking out our window. In winter Lake Winnebago freezes over and gets mapped by shanty villages navigated by roads with intersections and stop signs. All day, whining snowmobiles and trucks pulling ice shanties, some in the shape of Green Bay Packer helmets, little yellow and green pods whizzing across the ice. The buzz was all for the lake sturgeon, giant prehistoric fish who feed at the murky bottom of the lake. Some live past one hundred, some weigh over two hundred pounds, and to catch one, the fisherman needs a spear. He sits in a shanty without light and stares at a bathtub-sized hole bored in the ice, lava lamp blue, waiting for a glimpse of hump or fin.

I never experienced this myself, only listened at the bar to the tales of mythic battles, or when I was little, sidled up to classmates who brought to "show and tell" sturgeon eggs in a jar (caviar, I discovered later) or a photo handed round of an uncle holding a human-sized lump upright in a slick embrace. For my friends at school, sturgeon season was a drive across white expanse, ending in enclosure and proximity to one's prey, a drama close-up. For my family, though, the drama came from the long view, at a distance from where we lived on the ledge. Our view on the lake's activity was like witnessing the birth of a prairie town. We looked out not just on the rhythm of winter—every kind of blue turning to every kind of white—but on the rhythms of American towns: the ways of boom and bust, the way things can be born and then just vanish. What we saw also matched what I knew about my own father, someone who prized the white emptiness of a sheet of paper and someone who liked to draw on it—squares that became houses, groups of squares that became that thing called a subdivision, and lines that turned to roads.

2

The Architect

I

If you sat behind my father, say on a weekday plane ride across middle America, you'd see the small-town businessman in a button-down shirt, sleeves unrolled to reveal a meaty forearm, a heavy expandable wristwatch ticking the hours. Or, if you went looking for him in the pages of American fiction, you'd think of Babbitt, catch a whiff of Old Spice and the heartiness of a bar at the hotel convention. Or, hearing his life story—the swings of fortune, from riches to disgrace, from near-bankruptcy and back—you might think of the fiction of Dreiser, all those accidents of fate and American tragedies, the reverberations of rise and fall, like Sister Carrie in a rocking chair moving forward and back, forward and back. When he hands you his card, you half expect to see the one from the Monopoly game—the little man with a walking stick and wings on his back getting out of jail for free.

During high school, he worked for a lumberyard and at sixteen took out a car loan and used the money to buy a lumberyard to begin his business, Roger Peters Construction. He built his first house for his high school history teacher. Thirty years later the same teacher taught me at the same school. A thick-necked football coach still sporting the crew cut of his youth, Mr. P beamed when hearing my last name and told me he still lived in the house my dad built. I was impressed and a little put out. My great challenge at the moment was learning the proper formatting of a footnote. I didn't like hearing that at the same age my father was busy with more concrete accomplishments—zoning permits and foundations dug deep in the earth.

In 1950 he earned a full scholarship to architecture school at the University of Michigan. My grandmother Clem, who didn't see the point in education beyond the eighth grade, tried to dissuade him. I like to imagine her running behind him to the train, her gray hair piled as it always was in a coronet of braids on her head, her thick legs moving fast along the tracks. She couldn't catch up. Once he got to Ann Arbor he washed dishes to pay fees and joined a fraternity, a decision that looks to me now like another effort to purchase normalcy, a grab for glamour designed to shake loose the countrified boy he'd left behind. He rarely went to class because he was busy running his company from his dorm room. Some days his roommates were asked to vacate to make space for the local Ann Arbor draftsmen he employed.

After college he returned to Fond du Lac, bought land south of town, and built houses on it, mostly inexpensive ones marketed to the middle class and a few grander ones for doctors or dentists he knew around town. These houses lined curving roads with names evoking rural pleasures: Cherry Lane, Meadowbrook Lane. I remember Meadowbrook because for a year we lived there in one of his spec houses. I don't remember a brook. When I ask my mother about it, she tells me, with a trace of old exasperation, that it was nothing more than a brackish ditch.

He studied the other young up-and-coming men of the town and learned to act like them. I saw the effects of this all my life: He didn't like to drink but could nurse a cocktail long enough to fool you. He read Dale Carnegie's *How to Win Friends and Influence People* and in the car on the way to a party, grilled my mother, running through the names of all the men and their wives.

The year he bought our land and built our house, my dad owned, along with his home-building company, a small fleet of fast-food restaurants, one in Fond du Lac, others across Wisconsin and Minnesota. They were called Robbys restaurants and suggested a certain futuristic sleekness—low, the steel a shiny red, the roof shaped like wings. When the Robbys' jingle got airtime on the radio, we'd fly to the kitchen and sing along: "Robbys, Robbys, treats you like a guest, Robbys, treats you like the best, hamburgers, hot dogs, apple pie, and more!"

In the midseventies, he built one of the first condominium developments in the country in Rochester, Minnesota, and was nearly ruined. He saved the day in the nick of time with a loan from a priest friend who managed the coffers of the local parish. (It was his perception of the Catholic Church's benevolence, I think, more than his marriage to my Catholic mother that inspired him finally to convert.)

In the 1980s, he built and designed a mall at the south end of Main Street. The kids at school told me it was classy, with its pale slats of wood, skylights, and glass doors that slid like Japanese screens. There was a restaurant designed with an atrium over the dining room; a clothing shop, a furniture store, and a salon; and a bookstore owned by my mother and her best friend, an English professor at the community college. Together, my parents designed the store. A bay window with a built-in cushioned seat. A sliding ladder to reach the top shelves. By then, he had given up on homebuilding altogether and converted his Robbys restaurants to Hardee's, a franchised chain.

For years, he talked about writing his life story, but after he died, the closest thing to a retelling of his past we discovered on a slip of yellow legal paper, a list of buildings and developments and companies chronologically ordered. About his early childhood, there were a couple of sentences on money he earned for the family selling strawberries in town. Under the heading "The Sixties," there was one line: "Got married, kids," a skimpy account certainly of my origins, but pardonable since it says less about his regard for us and more about his attitude, a generational attitude even, that a self-made man shouldn't waste his reader's time on what anyone can do—procreate. Instead, he should concentrate on the feats of self-making, the real accomplishment. Ben Franklin claims he wrote his autobiography to his son, but in the autobiography itself, the sons and the daughters hardly make an appearance.

◇

A few weeks after my father died, a package arrived in the mail from an old family friend. Inside I found a manila envelope crammed with the print remains of a life. Newspaper clippings and Robbys newsletters. A snapshot of my father taken at the office, his hand resting on the keys of an adding machine. I had forgotten that machine but it came back—a ribbon of numbers unspooling from him at the desk to me on the floor. In one envelope I found, along with a cartoon sketch of a fast-food employee in a paper hat, an announcement from the *Fond du Lac Reporter* for the annual League of Women Voters house tour. A blurred photograph in the corner of the page showed a young couple in black turtlenecks leaning in against a railing. Behind them, our living room and a Navajo rug pinned to the wall. Below, a caption: Mr. and Mrs. Roger Peters, Rural Route 4.

But the document I found most fascinating came from a Rochester, Minnesota, newspaper, a front-page story about Roger Peters's remarkable rescue of Rochester Towers, his condo development: "A real estate miracle," one investor commented. "Nobody thought he'd pull it off." Finally, here was clarification of a murky stretch of my childhood. All I remember from this time is the echo of certain words repeated at the dinner table—"bleeding ulcer," "Mayo Clinic," "bankrupt"—and my mother's despair, conveyed, as it often was then, by a racket of pans and silverware at the sink. The year of Rochester Towers—1974—was the same year he'd forgotten to tell my mother he'd taken out a mortgage on the house, faithfully paid off by her just months before. The year 1974 was also the date I later saw printed next to her signature on the flyleaf of Virginia Woolf's *A Room of One's Own*. I inherited her copy in my twenties, and when I opened it for the first time I saw below the date a faint penciled scrawl: *He'll never change. He never will. There's nothing I can do about it.*

The day after I opened that package a friend of mine came over to dinner. He saw the clippings lying on the coffee table, flipped through the pages, and then read a couple of paragraphs out loud. I caught the tone: scoffing, a little bored. A successful New York journalist, he seemed amused both by the quaint local-paper prose and by the whole Horatio Alger tale (from farm to fast food). "Amazing, really. That those clichés are all there." He tossed the papers back on the table and changed the subject.

It was not just the wrong note to take days after a death; it was the wrong read of the man. My friend saw a figure of fiction, a type, and I had hoped he'd see a life.

I was angry that night, but later more forgiving. My friend hadn't yet lost a parent. He hadn't joined that club. He couldn't know how bruised and blank I felt. I forgave him too because I recognized his dismissal for what it was—a habit, a strategy of differentiation that had little to do with me or my past. I knew he had his own American rags-to-riches tale to contend with, a grandfather who'd risen from nothing and a businessman father who on those flights cross-country must have been as easily pigeonholed as my own: another cliché, another surface to scan like a bolded headline at the top of the newspaper page. I understood his need to distinguish his life as a writer in New York from the values he'd been born into. Over money, he'd chosen words. A writer trained to flinch at a cliché and to recoil at a story that could be too hastily skimmed, he wanted his stories (the ones he'd write and the ones he'd live out) to be read slowly, deeply, and from beginning to end.

It may be impossible not to swerve into satire when faced with the story of the American yanking himself up by his bootstraps. Writing the descriptions of my father's rise from farm to fast food, I was surprised by how hard it is to do. It was a writer's struggle as much as a daughter's. Tell it straight and I risked boring my reader. Tell it at a satirical slant and I turned a man I loved into a joke.

There is a beautiful illustration of this problem in the opening chapter of William Dean Howells's *The Rise of Silas Lapham*.

Published in 1885, the novel is a classic account of an American businessman's rise and fall. Silas, the son of poor farmers from the backwoods of Vermont, has made his fortune in the manufacturing of paint. He now lives with his wife, Persis, and two daughters in Boston, where he aims to penetrate the exclusive world of Boston Brahmin society.

To introduce Silas Lapham's story, Howells opens the first chapter with a device that will enable him to tell a predictable story at a satirical slant—and yet avoid transforming his character entirely into a joke. A newspaperman and editor himself, Howells begins the novel with an encounter between journalist and businessman. The ironic Bartley Hubbard is writing a piece on Silas for the "Solid Men of Boston" series in a local paper, a piece that will include all the elements you might find in a tale of capitalist self-making: the impoverished start, the hard-working parents, the devoted wife, a patriotic history (Silas took a bullet in the Civil War), the discovery of a paint mine in the back pasture, and the years of unstinting labor to make a go of it. There's even a lingering over the requisite framed photograph on the businessman's desk: a cluster of frowning Laphams in front of the old Vermont farmhouse "smartened up with a coat of Lapham's own paint."

From the moment he meets the paint king, it's clear the journalist regards this "solid man of Boston" as a joke. To Bartley "risen Americans are all pathetically alike in their narrow circumstances, their suffering, and their aspirations." Silas has barely begun his tale of growing up on his Vermont farm before Bartley interrupts:

> "Worked in the fields summers and went to school winters: regulation thing?" Bartley cut in.
> "Regulation thing," said Lapham, accepting this irreverent version of his history somewhat dryly.
> "Parents poor, of course," suggested the journalist. "Any barefoot business? Early deprivations of any kind that would encourage the youthful reader to go and do likewise? Orphan myself, you know," said Bartley, with a smile of cynical good comradery.

Lapham looked at him silently, and then said with quiet self-respect, "I guess if you see these things as a joke, my life won't interest *you*."

After the interview, Bartley goes home to his wife, who tells him she hopes he "won't make fun of [Silas] as you do some of those other people," and Bartley replies, "Nothing that he'll ever find out about." The article that does get published is crowded with little gibes and mock reverent flourishes: Bartley situates the paint mine "deep in the heart of the virgin forests of Vermont, far up toward the line of the Canadian snows, on a desolate mountainside" and calls Silas "one of nature's noblemen, to the last inch of his five eleven and a half." Silas is delighted with the piece. As predicted, he misses the joke.

I've always admired that first chapter of the novel. By introducing Silas Lapham through the newspaperman's irreverence, Howells finds a way to present a formulaic story and at the same time show his disapproval of a too scornful interpretation of it. In fact, the opening chapter might be as much an indictment of the snide journalist—and his purple prose—as it is a satire of the capitalist rags-to-riches tale. (Bartley had already appeared in another Howells novel, *A Modern Instance*, as a cad and philanderer, and the author of the kind of hack journalism Howells denounced.)

Setting the snarky newspaperman on his unsuspecting subject also ensures that readers will feel just a little protective of Silas Lapham—his life *will* interest us—even as we register the joke. And by seeming to dispense with all the Horatio Alger business through a proxy at the start, Howells can proceed with a tale that we trust will not be mere formula, not just another cliché tossed off, but a story and a man worth reading from beginning to end.

Yet while he may show more sympathy for his paint-king hero than his stand-in newspaperman does—or at least treats the type with more gentlemanly respect—Howells never does entirely transform Silas into a fully rounded, fleshed-out character. Whenever I teach the novel in literature courses, students invariably dispute this. Hasn't Howells humanized a stereotype by reversing the expected rags-to-riches plot? At the end of the novel Lapham's business has gone bankrupt, a failure that could easily have been avoided had he accepted a business offer, a real estate deal that if shady would have been perfectly legal. Lapham says no to the deal, loses it all, and ends up back where he started. The "rise" of Silas Lapham is not financial but moral. And this reversal, my students claim, transforms type into something more complex.

But I'm never convinced. Although it may be a reversal of the expected plot, it's not a more complicated take on the man. My students tell me that in doing the right thing Silas is an anomaly, but this view (morality goes against type) reveals more about their assumptions about American business practices than anything else. It is a notion I can forgive, since, like Howells, my students have good reasons for regarding the ethical entrepreneur as the exception to the rule. If Howells had the Robber Barons to contend with, my students have their own gilded aged phantoms: unscrupulous bankers with their mortgage fraud and predatory loans, and even a Ponzi schemer whose classic rags-to-riches rise doesn't end as Silas's does in rural retreat and moral conviction but in a prison cell for life.

No, in the end, however moral he turns out to be, I'm persuaded that under Howells's pen, Silas remains what Bartley would call "the regulation thing." The novel piles on an accumulation of evidence. Silas's provinciality and obsession with status. His penchant for bragging and his boorish monopoly of the conversation. His speech: a mingling of hearty colloquialisms ("I ain't a-going to brag up my paint") and hyberbole ("It's the best paint in God's universe"). His terrible taste and his indifference to literature or art. His narrow range of interests (horses, the newspaper, family, and paint) and his insular personal life (no society and hardly any friends outside the family circle). Even that body: the huge head, and his "great hairy paws." Hoping to impress high society at a dinner party, Silas stuffs those fists into an ill-fitting pair of "saffron-tinted" gloves. At his side they hang—like two "canvased hams."

And, then, at the very center of Howells's novel stands the crucial fact, maybe the most inevitable of all the facts put together, as predictably bound up with the future of the aspiring American as the farm and rocky fields are with his past. Without it, no social climb is complete. Silas Lapham is building himself a house.

After living in Boston for several years, Silas and his wife discover that they are living in the wrong neighborhood. The inhabitants of their street are either people just like them—wealthy but not prominent—or, it is vaguely suggested, people uncomfortably *not* like them. In a draft of this chapter, the ambiguity is made plain: one reason the Laphams want to leave their house on Nankeen Square is that Jewish families are moving in. The Laphams are also beginning to learn that money can't buy them a place among the old-moneyed families of Boston society. To aid his daughters in making a way for themselves—and marrying up—Silas hires the best architect in town to create for him a magnificent home in the better neighborhood on Beacon Street.

The house, a mansion on the hill, will have a view of the Charles River and of the fashionable street below. It will cost a great deal of money to make, and for much of the novel it will be Silas's great obsession—more compelling than his horses or the newspaper, almost more compelling than his paint. As a structural element in the novel, the house will also act as the spatial and symbolic pivot on which Howells's story turns. It will rise from the ground as Silas's fortune rises, and it will fall—accidentally burned to the ground when a cigar is left lit in one of the half-finished rooms—just as Silas's business falls apart.

In the figure of Silas Lapham I won't deny that I see traces of my father. I hear him in his speech, the mixed metaphors and rusticisms. Or I see him in a gesture: the way he could puff himself up, swagger a little when he was out of his depth socially, or the way he could lean, as Silas does, far back in his "leather-cushioned swivel-chair" when trying to assume a posture of patience or control. I see the fist on the desk pounding out a point, and I see his teetotaling Methodist heritage in Silas's nervous acceptance of a

The Architect

drink. Silas names a line of his paint after his wife—the Persis Brand. My father once horrified my grandmother by naming a short-lived ice-cream restaurant he built in Wisconsin after her: Clementine's Custard. At restaurants he called women "gals" and told old off-color army jokes at the bar, and at the kitchen table he held family meetings as if we were a franchised company, clearing his throat between words to ensure nobody could interrupt. Even Silas's saffron-tinted gloves jog a memory. I remember an Izod shirt my dad was given for Christmas, then, unfathomably, a token of status in our small town. On the first day he wore it, my mother noticed his scratching and scratching at the little crocodile above the pocket, as if he had mistaken it for a bit of dried jam or crusted-over ketchup, any one of the food particles that regularly found their way to his shirt or tie.

    I also see my father very clearly in Silas's real estate deals and frantic efforts to save the paint company at the end of the novel. During the bad times—most of the nineties—my father and my brother were in a similar race for survival: rushing from lender to lender, selling off one place just in time to pay back the loan on another. I never quite understood any of it, just as my students are never able to quite figure out Silas's business dealings at the end of the novel. (I'm half-convinced that Howells didn't understand business enough to explain it clearly himself.) My father kept a little Dictaphone in his shirt pocket and on car drives pressed it to his mouth, pausing so you'd only hear snatches of an unfathomable language, a mysterious vocabulary of square footage, easements, and interest rates. I didn't understand the words but I always understood the inflection, the shifts in tone. So did Howells, who may not have known how to explain a business deal clearly, but was good at depicting the adrenalin rush and the panic.

    Still in other ways, my father didn't fit the model of the American businessman at all. Nobody who really knew my father would be satisfied with so narrow a portrait. Vin, a friend of my parents, dubbed him "Roger the Artful Dodger," his way of explaining my father's graceful maneuvers at getting what he wanted and getting out of anything he didn't want to do. But it was a term one could just as easily apply to the elusiveness of his character, the difficulty we all had of keeping him stationary inside a definable box. At his funeral I was clear headed enough to detect from his former employees and business acquaintances a barely concealed eagerness to tell at last—or for the last time—their tales of Roger. The possibilities of this, of a Mr. Magoo caricature being the final word on my father, occurred to my brother before the funeral, and in his revision of my draft of the obituary he took the word *idiosyncratic* out, since it would be like an invitation, a prompt.

But there was no way we could stop it, the rush of recollections. How he had a gift for sleep—there were even doctors who diagnosed narcolepsy—and could, whenever he wanted, conveniently disappear, dozing at dinner parties, his elbows sliding, the cutlery clattering to the floor and waking him up. The time he came home without the car because he'd given the keys to a hitchhiker whose name he didn't catch but who would certainly return the car in a couple of days and who did, the car parked outside my dad's office with a thank-you note flapping from the windshield. The time he'd gotten a pilot's license but on his first and last solo flight forgot the gas and had to land in a field. And all the times when he was on the brink of disaster—the businesses in debt, the banks calling in their loans, and the way he could make the little red lines sinking to the bottom of the graph magically rise again.

Yes, my father fit, but then he didn't fit at all. If Silas's interests were limited to horses and business, my father's were expansive. He was not by nature jovial or optimistic; the heartiness he showed in public looked to me like something he'd once practiced in front of a mirror. He rarely bragged or showed signs of Silas's agitated scrambling for acceptance; he seemed oblivious to the opinions of others—not boorishly oblivious, as Silas could be—but so deeply distracted by his own circling and pacing out of an idea that he didn't always remember to look up. He would not have approved of Silas's insular private life—the entombing of the nuclear family—and often we'd wake up to find a stranger had moved in: Mickey from Japan, Ifyana from Nigeria, Greta, Tom, John, Kevin, and Bart, and once, startling my brother and me when we found her on the sofa one morning, a runaway picked up by my parents on the highway the night before.

Even to his children my father was a puzzle. In the fall he napped on the hump of leaves over his grandparents' graves; in my college dorm room, he charmed my friends by lying on the floor with us to listen along to Wallace Stevens reading "Sunday Morning" on a tape played in the dark. Disarmingly beautiful with round beseeching eyes, he could attend to his thoughts like a boy on a stream, a boy lost inside the refrigerator box, but could, like any child raised by a strident woman, disregard the tugs of others with nearly as much Zen-like concentration. His wrath could fill a room, his mood linger—an odor on the earpiece of the phone for a day after I hung up. His silences were maddening but just as often companionable: together, at a restaurant, we sat across the table, two books propped against one another in front of our plates. He couldn't stand not to have a book nearby, and my brother, David, remembers my father's desperation on a business trip when he discovered he'd forgotten to bring something to read. David was halfway through Truman Capote's *In Cold Blood*, and before he could stop him, my father reached for the book, noted the place where my brother had left off, and ripped the book in half.

Out of sight, we his children were often out of his mind—but in our presence, he could surprise us by how much he noticed behind his newspaper. He wanted to please. On a family vacation to New England, I begged to be taken to see Louisa May Alcott's house, but it was closed. He managed, after a furtive look around, to jimmy open a back window and slide me in head first to take a peek, a glimpse of what turned out to be the least old-fashioned of rooms, what must have been the break room: a hot plate and mimeograph machine, coffee cups stacked in the sink.

He rarely played with us, but for a few years, I remember a passion for the flying of kites, cheap paper kites his Robbys restaurant gave free to kids on their birthdays and that nearly always ripped on contact with the wind. We usually gave up early, but he'd stay out in the field until dark, holding tight to a string, the little Robbys logo unreadable in the night sky. On camping trips, he drove around the campground as if staking out a building site, turning and turning the tent until all the windows opened to a view. Some mornings, he'd stay in bed and stare at the ceiling, his eyes blinking, a tear tracing a slow course down his face. By the end of the week he was back in whistling-through-teeth exultation. Some doctors diagnosed him bipolar. Others couldn't decide.

If I'm honest, it is inside the rooms of Silas's house on Beacon Hill where I see my father most confined within the predictable American plot. I try to circle around this image—avoid it. I think of our house as something natural, wild. I think of it as having sprung organically from the woods and the rock. It was even designed to be thought of in this way. I want to keep commerce and its clichés out of it. I don't want to accept the idea that among the motives behind the making of our home, status might have been one of them. But there's no question it must have been. Like that mansion in Boston overlooking its pretty stretch of river, our house on the ledge with its views on field and lake was a mark of arrival, the materialization of a life built from the ground up.

Silas Lapham visits his house nearly every day, marveling as his dream takes material shape: first a foundation, then the ribs of a wall and the skeletons of stairs, then windows cut to reveal the view below. Often he brings his wife and daughters with him. On one of those visits, he offers them a seat in a corner where someday a bay window will open to the view. When his daughter Irene "curled her chin up" at the rough trestle bench he offers, Silas tells her: "Your mother wasn't ashamed to sit with me on a trestle when I called her out to look at the first coat of my paint that I ever tried on a house." Sitting in sawdust and watching the house come to life, board by board, Silas revisits the beginning of his story, and Penelope, his second daughter, teases him about it: "Yes, we've heard that story . . . We were brought up on that story."

For Silas the new house functions as a form of repetition, a means of replicating the excitement of the climb. He often refers to his early days as the most thrilling time of his life. This was true for my father as well, and I've always suspected this is why he pushed himself as close to the precipice as possible, why he liked to put it all on the line, and why he often seemed more irritable when his business was going smoothly than when it was going bust: he wanted to go back and do it again. The climb.

And one way to do it over again—although a short-lived exercise—is to watch a house rise from a hole in the earth. I saw this for myself. The smell of sawdust belongs to one of my first memories. The employees of Roger Peters Construction, including my grandfather Reinhold, came out and built the house in less than six months. From nearby quarries, they dragged huge pitted stones, the same kind that jutted from the caves and overhangs at the back of the house, to use as steps to the door. They dug a dirt road along the edge of the farm field and brought bulldozers and backhoes to lay claim to the rock. I was five years old. Sitting with my legs hanging over the edge of a yawning black pit—the foundation of our house—I watched as my father jubilantly climbed his way out of it.

But, even more than a return to the beginning, the house marks an arrival, a declaration of his new self, the kind Silas imagines will be accepted into Boston society. Our house was never lavish. My mother tells me it was built on almost nothing. She rummaged at old barn sales for every fixture and tile. The area where my parents bought land was not then fashionable, still mostly farms. My parents' friends didn't understand their wanting to live twenty miles from town. The land was cheap too, and neither of my parents would have been comfortable with the kind of extravagant display evident in every detail of Silas's house. My dad wanted our house to disappear, to fade into the background, to nestle into the rock and woods behind it.

But he must have also wanted it to be seen. There's the location, the enviable view. Houses on hills are meant to make a point. I didn't register this growing up. A few years ago, I opened the road atlas and noticed for the first time that the section of Highway 151 along which our house stands is marked with small green dashes. Green dashes are Rand McNally's signal for a scenic route, and all my life I've been unable to resist them. A lover of maps and picturesque bends in the road, I cannot take a road trip without demanding we exit the interstate and follow the back roads. Yet somehow I had never once looked at a map of where I come from, hadn't known that the place I was always looking to go, with its promise of a photo op, a view of real America, was the place I had lived for most of my childhood. For a moment, I lost my orientation. I saw my history from the outside. Through the window of a car speeding past on the highway, I looked up and caught a blur on a bicycle, a girl wobbling over gravel (me), and a house on a hill behind her (mine). I saw a lucky childhood—with space and a view and glass reflecting the light of American success.

My dad only built two houses for himself, unless you count the spec houses. Before marrying he built himself a weekend place on Green Lake, a little resort lake twenty-five miles west of town. A bachelor pad with just one room opening to a deck that floated out onto the lake. The little house was still standing when I was a teenager, and I saw it once—shabbier but otherwise, he said, the same. All squares like a Mondrian grid, the walls painted in midcentury oranges and yellows, the built-in cabinets for the hi-fi still intact, suggesting to me when I opened them Doris Day sliding to the floor. From the deck, his drunken friends threw, like Frisbees, his entire record collection, album by album into the lake. He took up sailboat racing and never told his friends he didn't know how to swim.

The house on Green Lake gives me the man—or the invention of one—and so does our house on the ledge. In glass and stairs and ceiling, I see a man in a black turtleneck leaning against a railing, a beautiful wife at his side, a beautiful room sunken and sun-lit below. It is a classic story: reinvention through the rooms one chooses to inhabit, so classic that American writers have been finding a way to tell the story—and often ironically—for over a hundred years. Think of Gatsby remaking himself inside his West

My parents, the dining room landing at the house on the ledge. (author's collection)

Egg mansion. Or think of Philip Roth's Swede Levov, the aspiring businessman in Roth's novel *American Pastoral*. A Jewish glove manufacturer from Newark, New Jersey, Swede is convinced that by moving his family into an old colonial house on land inhabited by Wasps for centuries, he'll acquire gentility—or, as he puts it, he'll "own the things money can't buy."

But no, when it comes to my father, I can't make it quite work. Not surprisingly, my father's version of Silas or Gatsby or Swede's story is just slightly off—tilted, askew. And this always happens with him. As soon as I've moved him inside the limits of a story—in this case, inside the confines of that American mansion on the hill—he slips to the edge of the frame. He steps out the door. And the difference has everything to do with the profession he chose. As much as our house on the ledge fit, as much as it was a mark of financial success, it was also a deviation, another act of differentiation. My father would not settle for just the purchase of culture. He'd find a way to contribute to it.

I like to think of books as if they were houses. Even when I was little, I did this, imagining chapters and scenes and plots as an arrangement of rooms. *The Rise of Silas Lapham* is no exception; it always translates to my brain as a floor plan and a remarkably symmetrical one, like some precolonial house with a hall down the middle and rooms of equal size on either side. Very neat. Almost too neat. The novel is structured as a series of pairings and oppositions. Two of almost everything. Two interconnecting narratives (a business plot and a courtship plot); two Lapham daughters (Irene, pretty and domestic, and Penelope, witty and a great reader of books); and two social classes, each represented by a family: the Laphams, a family on the rise, and the Coreys, a family with an old Boston pedigree possessed "of every polite taste and feeling that adorns leisure." Silas sells paint, while Bromfield, the patriarch of the Corey family, is trained to use it. He is a portrait painter, but since he finds it "absurd to paint portraits for pay, and ridiculous to paint them for nothing," he hardly paints them at all. Instead, he paints with words. He knows how to talk: about art, books, architecture, politics, history, nearly everything except business.

To my students, he is ridiculous. They don't get Bromfield's humor or his patrician manner or his arcane references. They don't understand why he and his wife are horrified at the prospect of their son, Tom, marrying one of those Lapham daughters. And they can't fathom how a man who doesn't work for a living might be considered respectable. "Bromfield is lazy, and he's a snob," they say. "Silas is the better man." They direct me to a passage after Silas's first encounter with Bromfield Corey. The status-conscious Silas is thrilled by Bromfield's attentions, but he is also uncomfortable: he tries not to let his wife "see in his averted face the struggle that revealed itself there—the struggle of stalwart achievement not to feel flattered at the notice of sterile elegance." Stalwart, my students remind me, wins out over sterile every time. Or, as another put it, "Silas has some get-up-and-go; he has those 'great hairy fists'; Bromfield just has words."

William Dean Howells was a poet, a novelist, a journalist, and the editor of the most respected literary journals of the day, the *Atlantic Monthly* and later *Harper's*. He moved easily among the cultured elite of East Coast society. Yet he was also something of a self-made man; he'd grown up in Ohio and began his journalism career as a printer's apprentice. He was an insider, but not quite, and had enough distance on the culture of Brahmin Boston to be able to register its flaws. My students are right to recognize that in *The Rise of Silas Lapham*, Bromfield Corey is another object of the satirical send-up: the man of talk and no action who's had all the get-up-and-go bred out of him.

But what I struggle to explain to my students is that while Howells is no Bromfield Corey, he's no Silas Lapham either, and if he'd been forced to take sides between these two social worlds—as my students always seem to want him to do—the novel convinces me Howells would choose the less stalwart man. It's often Bromfield who acts as mouthpiece for Howells's opinions (on urban poverty, real estate, art, and literature), and it's Bromfield who is the reader of books and literary periodicals, the consumer of the very cultural product Howells was in the business of making. Over money (and over fists), Howells would choose words. Just like my journalist friend back in my Brooklyn apartment, and just like myself. The novel is thick with conversation about the value of books, a constant stream of talk. Why do people read dime novels? What makes George Eliot a great writer? Why is realism better than romance? Why do some people own books and why do others, like the Laphams, just check them out from the library? But there's nearly as much talk about houses. The kinds of studs one should use in building a house, the colors a column at the door should be painted, why discreet old homes like the Coreys' are always more appealing than the showy palaces of the new rich.

"The architect" is another topic of conversation. Bromfield holds forth one night on the subject. He claims that architects (and musicians) are the "true and only artistic creators. . . . All the rest of us, sculptors, painters, novelists, and tailors, deal with the forms that we have before us; we try to imitate, we try to represent. But you create form . . . out of your inner consciousness." Embedded in this statement are Howells's views on literature. Dubbed by some the "father of American realism," he believed passionately that fiction must "deal with the forms that we have before us," that it must adhere to the ideals of representation. And yet the least representative of arts—architecture—is the one Bromfield regards as the truest, the ideal.

The statement also makes plain that architects, just like writers and painters, belong to culture's inner circle. Bromfield makes his pronouncement at a dinner party he and his wife are holding for the Lapham family. From the start, Silas is out of his element; the scene confuses him—the understated house looks "bare." Even the people look bare to him, the men unencumbered by those gloves a shop clerk convinced him to buy for the occasion and the young ladies comparatively subdued next to his daughter Irene in her ball gown. He's also confused to find included among the guests of such a prominent family the architect Silas has hired for the Beacon Street mansion. To Silas, the architect is a businessman like himself, but of a lower rank, not a man of wealth or power. He thinks of the young man as belonging to him: "It seemed that he had discovered the fellow, as he always called him, and owned him." Before building his house, Silas meets with the architect to outline his preferences. He imagines a grander imitation of the fashionable mansions in the neighborhood, but he has a "crude taste in architecture" and admires "the worst." The architect sets him straight at once and informs him that every one of his aesthetic preferences—from the molding to the floor to the design of the rooms—is wrong. Fashion does not equal taste. Though Silas regards his architect merely as an employee—no less of one than his clerks and secretaries back at the office—he will follow the architect's instructions to the letter because in doing so he believes he can purchase gentility, or, as Swede Levov puts it, "own the things money can't buy."

Of course, Silas misses the point: to enter the Corey world, it's much more important to *make* things money can't buy than to own them. As a man of taste, the architect belongs to the very social class Lapham so desperately hopes to join—and can't. This is not a point my father would have missed—it may have even been one of the reasons he built our house. He wanted a place at that table. To create the house on the ledge, he did not hire an arbiter of taste as Silas does, but acted as his own, and while he may have been inspired by other architects, the house was so fancifully and artfully designed that few would call the results fashionable, few would call them crude. Some might even have said (as I do) that he had succeeded in making an original form emerge out of his "inner consciousness." More than an emblem of status, the house was meant to be the map of an inventive mind, as much a work of art as the books my friends and I hoped someday to write.

I see this even in the first feature you encountered when opening the front door of our house: a wall of books lining the length of the room. To me, those shelves—the centerpiece of the house dividing back from front and upstairs from downstairs—are like some coded message from my father, as if he were equating one interior with another: the opening of a door into a room an entry into culture, like the turning back of a cover to reveal the first page.

To set himself apart, my journalist friend back in New York used words. I suppose so did I. Words and cities and books would save us from what we saw as the banality of commercial aspiration. We would take culture over money. When he chose architecture for a profession, wasn't my father also claiming for himself an entrance into a community of artists?

At the same time, if architecture gave my father credibility as an artist, it also protected him from that faint suggestion of laziness, the taint of unmanliness and of sterility that in American culture is often ascribed to the artist. My students' reactions to Bromfield Corey illustrate how prevalent those attitudes are even today. Reading Frank Lloyd Wright's autobiography, my father wouldn't have missed Wright's insistence that as much as he loved his lilies in the field and the feel of the pencil in his hand, his profession needed physical vigor—and virility. Looked at from my visual map of the novel—a house with a hall beautifully dividing culture from trade, parlor from kitchen—the architect is one of the few able to cross the corridor. Architecture enabled my father to move back and forth between two worlds, something I heard even in the structure of the sentence he used when introducing himself. "Architect by education," he'd say, "builder by trade." When Bromfield Corey sees the architect, he sees an artist. Silas Lapham sees a businessman. Both are correct. At ease in both social worlds, the architect is the invited guest conversant in the two languages spoken at the table. In fact, what distinguishes the architect from other artists is not just that he is working in pure form, but that because of the very nature of that form—a building—he can't escape the marketplace. He can't, as Bromfield Corey can, stick one of his creations in a closet. A house needs an inhabitant. It needs a customer.

There's a story about my father and Frank Lloyd Wright. In the 1950s, Wright visited the architecture program at the University of Michigan and, on a tour of a drafting class, stopped suddenly at my father's desk. Wright would have been in his eighties. My father was nineteen. Leaning over, Wright lifted the drawings from the desk, stared at them for a while, and then turned to the young man looking up at him: "I don't think you will be a great architect. But you will be a great builder."

I never liked this story—a boy's dream instantly crushed by the offhand comments of an old man. But that was not how my father remembered it. He told that story like it was a point of pride, the words of a prophet that had, in the end, come true.

3

The Second House

I have a photograph, a Polaroid taken a couple of years before we moved to the country. I'm three years old, dressed in a cowgirl costume, a pistol hitched to my waist, feet planted on the ground. Behind me a sidewalk ends abruptly in a mass of wildflowers and weeds. Lawn borders an unmowed field. One foot in field, another on pavement.

There's nothing special about this photograph. Thousands of Americans born in the 1950s and 1960s (and really anytime in the last one hundred years) can quickly and with the same wistfulness pull it from a box. All of my friends near my age can point to it and tell a similar story: Of the joy of getting lost in the corridors of a cornfield, gone to make way for a mall. Of a sky they might see over the Hudson now blocked by the steely reflection of a highrise condominium complex. We speak of the forces of destruction, vaguely conceived by us as a committee of ghoulish grown-ups in glass offices conniving to obliterate our playing fields. No matter how old we are, we are still children to ourselves when we tell these stories. We sit together and commiserate, and I forget, simply forget, that the man who laid the sidewalk in that photograph, the man who made the field behind me disappear, was my own father.

Our move to the country in the early seventies had offered my dad a way to return and to revise his rural childhood, but it was an act of nostalgia afforded by a remarkable capacity for commerce, a gift for going into figures, a gift for walking planks. A preservationist who loved the earth, he was a businessman good at paving over it. On Saturdays he manned the rototiller; on Monday he was applauded at the Rotary Club for housing developments at the edge of town and fast-food restaurants planted on what once were farmers' fields. In the creation of our house he was a purist. Inspired by a connection to the land and a vision of building in harmony with it, he had created a house so sensitively attuned to the landscape that it seemed to have sprung from the earth. He studied the trees and the angle of a window to catch a slant of the light. But in town, twenty miles down the road, he was a developer who built strip malls and so delighted in the word *entrepreneur* that when he said it I heard something dreamy, heard it the way other kids might hear "astronaut" or "prince on a great white horse."

I think of my father's story as belonging to America, a country where the civilizing impulse draws upon nostalgia for untouched, open spaces; where the zeal for wilderness so often colludes with the impulse to improve and access it. Even his profession I've always regarded as more peculiarly American than almost any other. "Build!" is a national injunction. And then the architect already embodies a divide: against commerce there is art; with creation there is destruction. The architect delights us by creating the places we live in and love (the sites of our nostalgia); he enrages us with the buildings that block our view.

In 1903, the novelist Henry James returned to America after a twenty-two-year absence. He hadn't been back to his native country once, not even for a visit. When he did finally return, he recorded his impressions in a collection of travel essays published the next year as *The American Scene*. Several chapters describe the transformation of his city and the shock of homecoming. Trinity Church, once the tallest building in New York, now stands squeezed between those "triumphant payers of dividends," the new skyscrapers. The grand concert hall of James's childhood has become a "nonentity." Worst of all, his boyhood home on Fourteenth Street and his grandmother's house on Washington Square have been rubbed out; there's not even a plaque on a wall. Memory is topsy-turvy, walls sliding like something in a fun-house mirror.

A year after publishing *The American Scene*, James wrote one of his best-known ghost stories, "The Jolly Corner." To me, it reads as a direct response to the losses already described in *The American Scene*. The protagonist, Spencer Brydon, is a middle-aged man of leisure who returns to his hometown of New York after thirty-three years living as an expatriate in Europe. He's come back to oversee two inherited properties, his boyhood home and another property nearby he plans to divide into a "tall mass of flats." During the day he visits this second property, one of those new apartment hotels going up "two bristling blocks" west of Fifth Avenue, but at night he roams his empty house, a mansion on the avenue that he affectionately calls "the Jolly Corner."

In a way, the story is a kind of resurrection. It saves what the wrecking ball obliterated, envisions the mythical past intact. James's childhood homes had turned to air or into a wall of factory brick, but here, a family home stands preserved, the black and white tiles on the floor as distinct as they were thirty years before. The empty rooms of the Jolly Corner are astir with memory: the "mere feel, in [Brydon's] hand, of the old silver-plated knobs of the several mahogany doors . . . suggested the pressure of the palms of the dead"; the "impalpable ashes of his long-extinct youth" float "in the air like microscopic notes." New York may be change, constant and swift, but for James, it's also memory embalmed—a creak on the stairs, the light from beneath a nursery door half-cracked. James gives us an elegiac fantasy: who wouldn't want to return to the first house, now vanished or degraded by the swing sets and alien furniture of others, and find it unchanged, empty, room upon room just for you?

But soon, the fantasy shifts into nightmare. While the family home inside is unchanged, outside on the streets of the city itself, Manhattan has been redrawn, a "vast ledger-page," a map of "criss-crossed lines and figures," a landscape built on "swagger things."

Like James, Brydon has returned to his hometown to find a landscape out of kilter: "proportions and values were upside down." In place of culture, privacy, and good conversation, he finds the sway of the almighty dollar.

Like Howells's Bromfield Corey, Brydon is horrified by the swagger things—but he's also drawn to them. Overseeing construction on his apartment house, he discovers an affinity for business. It turns out he's good at skyscrapers, good at climbing ladders, "walking planks" and "going into figures." Had he stayed in America he would have been a great architect, a land developer, a man of power and wealth. Stirred by a "rage of curiosity," a longing to know where his gifts for business might have led, Brydon takes nightly walks through the empty rooms of the old house. He goes on a hunt for his American self. Opening doors and turning corners, climbing stairs and crossing corridors, he stalks his game—and is stalked by it—until one evening he confronts his ghost, his alter ego, a grizzled figure dressed in the trappings of a millionaire with two missing fingers and a face so hideous that upon seeing it Brydon faints dead away. When he comes to, he is bathed in tenderness and golden autumn light. His head rests in the lap of the woman who loves him—both the man he has become and the man he might have been.

The year before my father died, I couldn't stop thinking about "The Jolly Corner." I badgered my friends to read it and foisted it on my students even when it didn't quite fit the syllabus. At the time I didn't get why it caught me, but now it seems strange I didn't see. It's all there, not just the divided man and his ghosts, but a pair of properties, one recalled down to the pattern of tiles on the floor, the other a real estate deal that will pay for the nostalgic look back. Originally James had titled his story "The Second House," his name for the apartment hotel Spencer Brydon owns. Crowded on both sides, a "mere number in its long row," the "second house" will be divided to make room for several families and be used by Brydon to keep his childhood home vacant. Earlier in the story, he announces to his one friend in the city, Alice Staverton, that he will never sell his childhood home. He will resist the "beastly rent values" to keep a "consecrated spot" standing. Opening doors to strangers will pay for the luxury of keeping a house intact and empty in a city defined by the crush of the wrecking ball and of the crowd.

Alice Staverton loves Brydon—all of him, the monstrous American he might have been as well as the European pleasure-seeker he has become—but even more, she understands him. "In short," she says, "you're to make so good a thing of your sky-scraper that, living in luxury on *those* ill-gotten gains, you can afford for a while to be sentimental here." She understands that by setting up a distinction between the swaggering values of the city and the hushed interiors of his past, Brydon has chosen to ignore the facts: that no such distinction is possible. The house on the corner of Fifth Avenue depends on the commercial development nearby. In fact, the mansion has always been connected to monetary gain; it was built with Brydon's father's money, wealth we assume was made in New York real estate. Even Brydon's cultivated existence overseas and his release from the demands of American striving get paid for by the same "beastly rent values" he moved to Europe to escape.

In this way "The Jolly Corner" reveals the irony—or call it the hypocrisy—of place attachment: the false barriers we can create between place (the creation of home) and property (the buying and selling of it). It reminds us of how easily our accounts of where we come from can turn to a mythic vision in which no money is ever exchanged, no holes dug, no skyscrapers built to overshadow the consecrated spots we call home.

When I tell the story of my childhood, I tell of gardening gloves dirty at the door and of my parents climbing the icy ledge to tap the maples, later boiling down their labor to a trickle, hardly enough to sweeten a pancake; of cobwebs milky behind glass and ginseng clumps in the woods. All true—the idyll, the great escape—but it is the poem, not the full report. I don't tell the story of the second house. I don't talk about how I spent as much time on the curb of a fast-food parking lot—a stopwatch in hand to time the drive-thru—as I did walking in the woods with my dog.

By the time I was fourteen, I lived split between the house in the country and my parents' businesses in town. At the south end of Fond du Lac, I worked for my mother at her bookstore, unpacking boxes in the back room or sitting alone at the front desk, drowsily reading the merchandise, the books half opened to keep the bindings from showing a crease. Customers were rare and intrusive; I couldn't hide my panic at their arrival, my relief to see them go.

The other job I had after school and during the summers was on the other end of town at my dad's fast-food restaurant. I filled ketchup containers and wiped the tables in the front lobby. Every August, I was hired for the annual Hardee's Corn Roast Festival. Farmers unloaded trucks of fresh sweet corn onto trestle tables arranged at the end of the parking lot. My dad shucked at the front of the line, while the rest of us worked the parking lot. In the mornings, I carried vats of melted butter from the kitchen, or from pickle buckets poured salt into sticky shakers hanging from the tables by a string. In the afternoons, my best friend and I took turns as the festival mascot, Corny the Cob. We crawled inside a giant yellow and green Styrofoam costume that looked vaguely like an ear of corn; inside, it was pitch-black and reeking of someone else's August sweat. All day we handed out candy to children who, barely visible through the narrow slits cut for our eyes, could be heard and felt, their buttery fingers grabbing at our knees, at the suckers extended from our fat Styrofoam hands.

Another summer in college I worked as a fast-food spy. After my parents' divorce, my father moved to Salt Lake City, where he'd agreed to take on, at a discount, a fleet of near-bankrupt Hardee's. He spent the next fifteen years trying to save them from going under, an effort accomplished (and in the nick of time) only through an accumulation of backed-into-a-corner gambles and the restraining influence of my brother, a steadier second-in-command. I lived with my father the summer after my freshman year, and my job was to drive from restaurant to restaurant across a mesh of numbered streets and to scout out the cleanliness of bathrooms, judge the warmth of the servers at the counter, and then record my findings on little white cards.

I was a harsh critic, and my father, flattened by his divorce and by what seemed like the imminent bankruptcy of his business, responded to my reports by dragging each of his managers into his office to scream at them. I heard my own words snapped back at me from the other side of the wall and saw the faces of his employees as they left his office. The next week, I drove to all the restaurants I had panned to steal packs of customer service cards clipped to the napkin holder on the tables. I filled out dozens of those cards, each a hyperbolic record of spotless tables and mouthwatering meals, praise in as many cursive scripts as I could manage. That weekend, the cards made it to my father, and I lay on the couch and listened as again he read my own words back to me. This time he was happy, and so was I.

One duty of the job of spy was taste-testing the food. I gained twenty pounds that summer. The back of my car was filled with half-eaten hamburgers, carcasses in crumpled wrappers. My skin filmed over in grease. My friends hear this part of the story and look a little sick. The farmers' market is their church, fresh kale their religion; instantly I am pitied, my father condemned.

I understand their point of view—even, some of the time, share it. Yet I know I can never get them to see it as it was. How he liked to hold meetings at the restaurants, in a corner booth, and how we spent long hours waiting for him—canned music, sizzling french fries in the background. And how it was not, as my friends imagine, just sterility. Sometimes he held meetings with us, his children. Across the Formica, he'd spread out napkins and scribble on them while he talked: arrows shooting off, a mass of circles intersecting to represent the family in sync or at odds, little maps of future deeds and opportunities. We sat under the shock of a fluorescent present, a brightly lit plastic world with no sorrowful history, beyond books or the emotions that come from the earth, from mud or trees.

 Nor can I explain to my friends how it felt at those corn roasts after the sun went down. Once we had finished cleaning the salt shakers and handing out candy, my friend and I took off our costumes, stopped in the bathroom to compare the butterflies on our training bras, and then went out into the cool of the summer night to admire the skinny chests of boys shivering in line at the dunk tank. Behind the Dumpster, we danced to Beatles tunes sung by a cover band on a makeshift stage under the stars. Out of the corner of my eye, I'd catch sight of my father. A beer in hand, his white button-down shirt a flag in the fading light, he stood with the farmers who'd just loaded up their trucks. I watched him—and then my mother moving toward him. Somewhere not far off was my brother with his friends, my sister with hers. Standing there, the moon rising, the asphalt still hot beneath my bare feet, I was home, as much at home as if I were behind a book in my mother's shop, or back in my bedroom, the moths against the screen, the leaves outside flashing white in the wind.

When I talk to people about my father's developments and restaurants I can get defensive, but he never was. He didn't see, at least not then, what he was doing as a developer or a businessman as incompatible with our house. He owned a long parcel of land not far from us on the ledge, and when we complained about the housing developments there, he looked up unperturbed, just blinked behind his newspaper, and said, "Somebody is going to do it, and I'll just do it better"—a standard refrain from developers, but in my dad's case, probably true. He hired a landscape architect to plant native trees on the lawns in town, trees to hide what he had made. Now when I go back to Fond du Lac, I drive past all the new construction along the ledge and am shocked—lawns stripped bare, houses not of the hill but defiantly on it.

One of my father's restaurants. (author's collection)

You saw the desire to do it better even in the houses he built in town, especially those that went up around the time ours did out in the country. From the outside, they were indistinguishable from all the other new construction in town, but inside I saw my dad's impulse to give his clients what he had given us—a vista. The flat, predictable fronts of the small houses built for working-class families edging Meadowbrook and Cherry Lane did not match the interiors; financial constraints demanded a choice, and the occupant, not the passerby, got all the aesthetic satisfaction. Even in the tiniest house, I saw signs of his struggle to give height. Wee bedrooms opened up to narrow balconies looking down on what he hoped would feel like air and space. It was a kind of gift, as if he were saying that we all deserve a house that doesn't house us in. Even the fast-food restaurants he saw as a service. He spoke of Robbys (and later Hardee's) in terms of postwar efficiency, and was proud of the restaurants, regarded them as something beautiful, built on the principles of a Corbusian simplicity. They belonged to modernity—food on the assembly line, a spaceship landing or about to take off.

Yet, in the years after my parents' divorce in 1988 and the selling of our house, I began to sense my dad's faith in the rightness of his choices weakening, his "somebody's going to do it, but I'll just do it better" nonchalance harder to pull off, and his easy management of the two selves (the back-to-the-land idealist at the drawing board and the man elbow deep in P&L statements at the fast-food booth) beginning to give way.

He didn't say so then. Not until much later, near the end of his life, did he reveal any regrets. He went on a long soul-searching trip alone to Dubrovnik. He sat every day on the patio of his hotel reviewing his life. On his way home, he met my sister and me at a Chinese restaurant in New York and told us about it, about how he'd had an epiphany: the house was the masterpiece and everything that came after it a mistake. Implicit was that my mother had been the ideal mate, she and the life they'd made the other masterpiece, and everyone after a mistake. Listening, my sister and I lifted our chopsticks and looked at each other across the table, telegraphing sympathy and the satisfaction of a long-held belief confirmed.

By the time our house was sold, the balance of my father's life tipped: increasingly one self was subsumed, sacrificed. He built a few more houses—one underground house with glass walling off what looked like the entrance to a cave—but soon commercial development and fast food took over. By my senior year in high school, he was hardly ever home—a hoarse voice on the line, a body half-asleep on a hotel bed or slumped in the corner of a phone booth at the airport. When home, he was a figure in the dark unloading his briefcases from the car, a shape under the sheets. There was no more garden. The subscription to the seed catalogs had run out. Without telling my mother, he decided we'd all move to Salt Lake City. My mother filed for divorce, and I came home from college to pack up his things. I stood on a ladder in front of the living room bookshelves and divided the books: Frank Lloyd Wright and Ray Kroc for him; Margaret Mead, Virginia Woolf, and the Nearings for her. Circling the legs of the ladder beneath me, our cat wove a figure eight before moving away—padding from room to room in search of the missing person, the man who'd disappeared.

After the divorce and after the house was sold, I maintained an uneasy vigilance. It was as if I were waiting—for a confrontation, a collapse. The climactic scene in "The Jolly Corner" is the moment when the artist, the sophisticate, the nostalgic, faces the businessman he might have been. My father's was a different kind of standoff, a crisis in reverse: The businessman coming face to face with the past he had lost, the middle-aged man confronting the young idealist. Where was the builder of houses, the planter of trees? Where was the boy in dirty overalls dreaming an escape? I sensed that my father was on a quest to find him—Citizen Kane seeking his Rosebud; Spencer Brydon hunting (and haunted by) the life he had forsaken—and for a while, I was with him on his hunt, moving along the corridors, peering in windows and out of them, climbing upstairs and down from room to room.

For most of the nineties, my father lived in a series of almost identical houses in Salt Lake City. They were a surprise to me. Most of them were rented and built by others; most were very ugly. I never understood his choosing them, much as I didn't understand the women he turned to in those years, women who spoke in a sugary western twang and bought my father thin gold chains to wear around his newly single neck. Usually he lived in one room at the top of the house, with a view of the mountains. The downstairs was furnished in the leavings of those women: lamps in the shape of bejeweled elephants and paintings of the sunset in the pinkest, sickliest of desert pastels. When we visited we slept in the basement, empty except for a television and an assortment of beds draped in white eyelet comforters.

One of those houses, a rambling stucco built by some other man for some other family, a Mormon couple and their brood of children, was so large that one floor was kept entirely empty, a hive of bedrooms connecting to bathrooms with triple sinks. One Thanksgiving I sat in one of those empty bedrooms with my father; we huddled together on the carpet looking at floor plans for other dream houses—underground houses, white glass boxes, tree houses, straw-bale houses, cabins on Montana rivers with huge doors on hinges that in the winter folded up into vertical shutters and in the summer folded down into horizontal decks. So many houses that were never built and were meant to be the glorious pinnacle of a life's work. To me, they always looked like deformed versions of the house he had built years before.

When they divorced and sold their house, my parents mislaid the plans, and I used to wonder if sketching those other dream houses was his way of getting back, an effort to reveal the contours of a previous life. For a few years, a model house in white plaster sat on his floor in Salt Lake, and once I caught him playing with it, opening and closing the miniature windows, transporting the plastic people—a misshapen mother, father, and child—up stairs, from room to room. Kneeling there, he was a boy inhabiting a future; at the same time, an old man revisiting an idyll—back in a basement with his young wife, two heads bent over blue paper unrolled before them, two heads touching over a future.

After the divorce I consented to a reversal of roles: I was the parent, he the child. His eyes seemed to get bigger and more wetly forlorn. In the past he had passed the phone over to my mother. Now we had to talk or I had to sit through long silences and wait for him to speak. For a year, night after night, he called me in college. I knew who it was before I picked up the phone. I sat in my dorm room smoking cigarettes, while on the other end of the phone, he heaved long sighs. His silences I filled with soothing-sounding platitudes and monologues on self-reliance. Out loud I read to him what I hoped were inspiring passages from my world religion textbook or from a Rilke poem. When he talked—a rush of talk—I told him he reminded me of a novel by Gertrude Stein, the language a mantra, a circle returning always to the same regret.

◇

One night, after rereading "The Jolly Corner" for a class I was teaching, I closed the book on Spencer Brydon and his ghost and lay in bed in my Brooklyn apartment listening to the bus keening to a stop across Lafayette Avenue. I stared at the pattern of stains on the ceiling overhead, until one memory lingered and sharpened into focus. I hadn't really thought of it in twenty years, but it read to me like the climax of the story, the moment when the American man at last stares down his American ghost.

After his split with my mother my father became a great traveler. He liked company when he could find it, and sometimes, we, his children, were all he could drum up. The bulk of time I spent with him in my adult life happened on those trips. Usually they were conceived last-minute, and usually they followed a predictable rhythm: euphoria turning to tension turning to a blowup turning to serenity and, if there was time, back again. A day with him was never steady, so that, say, on a vacation in Ireland, you might begin in a rage (jet-lagged in a rental car on the wrong side of the road, my brother up front gripping the steering wheel, my dad relaying churlish directions from behind his map), then find yourself in an Irish cottage next to two ancient farmers, purportedly distant relations, with your legs stretched sentimentally in front of their peat fire. By lunchtime, you'd be telling him to fuck off in a fish-and-chips shop, and by nightfall, you were together again, leaning over the railing of a bridge and watching as Dublin turned on its lights.

But the trip I thought of while reading Henry James happened in America, and it happened in a house of American swagger. On a plane my father met a man who belonged to a private hunting club outside of Pittsburgh, located on an estate that had once been owned by a Carnegie or a Mellon (I can't remember which) and only an hour's drive from Frank Lloyd Wright's Fallingwater. Somehow my father managed to wrangle an invitation—the man in the aisle seat probably didn't know how it had happened. He summoned me and my sister to join him there for Thanksgiving, and as usual didn't tell us anything about what to expect. We weren't even sure where we were going, since he always knew the more information he gave the less likely we'd go along with his plan.

It was our first Thanksgiving not spent at the house. I was working in New York City by then, and my sister was in college. She drove down from Ann Arbor to pick us up at the Pittsburgh airport, arriving in a beat-up Honda Civic with rusted doors and upholstery that smelled of marijuana and french fries. She'd cut her hair to look like Laurie Anderson and wore red combat boots laced to her shins.

Approached by a drive lined with trees, the house, like all Gothic piles, came as a revelation in the bend: white stone, with horse stables and a manicured lawn. The parking attendant saw us and ran, whisking the car—and then us—out of sight. The three of us were led upstairs to two former maids' rooms. Papered in cabbage roses, the rooms were low ceilinged and reserved, I assumed, for lower sorts. From the start, the place scared us, even my father couldn't hide it, and at first we refused to go down. We just lay there on the embroidered bedspreads listening to the sounds below: laughing horsemen back from the hunt.

When we finally nerved ourselves to go down, we wandered from one empty drawing room to the next (fires lit in the grates) in search of a drink and the familiar distraction of a Thanksgiving football game. We found the bar—hunting prints on hunter green walls, a discreet TV screen framed in wood paneling suspended overhead—but were told by the bartender that ladies drink only in the ladies lounge. The ladies lounge, a former ballroom—enormous, a basketball court gilded over—was empty. In the corner, we sat alone, as incongruous in our spindly chairs as the beer bottles and bowl of peanuts on the tea table before us.

Things only got worse once dinnertime came around. In the dining room, we were stopped again, a footman in full livery intercepting us just as we entered. Ladies in slacks were not admitted to the dining room. I had a skirt upstairs, but my sister hadn't brought one. We had to eat that meal in shifts. Course by course, we took turns trading our one skirt, me down for the turkey, then my sister (in skirt and combat boots), then me. At the table, my father waited, greeting each of us in turn with a feigned heartiness—as if he hadn't seen us in months, as if we were long-lost relatives home for the holidays, sleigh bells ringing over the river and through the woods.

Finally it was too much, and with my father mournfully following, we fled the dining room and charged out the front door of the house. A woman at the next table, with a Zelda Fitzgerald bob and a beautiful slouch, watched us go. I remember her look, not kind, but understanding, as if she caught it all: the lone parent, the divorce, the scene upstairs. Two sisters exchanging a pair of nylons in furious, whispering mutiny.

Outside it was nearly dark—a gray sky, the air autumn-sharp. We walked along a gravel path edging the property, horse stables on one side, a field on the other. My sister and I didn't speak, but in our minds we let him have it: *You've done it again, dragging us where we don't belong, and no heads-up as usual. And now we are embarrassed, and you know we won't be able to stay embarrassed because then you'll be hurt and then we will have to feel sorry for you—for your clumsiness, your pushiness. For having raised such ungrateful, humorless children.* I remember my stiffness—*other people would find this funny, why can't I?* These were the louder thoughts, but they weren't the deepest. The sentence ringing most insistently came in the form of a question, one I know my dad was asking too, one we were all asking in the year after the house was sold: Why are we *here* when we should be *there*?

Next to us, geese had congregated in the wet pools of the field, and up ahead, a flock of grouse, survivors of that day's hunt, moved in tight formation across the gravel path. On nights like this in the fall, when we were little, my parents liked to drive us to Horicon Marsh, a wildlife refuge near our house, where for a week or two thousands of Canada geese paused on their migration south. At sunset, cars lined the road adjoining the marsh. Already dressed in our pajamas, we sat on the hood of our car watching the show as if it were a drive-in movie.

But it wasn't my memory that broke the silence. My dad began to tell us about how at night on the farm he'd chase wild turkeys and pheasants out in the fields. Suddenly, unexpectedly, he began flapping his arms wildly. A loud yipping sound broke from someplace at the back of his throat. It wasn't a sound I'd ever heard from him before. Still flapping and yipping, he began to run, making a zigzag course down the gravel path in the direction of the grouse. The birds lifted from the ground in a great clamor of wings.

My sister and I stood paralyzed. At first, we thought he was trying to lighten the mood, but there was something ominous in the sound and in the way his body veered. And then in a quick second, birds squawking in alarm, we saw him trip and fall, hard, body flat on the gravel. We held our breath, as you do with children in the stunned silence after a spill, waiting for them to work out a wail or rise stoically from the dust. My father did neither: He just lay there in silence, head face down in the dirt. He didn't move; he didn't even turn his head.

When we got there and stood over him, he was still making the yipping sound but it was fainter and now sounded more like a sob. Get up, we said. Dad, get up. But he wouldn't. He only rolled slowly onto his back. On his face, there were tears and bits of gravel stuck to blood. He looked past us and up to the darkening sky. Get up. Get up, we said. We waited. We waited so long that after a while my sister and I were crying too.

I don't know what he saw in the sky that night—what grief, what ghosts. But I have a pretty good idea. Stretched on my bed in my Brooklyn apartment, I looked up and tried to see it all: the lost wife and the lost house, the embarrassed daughters, and the dreams made in fields that had disappeared. I saw his self-created monsters and the disappointment of the day: an arriviste who has arrived but finds he is still the imposter and will always be one no matter how hard he tries. What I saw most clearly was a little boy flapping his wings and wanting to fly. Above me was the American story of flight and desire, ending, as it so often does, with the hero plummeting to earth. Lying there on my back, I felt the eye-opening impact. In my body, I felt the thud.

◇

"The Jolly Corner" doesn't end with the crushing confrontation but with the stillness of an autumn afternoon. It ends with a woman's tenderness. Alice Staverton, who loves the whole of Spencer Brydon, is a type in James's fiction: all-forgiving, compassionate, ironic, and gifted with a kind of eerie awareness of what the man is thinking before he thinks it himself. And she is the one able to hold the story's ambivalence in her arms. Up to this point, the story seems a condemnation of American business, but in this final scene, and in Alice's response to Brydon, the tone shifts. Cradling Brydon in her arms, she welcomes back the man she loves from his nightmare, but she also defends the ghost he has seen: "Things have happened to him," she argues, "he doesn't make shift for sight, with your charming monocle."

Most of my life I was embarrassed by my father. I secretly—or, not so secretly—longed for him to be the architect artist or the back-to-the-land farmer rather than the businessman he became. When I think of that autumn weekend, my sister and I kneeling over my father on the gravel, I like to pretend we came close to embracing him, all of him, the man he was and the man he could have been.

The day after Thanksgiving at the robber baron's estate, we checked out of the club, climbed back into my sister's reeking car, and drove to Fallingwater a few miles away. None of us mentioned the events of the previous night. We drove as if someone were chasing us. When we stepped up to Wright's house, a light snow had begun to fall. We didn't go inside at first, just ran, delirious, around its perimeter. We were revived—by the snow, by a house so different from the one we had left and so much more familiar. Energized and upright, competent again, my father stood in a patch of snow between a wall and a waterfall and stomped his feet, looking up this time not at his monsters or ghosts but at a rise of glass, wood, and steel. Except for a small cut on his cheek, there wasn't a trace of the broken man from the night before.

The Second House

4

THE HOLY LAND

I like the names attached to the places where I've lived: Atlantis, Eden, Empire, the Holy Land. My hometown, Fond du Lac, was named by French explorers to mark the southernmost point of Lake Winnebago on the map. Literally it translates as "bottom of the lake"—my own Atlantis. Or I think of Empire and Eden, the little townships around Fond du Lac where my pioneer ancestors settled, my father's forebears in Empire, my mother's in Eden. In these place-names, I can trace my roots to the very heart of the matter—Empire and Eden like two signposts at the fork in the road of Western Expansion, often pointing in the same direction. But of all the names bestowed on my past, my favorite is "the Holy Land," the term locals used to describe the rural area north of town and east of the lake where our house stood.

A network of small hamlets—St. Anna, Mt. Calvary, St. Cloud, St. Peter, Johnsburg, and Eden—each with a church and a German-language mass, the Holy Land was settled during the second half of the nineteenth century by German Catholics. They came from Bavaria and the Saarland region, from Baden-Baden and from the borders of the Black Forest. With them, they brought their recipes for sausages and potato salad, a history you might still find heaped on your paper plate at a Packer tailgater. The descendants of these settlers all went to school with me, a handful of families whose names were painted on the mailboxes you passed on the roads behind the ledge: Freund, Simon, Schmitz, Thome, Wagner, Schneider.

When I went to high school in town and people asked me where I lived, I liked to say it—"I'm from the Holy Land"; I liked the ring of the words, the nod of recognition that followed. But when I said it, I knew it wasn't true. I knew I'd be discovered. We didn't fish, and we didn't hunt. During haying season, I'd be dropped off to play in the barn lofts of my classmates—golden tunnels through which I'd crawl panting, so allergic that a father or older brother would have to abandon his tractor and drive me home, his car wheels hurling up gravel as he turned into our drive. My brother, shy and skinny and alone on the bench, tried baseball but he was a left-hander in left field wearing, we discovered later, a right-hander's glove.

And then there was the house itself. Its oddity and modernity and its position on the hill exposed us, it told you about the way we talked; it told you about the bookstore in town and the restaurants where the parents of some of my friends worked. Most of all it told you we were missing a history. The Schmitzes and Schneiders living in their white farmhouses were all related to one another, citizens of the Holy Land for generations. They belonged to a continuum. My parents seemed to have sprung from a world wholly of their own making, liberated of a history and emerging newly formed from our house like a Botticelli figure from its shell.

Or if they had a past, it was unrecognizable. People thought we came from Chicago, from out east. I had to tell them again and again that my father had grown up only a few miles away on a farm, that my great aunts were Catholic nuns living right in town at the St. Agnes convent. I impressed upon them my parents' humble beginnings, bragging about it the way some people crow over a *Mayflower* pedigree. We were, I swore, as local as they were.

But it didn't matter. We were outsiders the day my mother erected a fence to block the old snowmobile route that ran through our woods. And even if this had been forgiven—or even if my brother had suddenly exhibited a talent for sports—there were still the facts of our origins. At the time, I didn't understand how deeply imprinted the regional boundaries were. My father may have come from only a few miles away, but it wasn't the Holy

Land proper; his parents were Protestants, some of his ancestors Irish and English, and his grandparents were buried in the wrong cemetery. That my mother's family, German Catholics like the rest, came from Eden, a town at the edge of the Holy Land, made no impression since all this had happened too long ago. Her grandparents had moved to town in the late 1800s, and town was still, even in my childhood, another country. Authenticity, I had to understand, was a badge earned by staying put.

As much as I recognized our separation from Holy Land society, I never felt a separation when it came to the land. In fact, my awareness that we were not like other people only seemed to fortify my bond with the place itself. The field and the woods—especially the woods—were somehow holier and more deeply mine because of it. For a while (I was nine or ten) I lived under the conviction that nobody before had enjoyed such daily acquaintance with the hickory nuts under foot or had fingered the pocked indentations of ledge rock as lovingly, not the farmers who'd planted the apple trees on the other side of the woods, not the ancestors of any of the Holy Landers who went to school with me. During this phase I took to naming things: my tree, my rock, my path, my orchard. I believed the woods belonged to me in a way it could never have belonged to anyone else. At night I liked to stand at the edge of the woods—or even walk a little way into it—and listen to the leaves loosening in the wind and behind that another sound, what I thought must be the nocturnal rustlings of animals registering my familiar presence in their sleep.

My mother never commented on my nature-girl phase—and my father didn't seem to notice it—but it must have gotten on everybody's nerves: the dreamy diary-keeping and the thumbed copy of *Anne of Green Gables* in the glove compartment of the car and all those theatrically announced "ambles," as I'd have put it then, to the apple orchard in spring or to my favorite tree in the fall. My mother was patient. She must have figured I'd outgrow the worst of it.

And she was right. I did. But never entirely. Too many instances of adult joy can be traced back to it. I'll be parked at some gas

The southern end of the house. At the edge of the porch was the path leading into the woods. (courtesy, Susan Peters)

station off the interstate, and there at the wooded edge of the lot behind a chain link fence I'll catch sight of it: a firefly alights on the curb and then, as if beckoning me, moves deeper into trees. I'm drawn—back to a woods so black that not even the lights from the gas station can penetrate, back to a sound louder than the trucks rattling on the freeway behind me. I hear it: A wild thrashing of leaves, a reminder not so much of loss as of its opposite. Expectancy. Unknown possibility. A girl under a tree at night who looks up to a future swelling with stars.

But when it comes to that sense of proprietorship I had then—my path, my tree, my bird—it gets more complicated. On one level, a custodial relationship to place is not a bad way to get started on an education in beauty or in environmental sensitivity. By relating so personally to the landscape around me, I was learning to look closely at things. This is not—as any spiritually enlightened person will tell you—the ideal way to go about loving a thing (or a person), nor would many environmentalists argue it's the ideal way to go about saving the earth, either; too much concern over one's own trees and you risk forgetting about all the rest. But I still hold it's not a bad way to *start* loving.

I remember once standing with a friend of mine in front of a painting at a museum and overhearing a woman behind us: "It's always like this with me," she said. "I don't really pay attention unless I pretend the painting is hanging in my living room. Then I can look at it, the details." This horrified my friend, but it didn't bother me as much, at least not if I deciphered her comment as a confession that to see a thing she needed daily intimacy with it. Even my friend's complaint—"another of those types who can only decorate with beauty, domesticate it"—I could read in a more positive light. Wasn't it a domestic impulse that had first led me to wildness? Wasn't my careful raking of a web of paths in the woods an uncovering? Under mulch and bark and a green mat of moss, a colony of ants, and sometimes even a snake, Dickinson's "narrow fellow in the grass . . . unbraiding in the sun."

No, what bothers me really about this phase has less to do with my attitude toward the trees or the woods. It's my attitude toward other people that troubles me. More than anything, the sense of ownership I had then was marked by a need to exclude, the arrogance of believing nobody then—and almost nobody before or again—could know or love the woods as I did. It's an arrogance I like to think I outgrew, as I outgrew *Anne of Green Gables* and diaries that locked with a key. But sometimes I'm not sure I ever did.

When we first moved to the country, there were few other houses on the ledge. Today, the slope looks more and more like suburbia: lawns bright green and mowed in alternating golf course stripes; trees absent or pruned unnaturally (a Christmas ornament or a chocolate kiss), their branches clipped so you can't see movement, you can't see wind. Many of the houses are enormous and most are sided in variations of what seem the same color—a putty tan that aspires to something natural but can't hide the plastic underneath. Ownership is flaunted: properties once bounded by hedges or trees (or nothing) are now marked off by a fence with spikes or a row of lights that stay on all night, eclipsing the moonlight and turning the grass a frosted blue. Few of these new houses are built back into woods or against the rock, but are installed in front of it, the windows bulging like eyes, the houses screaming their supremacy, as if to say, "Look, we have a view"—as if to say, "We make no apologies for ruining yours."

I take these drives along Highway 151 and grieve over the smallest change: The absence of an old billboard that stood in a field of tall grasses all my life—it seemed rooted there—and the gas station that's taken its place. Even the road itself, whose slightest shift in terrain I knew in my feet and my hands, in the press of the brakes or the steering wheel, has changed course. One section has been diverted from the old route snug along the lake, bypassing the curve where bait shops, picnic tables, and taverns hugged the shore. In the old days to make your way from Highway 151 to another highway going to Milwaukee, you'd need to crawl along through town. Now, the highways are connected, so that a stranger passing through gets no glimpse of Main Street, no hint of the region's history. He sees the flash of a pretty lake—but where? For most people, my home is not on the map; it is the vague in-between, a word mangled by the GPS, a directive you follow and then forget.

My reactions on my trips home worry me a little. I hear myself, and I don't like how I sound. Back in the judgments of my childhood, I separate out the good from the bad and always put our house and its aesthetic on the right side of things. I click my tongue. I tick off mistakes. I sound young. Even worse, I sound depressingly old—an old snob wishing on others a patience for stoplights and the frustrations of a folded map. How did I become this person, so easily scandalized by vinyl siding? When did I start shaking my walking stick at the modern world?

The Holy Land

◇

My drive along Highway 151 is an old story. Henry James tells a version of it when, in 1904, he describes a walk up New York's Fifth Avenue in *The American Scene*. He writes (and mourns) his way from south to north, cataloging the effects of the American spirit of the "perpetually provisional." At Fourteenth Street, manufacturing lofts cast shadows on the site of his "ruthlessly suppressed birth house"; at Thirty-Fourth Street, the old brownstones have been replaced by department stores, apartment buildings, and that defining space of mobility, the American hotel; further north, near Central Park, the marble mansions of the new rich line the streets, gilded temples that will, he recognizes, soon be substituted by even larger and more lavish ones. For James, Fifth Avenue is the great boulevard of impermanence, the perfect expression of the "what goes up must come down" attitude that defines not just New York but all of America.

The gloom in these passages is familiar enough. It's the kind that seizes me when I drive along the ledge and the kind I feel whenever I look out the window of a plane—down below the suburban outskirts of every American city, fresh sod and row upon row of houses, three-thousand-square-foot behemoths born of another real estate boom. (A lover of metaphor, James might even have laughed at the names we've given them: the McMansion, the Hummer House, the Garage Mahal.)

But most striking in James's elegy for New York is the stark reminder he offers of the perils that can befall us when we are in retrospection's grip—he shows us the way nostalgia can go bad, the way it can settle into sentimentality and harden into snobbery. You see it in his shuddering over Central Park and its democratic ideals and in his wholehearted approval of that less democratic institution, the private country club; you see it in his belief that right houses have been replaced by wrong ones, and more disturbingly, you see it in his conviction that the wrong people have moved to town, not just the new rich swaggering up the avenue but the throngs of immigrants, Jews and Italians, stepping off the boat at Ellis Island. James shows us nostalgia at its xenophobic worst; observing the "gross aliens" pouring into the city, he is left with a sense of having "seen a ghost in his supposedly safe old house." Listen and you'll hear under the elitist prose, the squeak of a child woken to a nightmare, one where vistas transform into vacant lots, dirty boots stomp in the nursery, and strangers have taken possession of the house.

Yet there is one moment in *The American Scene* when James doubts himself. It is the moment when he asks the question that can unsettle any nostalgic, especially one with a preservationist bent. Aren't all of us who believe in an authentic home and in ourselves as the authentic natives ignoring the facts of our own arrival? Don't we all have our ghosts in the supposedly safe old house? "Which is *not* the alien," he asks, "and where does one put a finger on the dividing line, or, for that matter, 'spot' and identify any particular phase of the conversion, any one of its successive moments?" What James doesn't say—but implies—is that where we mark the dividing line between right places and wrong ones, between those who belong and those who don't, is with ourselves—our stories, our consecrated spots.

In a passage on Thoreau and his last days at Walden, the philosopher Stanley Cavell writes that when it was time, Thoreau left Walden "without nostalgia, without a disabling elegiacism." Nostalgia, Cavell explains, "is an inability to open the past to the future, as if the strangers who will replace you will never find what you have found." In my own refusal to give all those strangers of the future—all those inhabitants of the new houses on the ledge—an authentic connection to the places of my childhood, I recognize my own disabling tendencies: I want to lock the place inside my private past.

But there is another danger as well. If I've denied entrance to the strangers of the future, haven't I also denied entrance to the strangers of the past, those who had come before me? In nostalgia, we can grow forgetful. Dreaming the primacy of our own pasts, we don't always people the void predating our arrival or plant in our minds the trees that came before us, trees we never believed existed because we weren't around to see them planted or to see them fall. We freeze a place in time and forget that once we were the villains in the story. The neighborhood in Brooklyn where I live now was, when I moved there in the late nineties, in the throes of gentrification. Only weeks after moving in I felt resentment, as so many interlopers do, at others doing the same.

<>

There is a scene in the novel *Lucy* by the Antiguan writer Jamaica Kincaid that always reads as a finger pointing straight at me—or more accurately, pointing at all of us middle-class Americans holding tight to memories of our first places, our consecrated spots. Lucy, a young Caribbean immigrant, has moved to America to work as an au pair. Her relationship to her new employer, Mariah, is complicated, swinging between affection and a cynicism that can sometimes erupt into rage. On one hand, Mariah appears to Lucy like some golden princess out of a fairy tale; Mariah is generous, even at times playing the role of surrogate mother. She tries to help the girl and tries to educate her. She talks to her about feminism and about Freud. When Mariah invites Lucy to the park to see daffodils for the first time—intended as a gesture of kindness—Lucy is infuriated and tries to explain that the flowers remind her that as a child at her British-run school back in Antigua she'd been forced to memorize a poem (Wordsworth's "I Wandered Lonely as a Cloud") about these daffodils, flowers she'd never actually seen. Lucy's reaction is a charge against the colonizing practices of the British-run schools she attended, but it's also an indictment of Mariah. From her cocoon of privilege, Mariah obliviously assumes that everyone is like her, that everyone will love what she does, an assumption that shows her to be—however unwittingly—a colonizer in her own right.

When I teach the novel (or really any of Kincaid's works), my students, mostly white and middle class themselves, either get very quiet and stony faced, or they fidget in their chairs. "It's as if," one said, "everything I like about myself is turned inside out." They recognize themselves in Mariah—and I can't help but think Kincaid assumes many of her readers will do the same—and they understand the question the novel is asking of them: What happens when the middle-class virtues and privileges (an education in Freud and feminism, a desire for a nice house and nice kids, even the love of nature) are observed from the perspective of the excluded outsider? What assumptions get overturned? Asking this question is the point, one of the reasons I teach the novel. We're meant to squirm at the questions—and then we're meant to think about them.

The scene that really gets me, though, happens at Mariah's country house on the Great Lakes. The house has belonged to Mariah's family for generations. She loves the place as passionately as she loves daffodils, and she wants Lucy to love it as well, wants "everybody to enjoy the house, all of its nooks and crannies, all its sweet smells, all its charms, just the way she has done as a child." Lucy finds Mariah's attachment puzzling, but what puzzles her most of all is Mariah's outraged reaction to "what seemed the destruction of the surrounding countryside." Mariah and her friends give money to preservationist organizations and even hope to someday write a book on the "vanishing things." Lucy reacts to all this with a question, the same question really that Henry James asks about his own attachments to Fifth Avenue:

> Many houses had been built on what they said used to be farmland. Mariah showed me a place that had been an open meadow, a place where as a girl she went looking for robin's eggs and picking wildflowers. She moaned against this vanishing idyll so loudly that Louisa, who was just at the age where if you are a girl you turn against your mother, said, "Well, what used to be here before this house we are living in was built?" It was a question I had wanted to ask, but I couldn't bear to see the hurt such a question would bring to Mariah's face.

The Holy Land

The farm we looked out at every day from our house belonged to one of the reigning families of the Holy Land, the Schneiders. They were good neighbors, and over the years they looked out for us. Betty, one of the teenage daughters, saved me from drowning in a neighbor's pool. Mr. Schneider acted as mediator after that first misstep in local relations—the barbed wire strung across the snowmobile trail. And it was Ed Schneider, a boy my age, who once stepped up from the back of the school bus to gallantly intercept my new pink Kotex purse as it was flung from boy to boy over my head.

The Schneider kids, though, were never exactly friends. They were beyond us—wilder, older seeming. At school we heard about their parties: the famous rope swing that hung from the barn ceiling and lifted you through the open doors to deposit you, drunk, in a back pond and the rumors that the police sent out special signals on those Saturday nights alerting the nearby patrol cars to be on guard. We observed these parties firsthand from our house up above—all night the barn door blazing music and light, and cars wheeling in and out of the drive.

But what had made them "other" was not their purported wildness so much as their authenticity. They were exotic because they were the real thing. Mr. Schneider you saw in all the right places: on the beach road hauling his ice shanty down to the lake and drinking an old-fashioned at the bar before a Friday night fish fry. Mrs. Schneider caught one of the biggest sturgeons on record and won the women's softball championship three years in a row. When I envisioned her dressing a deer, she did it absentmindedly, effortlessly, the way other mothers might peel a potato and drop it into a bowl. The difference between us was as different as our houses. When the older Schneider girls, Nancy and Betty, came to babysit for us, they were curious but uneasy. All that glass and the absence of partitions disoriented them. When they stayed with us, we ate our TV dinners in the shelter of the little bedrooms in the back, all of us lined up on a single bed against the wall.

As I got older, these differences no longer seemed to matter. In my late twenties, I connected again with the Schneiders. Betty and I became close friends. One summer, I came home to live with my mother and stepfather for a month, and saw her nearly every day. By then, the house on the ledge had long since been sold, and "back home" was now a mile away, a white painted cottage on the lake my mom had purchased after her divorce. This house had dormer windows facing Lake Winnebago and a tiny kitchen garden planted in well-tended symmetrical rows, a rebound acquisition I liked to call it, in every way opposite from the house my mother had loved the last time around.

Connecting again with Betty surprised me a little. In her company, I had suddenly become the native I had always yearned to be. She liked to talk about our shared past. The quirks of every one of our school bus drivers, the tiny school we'd both attended through the third grade, and the inevitable rotation of taverns we visited after we turned eighteen. Whether you liked to drink or not, bars served as the center of any teenager's life in the Holy Land. Every weekend, a drive on icy country roads between St. Peter and Johnsburg to a little wooden shack appearing over the rise on a hill, a Schlitz sign creaking in the wind. Inside, under a haze of smoke, you learned how to play pool and how to cock a hip (you hoped alluringly) at the jukebox.

I liked the reminiscing, but still I was surprised by it. By then I'd lived in New York City for over ten years and should have seemed even more of an outsider than before. It occurred to me that the requirements for authenticity had changed, no longer defined by staying put, but by a hunger for shared memory. The presence of so many new houses meant the old rules no longer applied. Of course, lots of people were still around who could talk to Betty about those early days, but it was as if my memories seemed more pure because they had not been altered by the new taverns or been crowded out by all the new people who had since moved out to the ledge. In leaving I'd frozen the Holy Land in time.

And then there was a simple fact: for years, our house had been a daily feature of Betty's view, the lights behind trees up on the ledge as much a fixture of her childhood as the square of a white farmhouse below had been a constant in mine.

The friendship with Betty also meant that the mythology I'd created as a child—the wild parties, the glamour of a barn door open to everyone but me—required revision as well. I went to a party in the barn that summer, beer and a few people in a circle of lawn chairs. It was tamer than I imagined—and it was better than I imagined. That day they'd held a garage sale in the barn—tables mounded with Holy Land effects: costume jewelry in a button tin, tea towels, and a milking stool I took home with me to New York and now use as a three-legged stand for a ficus plant.

From a rack against a wall, someone started pulling out dresses and old men's suits and then trying them on—spontaneously, a costume party. The famous rope swing hung from the central rafter, and we moved the tables to the side of the barn so that we could each, dressed in a polyester pantsuit or a Sunday hat, take a turn. When it was mine, I remember floating—the swing extending out one door toward the lake, and out the other toward the highway and the ledge up above. Through one door, I saw the familiar blue of Lake Winnebago, but closer now, telescoped, enlarged. Through the other door, I swung in the opposite direction and looked up. My past tilted. I saw our house as I'd never really seen it before, from a neighbor's point of view. It was dusk, the sun setting over the lake and the moon just coming up. From some old speakers in the hayloft, Neil Young was singing "Helpless," his elegy to the Canadian town where he'd grown up. Soaring from view to view, from lake to our house up above, I heard what I saw:

> In my mind I still need a place to go
> All my changes were there.
> Blue, blue windows behind the stars,
> Yellow moon on the rise

After everybody left, Betty and I sat on the lawn in front of the barn and looked up at the moon, a sickle over the ledge, over our old house. Betty told me about how much she'd always liked watching the moon from where we were sitting, and then she revealed something I had once known but had somehow completely forgotten. How I could have done this I cannot say.

Before my parents bought the twenty-three acres on the ledge, it had belonged to the Schneiders for three generations. That night Betty told me about how as a little girl—she was nine or ten, the same age I was when I haunted our woods—she had spent long afternoons there. It was her secret spot, where she'd go to be alone. She told me how she hated the thought of us, hated the trucks that came to dig up our driveway along the field, hated the hole in the earth. Secretly, at night, after all the construction workers had left, she would walk up the hill to pull up the pink flags, throw tin cans in the gravel pits, and stomp on the mounds of dug-up earth. And then, after we moved in, she hated it for a little longer—our house now in contest with the moon, a light where before there had been just a line of trees, a jagged outline she had known by heart.

During the month I spent living with my mother and stepfather I caught wind of a rumor. Gracie, the woman from Chicago who now owned our house, was thinking of selling it. The rumor turned out not to be true, but the next time Gracie came up for a visit, I casually—or at least I tried to sound casual—mentioned that if she ever wanted to unload it to let us know. When I mentioned the idea to my brother and sister, they reminded me that not only could we not afford it but that the prospect of returning to the house for real, even for a vacation, was impractical, even slightly creepy. Where would we sleep? Our bedrooms were too small for a couple, and when and if we married, would we bring our spouses and move into our parents' room?

My sister reminded me of an old anxiety of hers. As children we rarely had friends our age over to visit and played mostly with one another. It was like the Brontës, she used to say—the secret games, the secret languages—and she half-jokingly worried we'd end up unable to live with anyone else. We'd end our days hiding in that house, like something out of the movie *Grey Gardens* or like the elderly sisters and brothers we heard about who still lived together in some of the farmhouses nearby. There we'd be: eighty years old, spiteful, still vying for the bathroom and the remote control, still sleeping in our single beds.

Even if living there again was too weird a possibility, I still wanted to find a way to keep the house from being demolished, the field from being divided up. Certain this would happen, I tried to think of something, even proposed to my brother we try to buy it and turn the house into a nature center. I pictured display cases in the back bedrooms. Under glass, bird feathers and fossil remains. Paths through the woods with a little stand as you entered for holding the map.

But when I mentioned this business about "unloading" to Gracie, she just laughed. "I'm not selling," she said. "And it's funny you should ask. Just got a call from the Schneiders asking me to promise if I ever did sell it, they'd be the first people I'd call." For a second I heard inside my head a child's voice: insistent, greedy. But it's ours! Hadn't the fact of our building the house made it so? And in that instant it didn't matter that Betty had mourned our arrival, that her father had once sold the land to us. It didn't matter that they had come first.

Just last year I had another conversation with Gracie on the phone. She'd been remodeling the house, and I'd driven up the gravel drive to take a look. The outside seemed much the same, but I'd heard that inside they'd ripped out the old carpeting, the unfinished wooden floors, and put in Zebra wood. They were aiming, my mother told me, for a Japanese effect. As I was talking—a compliment on how nice it all looked—I found myself stumbling over words:

"I just saw our house," I said. And then I tried to save it. "*The* house I mean . . . No, I mean *your* house." There was a long pause. Who knows what it signaled. Frustration? Pity? When she finally spoke, her voice was gentle but firm: "My house," she said. "Mine."

◇

In the sixth grade I was invited to a party at a house out in the country east of town. The house belonged to a girl named Robyn, the most popular girl in my grade, and it sat in the fold of a valley with a creek running down the middle. Soon after that party I learned the word *fecund* in an English class and immediately thought of Robyn's fields. I don't remember much about the house itself except that it was newly built, impressive, and seemed commensurate with Robyn's feathered hair and golden skin. I do remember the landscape. Behind the house were horse stables, a separate cottage for a French grandmother, and a swimming pool sunk into a meadow. At the edge of the pool, red-winged blackbirds clung to spikes of prairie grass.

To me the place was a marvel, an enchanted landscape. Nothing, not the half-cooked pepperoni pizza or the squealing twelve-year-old girls or even the soundtrack of the movie that played over and over all afternoon ("Grease is the time, is the place, is the motion"), could convince me I hadn't landed in some exotic elsewhere. A chateau. The South of France. All day I waited for the French grandmother to join us, expecting a swim cap with flowers, a supple European dive.

At dusk I heard the car horn outside and came out trailing my wet towel. My father was waiting for me in the car. This was a surprise since he rarely picked us up, and when he did he never came on time. I saw him step out of the car and then into the field bordering the driveway. I could see he was in a trespassing mood, and I worried. But he didn't do what I expected—didn't peer in the windows or clomp through the shrubbery or frighten the mysterious grandmother in her deck chair.

When I got closer, he began pointing. He pointed behind him. "This is Artesian Road," he said. "The road where I grew up." He pointed up the hill to where the one-room school had been and next to it the Peters farm where his mother, a sixteen-year-old country schoolteacher, had boarded one year and where she met my grandfather Reinhold. He pointed in the other direction

The Holy Land　　　　85

to the house where he had grown up and then past it to the rise of a hill. "Back there," he said, "was my grandparents Keys's house." And then he pointed to Robyn's house and her fecund fields: "This land was ours once," he said. "All part of my grandfather's farm. I used to ride horses here."

I hadn't realized any of this, and at first I wasn't entirely pleased to lose the South of France and see it replaced by another kind of elsewhere: my father's ordinary past. But even then I grasped the significance—someone had built a house on my father's consecrated spot. I wondered if he might cry and was prepared to accept an act of trespass since this time it might be justified. But he didn't cry or walk up to the house. He just turned to me and offered up another of the developer's refrains. This time it wasn't "someone's going to do it and I'll do it better" but the other phrase he relied on: "Well," he said, "people have to live somewhere." And then he got back in the car, slamming the door a little harder than usual. On the way up Artesian Road he slowed in front of a stone house next to the ruins of a crumbling silo. Once a showplace with barns and stables and four hundred acres of fields, the farm was now just a house on a half-acre with a boarded-up sunroom and fifty windows that looked as if they hadn't been washed in years.

My father was a developer. When it came to matters of place, he was never a consistent nostalgic. My sister used to say that he was the most—and the least—sentimental man she'd ever met.

On the day his grandfather Keys's farm was sold, my father remembered an uncle or cousin "pitchforking" all the family photograph albums out one of the house's fifty windows, then loading them onto a truck and carting them away to an auction house. He could never get over this betrayal and talked about it every time he came back to Wisconsin for a visit. How could they do it? Worst of all, how could he have let it happen? For years I imagined myself sifting through a box at the Chelsea Flea Market in Manhattan and coming across those photographs of my father's people. I saw what I'd never seen, only heard about. A daguerreotype of a man in a bearskin coat. Giant elms, long since stricken, shading a family picnic. The beloved hired hand, his face shadowed by a tipped hat. And a white-haired woman posing beside a hollyhock. My great-grandmother Keys was famous for her hollyhocks. Not a dead black leaf, they said. Taller than a tree.

I envisioned delivering these photographs to him, meeting him at some restaurant and calmly passing an envelope across the table. I saw his face as he opened it.

Years later my great-aunt Elizabeth handed over a box of photographs and a collection of hand-tinted postcards. I called my father in Minnesota where he was working at the time and listened to his excitement over the phone. Aunt Elizabeth's pictures belonged to the Peters side of the family; these were not the photographs he'd been looking for. Still, it was something.

The next day I drove across Wisconsin with a cardboard box in the back of my car. When I got there, he was impatient enough to meet me in the parking lot, but I noticed that once we brought them into the hotel and he began leafing through the pictures, he hardly paused long enough to read the penciled caption at the bottom of a photo. He sat on the bed and tossed them one by one across to me as if we were playing a game of Old Maid. He was distracted—business trouble. He was tired. Before long he was asleep, one arm nearly crushing the pile of pictures next to him on the bed. Later when I asked what he'd done with the box, he didn't seem to remember, and I was sure he'd forgotten it at the hotel or left it spinning around the carousel at the airport, a lone parcel that nobody bothered ever to come back and claim.

In those years when I wandered the woods, there was one population I did welcome into my private bower. These were the first people, the "real natives." Anyone from the present and anyone from the recent past, I excluded, but the further back I went, it became easier to imagine someone else following the same trail along the ledge. I had, however, only the most indistinct notion of who these authentic inhabitants actually might be. A French name for the town, the Native American name for the lake, and a fourth grade history lesson had conjured for me a violent and romantic history: beaver pelts dripping from canoes, voyageurs gliding past.

Later, I read a biography of the Danish writer Isak Dinesen, but got stuck on the part where Dinesen's father, Wilhelm, sets out for the American wilderness. He lives for a year in the Wisconsin Territory with Chief Oshkosh and his tribe, the Menominees. Oshkosh, a town I associated with torturous hours at the orthodontist and baby overalls with snaps, was across the lake and had been named for the chief. I could see the lights from our lawn. For a moment I looked up from the page to a changed view, the glow across the lake a journey beyond—to woodland campfires, Danish manor houses, Meryl Streep in a cracked voice speaking the opening lines of a movie I loved. "I had a farm in Africa."

Growing up, my history was a jumble: a mess of disconnected references, vague images of Pocahontas and a French missionary portaging a path beneath the ledge. But as I grew a little older, my understanding of history improved—although not by much—and with more clarification there came a shift in identification. When I first started learning local history in school, I connected less with the natives on the shores and more with the voyageurs and missionaries stepping from their boats, a perspective I realize now that the majority of white American schoolchildren (and adults) have probably shared for hundreds of years. But it was the seventies, a time when some efforts were being taken to rewrite the history books and to change our point of view. Once this happened, my perspective reversed, and over time nostalgia swelled into outrage.

Down one of the lake roads nearby was Camp Shaganapi, an abandoned Boy Scout camp with a crescent of sandy beach and a wild woods so beautiful that a slew of developers had coveted it for years. They were thwarted, one by one, as yet another burial site was discovered along the shore. In school we learned about the Ho-Chunk, sometimes called the Winnebago, and the Menominees whose land covered much of eastern Wisconsin, from Winnebago to Door County up to Green Bay. The Menominees had built their wigwams all along the ledge, often positioned like our house, just beneath the bluff. We learned about the mound builders, early natives who had created those enormous effigy mounds in the shape of animals along the top of the ledge, a sign, my teacher said, that they revered the ledge as sacred. Holy Land.

And then there were the names of the towns. Not far from all those German settlements—St. Peter, Marytown, St. Anna—was a string of villages along the lake that had first been gathering places for Native Americans and still bore names that told you so. I learned that Pipe and Calumetville, towns I knew as nothing more than a few houses on the side of the highway, had been named for the stone pipe the Menominees used. (*Calumet* is the French word for a long-stemmed tobacco pipe.) Recently, I saw that the author of my old WPA guide to Wisconsin even seemed to know what went in those pipes: "Hudson Bay plug tobacco, sumac leaves, and aromatic red osier bark." In Calumetville, the Menominee chief Little Wave had once established a village and I tried to picture it, a clearing in place of the tavern and gas station that stand there now, a forest where fields now slope to the lake.

But I remember experiencing my greatest excitement—and confusion—the day our teacher explained the origins of the two little villages north of us on the highway, Brothertown and Stockbridge. Two Native American tribes had come to Wisconsin much later, in the 1830s, from New York. The Brothertown tribe, descended from the Pequot, the Mohegan, the Narragansett, and the Montauk, were Christianized Indians who had banded together while living on lands they were deeded in upstate New York near the Oneida nation. The Stockbridge Indians were Mohicans, a people who once had called all of the Hudson Valley home, but by the end of the seventeenth century were pushed out. They lived for years together in Stockbridge, Massachusetts, where they too became Christians but then were forced north to Oneida land, not far from the Brothertown tribe. And then, in the 1830s, both groups were forced west again. In the Wisconsin Territory, they purchased land from the Menominees and moved to the eastern shore of Lake Winnebago.

It was a confusing story for a child (or an adult). It was also thrilling. I'd read James Fenimore Cooper's *The Last of the Mohicans* that year, and although I didn't really like the novel (or entirely understand it), I was excited to discover that the last of the Mohicans had not, as Cooper's novel told me, been killed while holding up a drooping damsel at the edge of a cliff, but had once lived down below on the shores of the lake. Cooper had gotten it wrong. While he sets his story accurately in Mohican territory, Cooper based his characters and plot on a different tribe, the Mohegans. From the woods I looked down and pictured it: the last of the Mohicans revived and standing, spearing a sturgeon somewhere out on a frozen lake; the limp Cora, Cooper's heroine, now upright and waiting for him on shore.

But as always, my romantic visualizations would need revising. I later learned that the Stockbridge Mohicans had been embroiled in a land dispute with the Menominees once they arrived in Wisconsin. The Menominees claimed that when they agreed to sell the land to the Stockbridge and Brothertown Indians, they had done so under an assumption the land would be shared; there would be no ownership, no division of land, no property boundaries at all. No "me" or "mine" or "I came first." But having endured so many property disputes back east, the New York tribes had learned that "good fences make good neighbors" and settled for a smaller parcel of land they could call their own.

In the end, property lines didn't matter. Almost as soon as the Stockbridge tribe arrived, white settlers discovered that the land between Lake Michigan and Lake Winnebago was a fertile paradise. The Brothertown and Stockbridge would be sent farther west again. When some refused, they were offered citizenship and the chance to own their property on an individual basis, but that meant revoking their tribal status. Those who stayed ended up struggling and sold their land, and the rest, along with the

Menominees, moved farther north to a reservation west of Green Bay.

The more I learned about Native American history in school, the more clearly I understood that the fate of the Mohicans and the Menominee—forced migration, a constant loss of homeland—was repeated across the country, tribe by tribe. I remember the sorrow at hearing all this, and I remember how I'd come home from school at night and rail at the dinner table about all "those people"—the land speculators who'd taken the Menominee and Stockbridge land, those farmers who'd come to cut the trees, come to unearth arrowheads and throw them in the rock pile. And then, on the bus home one day, looking out at the fields in the rain, it hit me just as it had hit me that day with Betty on the lawn. "Those people" were mine.

A few years ago I came across a translation of an old German book. Published in the late 1840s, the book was written by a German schoolteacher, Dr. Carl de Haas, and it was called *Nordamerika, Wisconsin, Calumet: Winke für Auswanderer*, later translated from the German as *North America, Wisconsin: Hints for Emigrants*. I'd heard about the book and knew that during the height of German immigration between the 1850s and the 1890s the popularity of *Nordamerika* accounted for a flood of Germans moving to Wisconsin. De Haas had bought forty acres near Calumetville, the little town down the road from us, the same little town where the Menominee chief Little Wave had once lived and where he filled his pipe with sumac and red osier leaves.

I couldn't get over it. It seemed impossible to me that surges of people had been called to that little juncture in the road—*Calumet* is even included in the original book title—now just a scattering of houses and a tavern where on Sundays my mother and stepfather go to watch Packer games and eat Sunday brunch. I wondered if my German ancestors had read *Nordamerika*. It seemed probable. All I knew about my father's forebears in

Germany was their poverty: A story about how they'd dined by emptying sacks of boiled potatoes straight onto the table and then bit into them like apples. Or the story about Anna Peters, a great-great-grandmother who on her passage to America lost her husband—he was buried at sea—and how when she arrived in Wisconsin, a widow with a baby, there was nobody waiting to meet her.

Back in Germany had Anna read *Nordamerika*? And if she had, what did it tell her to expect? In an old New York German newspaper, I found a report of someone who had read the book and been inspired to leave Germany because of it. The article had been written in 1900, more than fifty years after the book's first printing. The author, Rudolf Puchner, remembers how on reading *Nordamerika* for the first time, he "admired it, just as the wise men from the East admired the star above them to show them the way to the Holy Land." And he remembers that on the ship across to America he sat facing the setting sun and tried to picture Wisconsin. What he saw in his imagination came, he claimed, straight out of De Haas's descriptions: "the majestic calmness of the virgin forest" and the "superb" Menominee slipping through a thicket; the "glimmering waves of lake Winnebago" and the "stag at dawn" approaching "the lake to drink the clear water"; "gay-colored dots of wild duck gliding to the distant shore."

It's a romantic portrayal and not an entirely accurate one. Winnebago's waters are never clear; in fact, in the Algonquin language the name *Winnebago* means "stinky water." The lake is so shallow it glazes over with a layer of algae for a month in the summer. And by the time Anna Peters or Rudolph Puchner had arrived in Wisconsin, most of the Menominees were already on their way into exile—to the reservations farther west or to the one near Green Bay, a sliver of what had once been a vast territory.

What's also odd about the passage is that Puchner's dreamy depiction of eastern Wisconsin doesn't reflect the tone or content of De Haas's book. De Haas remarks on the attractions of the area, but he doesn't wax poetic. *Nordamerika* is a practical guide: the proper cutting of those virgin forests and the kind of timber to use on a barn, the price of a stove in Milwaukee compared with one in Fond du Lac, the quality of the soil and the working of a plow. My favorite passage is the Calumet schoolteacher's advice on marriage: Should the immigrant arrive single, he must marry quickly. This, he promises, is easily done in America; it can happen in a day. Just walk to the wharf in Milwaukee and from the line of immigrants stepping off the steamer, select a pretty girl.

De Haas's *Nordamerika* was written for and about settlers. Its aim may have been to present a picture of Eden, but more than this it was intended to explain how to gain dominion over Eden. In De Haas's accounts, there are no stags at dawn. And no warriors emerging from thickets. Those superb Menominees are barely talked about: De Haas assures his readers that the few one encounters are "shy and timid." They wear paint on their face. That's about it. The Brothertown Indians who live just down the road are by contrast "a civilized people, Christians." He notes that they have lost their native language, a detail that in its noncommittal flatness almost reads to me as approval.

Puchner's rhapsodic take on De Haas's text, his transformation of an informative guide into a tale of untouched paradise, might be nothing more than rhetoric, the nineteenth-century writer giving his readers what they expect: lofty diction, a flourish or two. But to me it reads as something else. Misreading (or misremembering) *Nordamerika*, Puchner recalls one of the original impulses that sent him to America in the first place—Eden—and it reveals a longing for the idyllic past. By the time Puchner was writing his recollections in 1900, eastern Wisconsin had already been altered by settlement. Wilderness was gone.

Reading Puchner's description of the Holy Land, I can't help but think of those walks I used to take in the woods. My ambles. The search for a wilderness pure, nobody there but the "majestic calmness" of the forest, and the only person invited to join me the true native, a mound builder emerging from behind a tree. I think of my drives along Highway 151—how I can't help but hold my hand up to hide the signs of occupation, how I squint to see the lake and the woods as they once might have been. The last time I was home I did something I'd never done before. In sacrilege to a fierce and lifelong attachment, I lifted a hand to hide our house— Gracie's house. It was a brief impulse, unconscious, but in that instant, in a quick black blur, "me" and "mine" were gone.

Other than my mother's house on the lake, the only place in the Holy Land I visit regularly now when I go back to Wisconsin is a farmhouse a quarter of a mile down the highway from our place up on the ledge. The house belonged to Ann Hanson, a painter, photographer, and self-trained landscape architect who had mentored my parents when they first moved out to the ledge in 1971. She was the person who introduced my mother to the work of the landscape designer Jens Jensen, and the person my father hired to create the little rock gardens bordering his housing developments in town. Ann and my mother were close friends, linked by curiosity and a compulsion to arrange a view. Looking out at a garden, they cocked their heads, studied it as if they were holding up a painting at arm's length. Plants were just another palette: colors lifted with a shovel, the yellow dahlias against the barn dug out in May and replaced by the purple monarda in July.

In the thirties she had studied at the Art Students League in New York, and after the war she and her husband, Fred, a science teacher at the high school in town, bought an old farm along Highway 151 on the other side of the apple orchard. A hillside with a creek meandering down from the pasture and an old barn, weathered to just the perfect gray. They raised four children there, and over the next sixty years, transformed the beautiful property on the hill into their own Clearing: curved paths, a stone gardening shed, and perennial rock gardens climbing the hill. When they bought the farm, the house, a traditional white rectangle, asserted its angular uprightness against the curve of the hill. By removing a floor, they lowered the structure so that it would settle into the hill. They painted the house a dark red, the color of red osier dogwood, tended to the ancient trees already there, and planted so many new trees that now, seventy years later, when you drive along Highway 151, past the clipped lawns of housing developments, you are surprised by a blur of forest, a shock of natural disorder—wildness achieved by painstaking design. Even the inside of the house reads as a rejection of affectedness or excess. Until she died at ninety-seven, Ann could still walk you through the house and tell you the origins of every board on the floor yanked from a barn or rescued from the old beams of the attic.

Ann was tall—her neck and shoulders made you think of Georgia O'Keeffe, her profile of Katharine Hepburn—and she was gifted at nearly everything, including the art of slowing time. As children we'd walk to the Hansons' through the woods, then across the apple orchard and down along her creek in the back pasture and find Ann somewhere in the garden on her knees. Dusting off dirt, she'd lead us on her own version of the house tour, first to the pond, where she'd take twenty minutes educating you on how to look at the interior fold of a lily or explaining the novelty of one of Fred's benches built to encircle a tree. She did not speak to you as a child or seem to register that you were one. She talked—and this confused me—as if plants and trees might matter more than people.

Ann's opinions were strong, so strong that sometimes after talking to her, you couldn't remember what your own had been— wiped out by the force of her conviction. My sister and I used to bring our boyfriends for Ann's inspection, a necessary and always nerve-wracking ritual since we knew that these men, most of them East Coasters, were likely to fall short, especially when it came to a sympathy for vegetation. There was Jim, the man my sister later married, who made the mistake of confusing a fir and a spruce. Or there was my friend Tim, who became so close to Ann that for years they kept up a lively correspondence, but on first meeting was summarily rebuked: "If you care so much about plants," she said, aiming her cane for the toe of his boot, "then why are you standing on one?"

Sometimes, though, Ann confused me, especially when we started talking about all the changes happening to the Holy Land.

She didn't approve, any more than I did, of the pseudo-estates with their fences and floodlights, their lawns fertilized to an emerald perfection. The runoff from those lawns left a worrying layer of bright green scum on her pond. Like me, she preferred the old apple orchard across the road to the housing development that had taken its place. But there was a limit to this kind of conversation—and before long she'd change the subject, draw me to the window to look at a tamarack changing colors or below it, a bird investigating the gravel path. Once, sitting in her bay window, I asked her about the highway down below. It ran so close to her house that you couldn't hear the water from the stream under the rumble of the passing trucks. Widened in the fifties, the highway had once been just a country road with hardly any traffic. How did you feel, I asked, when they built the highway? "I cried for a week," Ann said. She gave me a look, almost of reproach. "And then I stopped." It wasn't that she was resigned to the development of the Holy Land, but she seemed to find nostalgia a dangerous business. She was in her nineties. Time was precious. Why waste it on the past?

On one of my last visits, I found Ann waiting for me at the front door. She'd hung a camera around her neck and wound the strap of her walking stick to her wrist. "I have a project," she told me, "and need your help." All week she'd been studying a branch on an old tree at the top of a hill in her meadow, and had been waiting for someone to help her photograph it. I would support her up the hill and hold the camera steady. We took our time, me on one side, the cane on the other. Once we made it to the top, she was just as slow about setting up her photograph. She needed to get it right, she explained, because she had only one shot left on her roll of film. From different angles she framed the branch with her hands—thumbs touching, forefingers in the air to form a half square. Before pressing the shutter, she asked me to hold her elbow steady so her hand would not tremble.

I read that afternoon as a message, a hint about how in the future I might train myself to see. Those unsteady hands held up not to block out the built landscape, but to frame and focus the beauty around it. On the way back to the house, we stopped at the crest of a lower hill, the familiar view of highway and field and lake below. Ann pointed to a grove of trees down near the lake. "There was hardly a tree down there when we first came here. Bare earth. In some ways this view is wilder than it used to be—and even more beautiful." She cocked her head in the direction of our old house. "Not so long ago, even your woods was once just a field of dug-up stumps, you know. Look at it now." She didn't have to say anything else. Here was another message, and I heard it. Be wary of locking the history of the Holy Land (and the history of America) into too simple a march of doom, too straight a descent—from the wildness of the Menominees to the ugliness of the three-car garage. My eye, so alert to every mark (or mar) on the landscape, had missed seeing the improvements: the lawns returning to prairie grass, the wildflowers left to spread along the highway down below, and the trees growing where before there had been nothing but tired overtilled earth.

5

Leaving

I

Fifteen years ago I was teaching a night class at a community college in the Bronx. It was a remedial composition course. Most of my students were immigrants and had been in America only a year or two, yet already the first flush of anticipation had paled, the dream hard to conjure up. Taxi drivers and hotel maids and short order cooks, they worked all day and came to my class so weary that I usually let them break for a ten-minute nap.

One evening we were all so tired I couldn't think of what to do—it was the "art of description" unit—and I ended with a personal essay assignment: "Describe the house of your dreams. Be specific." It was not an inspiring assignment, but the results were magic. Fluency. Transitions. That quality I'd been harping on all semester—detail. It was as if for years, they had lain awake at night imagining the exact color of a wall, the shape of a swimming pool.

Their enthusiasm for the topic shouldn't have surprised me. Writing about their dream houses they were reviving a fantasy that had begun to fade, coloring it in, giving it shape, organizing it into hallways and rooms, turrets and gardens, a three-car garage. But while I may have been happy with the results of their essay, I wished I hadn't assigned it. I didn't like it that I might be encouraging false hopes. I didn't like to see them disappointed.

Some of those students would follow me the next semester to the American literature survey I was teaching, and I thought of all the books they'd read there, all the fictional houses they'd be introduced to, and how none of them ever seemed to end well. Think of Lily Bart in Edith Wharton's *House of Mirth* whose marriage quest is never about the man and always about the drawing room she might someday acquire through him. She ends alone in a tiny room in a dingy boardinghouse. Or there's Gatsby, who gets his mansion, his glittering showplace, but ends floating dead in his swimming pool. Or Swede Levov in *American Pastoral* whose old stone house in the waspy New Jersey countryside won't end in happy-ever-after but in the loss of a child, a divorce, and a For Sale sign on the lawn. It's hard not to be cynical about dream houses. It's hard not to see them, like Silas Lapham's house on Beacon Street, going up in smoke.

If I had to date my own knowledge of an ending—my sense that our house would not be mine forever—I would choose an autumn Saturday in 1979, a day that began in conflagration and ended with a poem. I was thirteen.

Every year we rented the field between our house and the highway to farmers. Some years they planted alfalfa or corn. I even remember a late summer of sunflowers. But usually they planted hay. On that Saturday, most of the hay had already been baled and carted away, but there were six or seven cylindrical bales, taller than I was, still clustered at the corner of the field. That morning my father had walked to the middle of the field and lit a match. Restless, bored, as he often was on weekends at home, he'd set out to burn the last traces of grass. He had the look—the manic look. At breakfast, there'd been an argument. "It's too windy," my mother said. My father ignored her. "Don't I know what I'm doing? Didn't I grow up on a farm?"

My sister, brother, and I climbed a bale in the corner of the field, and for a while we watched him—the excitement in his body, the way he bent at the knee as he lit the grass, the gold underfoot turning black. But after a while we turned away toward the woods, distracted by our own autumn high: the stretch in our legs as we jumped between bales, the smoke in the air and maples half green, half a flaming red. Somewhere in the distance we could hear the whining of a chain saw. And so we didn't notice it at first—how our hair whipped against our faces, how the wind had picked up.

We turned only when we heard her, my mother, yelling. Then we saw the fire, out of control and heading for the bales, heading for us. We couldn't hear what my mother was saying, but we saw what she foresaw: bales taken one by one, a burst, a roar, and us caught inside. I remember our leap in unison to the ground, and then the run to the house. She met us at the door, then disappeared inside to call the fire department, while we stood on the lawn under the oaks and watched: below, our father in unfamiliar contortions, stomping, whacking at the grass with an old broom.

Then sirens and a wall of fire engines along the highway, and from them figures emerging, volunteer firemen who'd had to abandon their chain saws, their rakes and storm windows, who'd had their Saturdays stolen by a neighbor foolish enough to burn his field on a day like this one, a neighbor they never would see as a farmer's son, never see as one of them, especially not after this. He was a farm boy who no longer remembered how to read the wind. I saw my mother walk to my father's side. They stood there together—like naughty children as wary of punishment as they were relieved at their rescue—and faced the men advancing from the trucks.

The men worked all day to put the fire out, and were still working when my sister, mother, and I left in the late afternoon. Ellen, my mom's partner at her bookstore, offered to drive with us to Milwaukee to see a movie. By then, the firemen had managed to control the fire, and it didn't seem likely it would make it to our house or cross the road and take Mr. Schneider's barn. I knew we were abandoning my father, but I was happy to get away. I didn't want to witness any more of the gruff good fellowship he put on in front of the firemen or have to overhear the final apology. And I knew that look on my mother's face, that combination of fury and sympathy he always aroused in us. As we left, the firemen were coiling up their hoses, and I saw my father behind them, leaning on his useless broom.

On the drive to Milwaukee, I remember my mother's eyebrows, singed to an uneven bristle. My siblings tell me I am wrong about this, that she lost her eyebrows after a different fire and a different argument with my father, one of those fits of stomping martyrdom that could overtake her when he refused to put down the newspaper and get out of his chair; she went down to the basement to fix the water heater herself, and it blew up in her face. My sister and brother are probably right, but I still see it the same way: her profile when she turned to Ellen in the front seat, the naked brows and the wide-eyed startled look they gave her. And I can still hear the murmur of their conversation, the gist of which was the familiar refrain: "he'll never change, he never will."

But what emerges in sharpest relief from that day is the movie we saw once we got to Milwaukee. The movie, *My Brilliant Career*, was showing in the little art theater where we went to see the foreign films that never played in Fond du Lac. Based on a 1901 novel by Miles Franklin, a young Australian who wrote the novel when she was still in her teens, the film follows Sybylla Melvyn (played by Judy Davis), a high-spirited dreamer who longs to leave her parents' dried-up farm in the outback of New South Wales. Sybylla plays the piano. She writes poetry. Later, she turns down a proposal of marriage for the sake of a "brilliant career."

From the first scene, I was hooked. A windstorm. Barn doors creaking. Dust whipping through the chinks of a sad little house where a young girl sits upright at the piano. This wasn't my childhood. This wasn't our house or our landscape. But I have always been able to take a book or a movie and make it pertain. Instead of drought, I saw fire. Instead of dirt, I saw smoke blowing through the cracks of a door. Instead of Sybylla's father, beaten down by dust and drink, I saw my own father lighting matches and tossing them to the wind.

The scene that mattered most, though, came at the end of the film. Sybylla has written a novel. In the final shot, she ties the pages up with string, wraps them in brown paper, and at sunrise walks a country road to the mailbox to send the package off to a publisher. To me, this was a perfect ending. On the two-hour drive back to Fond du Lac, I reviewed the movie scene by scene, lingering on the last. I forgot about the fire, the field, my father waiting. I was thirteen and still in my melodramatic diary-keeping phase. My reaction to the film's ending is even recorded in the diary I kept then: "heart-stopping, achingly lovely," the words underlined twice.

When we got home, it was dark. The firemen were still there. The field had caught a second time, and they'd had to come back. Squaring her shoulders, my mother headed for the field, now lit by the headlights of the trucks. I went up to my room. *Seventeen* magazine was publishing teen poetry in those days, and that night I decided I would send something out. The poem I chose was about a girl who refuses the red balloon her mother buys and instead selects a gray one. It magically lifts her above the treetops, while below on a park bench, still holding a red balloon, the mother waits forlorn. The girl floats off and gazes down to where her mother has shrunk to a speck. There's no missing my theme. Flight. Teen melancholy asserting itself against a midwestern mother's good cheer.

I typed up the poem and set my alarm for 6 a.m. The next morning I walked down the gravel driveway, ignoring the charred field, the little whorls of ash rising in the wind. At the end of the drive, I put my envelope in the mailbox, pausing to admire the sunrise, just as Judy Davis had in the film.

An acceptance letter with a check for twenty-five dollars arrived in the mail a few weeks later. I was convinced that the ritual (the walk, the sunrise) accounted for my luck. My family greeted the arrival of the check from *Seventeen* with astonishment. My father gave me twenty-five dollars in cash, had the check framed, and hung it on his office wall, beneath a photograph of a large mud-splattered hog, the caption of which read: "You can't teach a pig to fly." As far as I know the poem was never published. I didn't have a subscription to *Seventeen*, but every month—for almost two years—I went to the drugstore and looked for my poem in the back pages of the magazine.

I've always linked these three events (the fire, the film, the poem) in my mind. I suppose this is because I saw them each as a kind of crossroads: a beginning and an end. With adolescence came a need to change how I thought about home. Someday I'd have to leave, and this demanded a shift in perspective, the dismantling of what had become a kind of idyll. I needed something extreme: the reconstruction of a place I loved into a dried-up backwater, wind in the familiar cracks. Even the poem seems like a farewell gesture, not just in the subject I chose—a girl floats away from the ties of the past—but in the very act of making the poem. Words could be another kind of home, a structure in which I might build my own place to live.

As for the fire, it seemed a forewarning, one of the moments in my parents' marriage I could point back to as the last straw—something about the way my mother looked when we drove away, something about the way she looked when we came back. But this wasn't the actual end. My parents were together for five more years, and the house wasn't sold for another ten.

Probably my brother, David, would choose a different climactic scene: The night my father roused my brother and me from our sleep at three in the morning and led each of us, first David and then me, to the kitchen table where my mother sat waiting. My sister, Susan, was away at camp. My father had arranged another of his family meetings, this time a dramatic performance, a forced confession in the dead of night. The kitchen was lit up, and my mother sat at the table crying. He made her tell it: she was leaving, it was over.

The house on the ledge hasn't burned down. It still stands, much the same, although the trees my parents planted along the fence dividing the field and our lawn are so tall I barely recognize them. Someday, though, the house will disappear. A few years ago, I borrowed keys from Gracie and brought an architect friend from New York to see where I had grown up. He was impressed, and since he is the sort of person whose good taste is of the irrefutable sort, I was relieved. But when he began to marvel at the perfect curve of the interior walls, I had to explain that the leaning walls were not intentional but the result of forty years of rock pressing up against the back of the house. My father, in his slapdash way, had built no retaining wall. Over time, that old glacier has shifted the foundation, so that now the inner walls are bowed like the prow of a ship.

    I don't entirely mind this fact. We always felt the ledge pushing us forward into the future, into that expanse of field and lake. Maybe it is only right that the ledge is pushing the house toward its demise. My father probably wouldn't have minded this, the straining walls that foretold eventual collapse. Like Frank Lloyd Wright, he believed that houses should succumb to the earth as much as they should conform to it. I remember my first encounter with our house when I was five years old. Legs dangling over the edge of a great hole in the earth, I listened to the scrape of metal against limestone, earth sounding its indignity. I can't help but think the ledge is finally taking its revenge.

At the end of his life, my father lived easiest in hotel rooms. For almost a year he lived in an Americ-Inn he owned in a small town in southern Minnesota. The epiphany in Dubrovnik didn't stick, and against our wishes—he was already sick then and supposedly retired—he decided he would risk it all (yet again) to build on land he owned next to the hotel a commercial development with apartments on the second floor. The idea was to create a mixed-use property, one that would offer a Main Street feel. The drawings he showed us depicted, in colored charcoal, figures mingling under an awning. There were streetlights and café tables out under the stars.

    He was consumed by the project, and for a year he disappeared. When I finally went to visit him, I saw that he was happy and that one reason he was happy was because he was living in a hotel. He liked the little shampoo bottles and the maid service. He liked rising at four in the morning to chart a miraculous recovery or push himself to a success near at hand. The bed piled with beaten briefcases, the air dry and still. The whiff of crisis and the hum of the air conditioner ticking a deadline. He liked the atmosphere in the lobby, the smell of bleached towels and chlorine on the skin and in the hair of all those people on their way to somewhere else.

In those final years, I saw my father rarely. It wasn't that I was too busy. He was. I could barely keep up with his projects, now just paper history stored in a row of steel filing cabinets. There was always an assortment of strangers living in his house in Salt Lake City—unemployed construction workers, the teenage children of some ex-girlfriend who'd moved east—and he remained an avid mentor to anyone who reminded him of his earlier self. He kept scribbled in his Day Planner the phone numbers of dreamers: a Chinese inventor he met on a plane who'd built a bicycle that when pedaled generated electricity, a Pakistani taxi driver who delivered him from JFK on one of his last trips to New York and wanted to open a restaurant in Queens. He loved a go-getter. When we were teenagers, he made us take a psychological test that would register our entrepreneurial faculties. I scored the lowest. To comfort me, he showed me the spiking graph in the social empathy and language skills quadrant, pointing to the attached printout where it said that while I might not start my own company, there would always be a place for me in marketing or sales.

When I did see my father in the last few years, it was usually on a trip together. By then he'd thrown himself into charity work, traveling to Kenya and South America to build wells and make microcredit loans to rural women breeding chickens or growing vegetables from the greenhouses he funded. I joined him on one of those trips, a well-building project in Bolivia and Peru, and it was there that I began to notice a change.

On a gray day, we took a trolley ride up to the ruins of Machu Picchu. At the top, we saw ruins dissolving in mist, the cliff edge falling away. I wanted to race from room to room, rock to rock, and waited for my father to follow. But when I turned, I saw his eyes were closed, his body pressed against a wall. The person who'd been there just before, always before—the boy who leapt up ladders, who drew floor plans with excited feet, and who couldn't help but go dangerously, rock-skiddingly close to the edges of things—was fading, just like the walls and rocks around us. In his place, a seventy-year-old man paralyzed with fear. Faced with one of the most beautiful houses on a ledge in the world, all he could do was close his eyes and mouth the words—*Get Me Down.*

When he got sick, he moved from his hotel room in Minnesota to an assisted living complex in a mountain valley outside of Park City, Utah. None of us could believe how well he took to it at first. He didn't mind the bland food—it was like the food he'd grown up on—and he even managed to get excited about an outing the residents were taking to a local cheese plant. When I visited him at his apartment there, I discovered he'd made a friend, a Mormon rancher older than he was, a woman he said reminded him of his cousins, the girls he used to play with on his grandfather's farm. When she left, he called me up and cried.

For a while he treated the place as if it was another hotel. He asked us to order books on the design of elder-care facilities and began to talk of how someday he was going to build one. Leaning on a walker in the hallway, he pointed to a door, a wall, and described his plans to rip open the wall, move the door, and install sliding glass and a patio, a deck with a mountain view. Nearby, eavesdropping, stood the manager of the place, a man I'd already recognized for his faintly menacing presence in the hallways, like an undertaker at the door. He patted my father on the shoulder—"Making plans to change the world are you, Roger?"—and gave me a knowing smile. By then I recognized his type: pacifying baby talk for the residents and an obsequious wink over their heads. Of course he could have no idea that my father had already been in touch with the owners of the place, knew its dismal financial history, and quite probably had every intention of doing something about it. The manager misread my father's oddness as dementia, and for the first time I understood how in old age, eccentricity could put you at risk. Nobody will know the difference, and you'll suffer for it.

When he got very sick, he was moved to a rehabilitation home in Salt Lake City, the kind (although I didn't know it then) that is just a cover for a place where people go to die. I flew from New York to visit. He'd become obsessed with a plot of land he'd once almost bought on a river in Montana and made me look through his old Day Planner to find the number of the man who owned it. The guy had once been a friend of my father's, and when I called him he was kind, repeating into the phone things like "when you're better, we'll talk about it." But my father wouldn't give up; every day he made me call. He wanted to build a house on that river, a little house just like the bachelor house on Green Lake: a room and a deck over water. Some days, he seemed confused and was convinced that he'd been wrong; the land was in Minnesota. By then, it occurred to me that there's the opposite risk to a life of eccentricity: your children won't recognize signs of dementia when they come.

But most of the time he was just the same—clear headed, stubborn, surprising. The most surprising moment occurred one afternoon when he met with all of us children in the cafeteria and announced that he wanted my brother to scout out the old Rienzi Cemetery back in Fond du Lac for a potential gravesite. This came out of the blue. A few days later my brother returned with a drawing of the cemetery—winding roads and little square numbered plots, a map that on first glance could have been the plan for a housing development or a campground that on vacations my father would study until he'd figure out which site was the best one, then huddle with us in the car outlining his strategy for moving into it once the occupants drove away. Usually a child was sent to stand sentry at the campsite in the early hours of the morning to make sure nobody else would get there first.

Along with the map, my brother brought exciting news. The most beautiful part of the cemetery—ancient oaks and maples, a view of Lake Winnebago—was the old section up on the hill. This was where the Civil War soldiers and the old Protestant families and the first settlers of Fond du Lac were buried, and it had long since been filled. But my brother had made a discovery: One family plot was still empty and available, expensive but available. The family who'd owned it over a hundred years ago had disappeared and stopped paying their yearly dues. Even better, the land for sale was just across the path from the Keys family plot, where my father's grandparents and great-grandparents and even Schmitty, the beloved hired hand, were buried.

Nearly every time he came back to Wisconsin, my father visited those graves, usually with Dr. McBride, his best friend. Rienzi Cemetery was at the foot of the ledge and just down the hill from where he'd grown up in Empire. He and Dr. McBride would sit with their backs against a headstone, their backs to the ledge, and look out through the red and yellow maples to the blue of Lake Winnebago below.

After learning about the vacant plot at Rienzi, my father could barely contain his excitement. I could sense the pacing impulse in the way he drummed his fingers on the armrest of his wheelchair. Few would understand this—most would find it morbid—but my brother and sister and I were just as excited. We were enough our father's children to appreciate the one last great real estate deal, especially one that held so much sentimental promise—a chance to go home.

The week before my father died, my brother drove him up into the mountains to see the house he was building—another house backed into a hill. Bookshelves to the ceiling. Sawdust and the skeleton of a staircase, windows missing their glass and open to the valley below. All his life my brother had been the devoted son. On the day after he graduated from college, he'd gone to work for my father and had stood by his side for more than twenty years, through all the travails of bank loans and near-bankruptcy. But he was the son of a midcentury father, the kind who found it easier to voice approval to his daughters than to his son. The son just got a slap on the back. That day, though, my father had no trouble saying how proud he was. In fact my father liked the house so much my brother almost began to worry that he had designs on it.

For the rest of the week, he refused to stay inside his room at the rehab center. One day, he even escaped, wheeling his chair down a side street. He got lost, and from his cell phone called me in New York asking if I could find a map of Salt Lake City and figure out where he was. Finally, the nurses gave up and let him spend his days outside in front of the building. He sat there every afternoon with his newspaper dropped at his feet, his face turned to the sun, and his skin burnt a deep brown. Like some Greek tycoon, my brother said, and I pictured it—not a deck chair on a yacht out to sea, but a wheelchair alone on an island of grass at the edge of a parking lot.

The Apartment

6

Reid Terrace

When I think of Fond du Lac, I portion it off. My father gets the restaurants and those streets where he built his houses. He gets the office across from the old railroad depot where he ran the construction company and the office he'd later move to down the hall from my mother's bookstore.

But the older section, the business and residential district downtown, invokes my mother and her parents, Lester and Kathryn Herbert. At Gilles, the frozen custard drive-in restaurant at the south end of Main Street, I flash the headlights for the waitress and think of a progression of high school dates—my mother's, my own. Visiting the city park along the lake, I stand in front of the old band shell and see in my mind a photograph of Lester, on a Sunday outing with two of his nine older sisters. These two were nuns—Sister Martine and Sister Norberta—and I see them, on either side of my grandfather, their black habits flapping in the wind. Or on Main Street, a jagged outline of classic brick buildings two or three stories high, I pass the empty storefront where Lester worked for sixty years, then turn onto Sheboygan Street and see him standing on the wrap-around verandah of the Elks Club, a Manhattan in his hand.

The street we always showed off when visitors came to town was Division Street, one block over from Sheboygan. First, the grand old houses where the doctors used to live, with gables and deep porches. Then the old Boyle Catholic Home, one of those solid Italianate brick edifices that would have signaled "institution" in the nineteenth century and now stands empty, waiting for the day when someone will have the money to turn it into condos. My siblings and I would go there every week with my mother or with my grandparents to visit two more of Les's sisters, Great-Aunt Dora and Great-Aunt Marie. We were led down long dark-paneled hallways and into an ancient elevator, an iron gate slamming shut, a slow whining ascent, and at each floor, figures visible through the grate: a woman in a rocking chair weeping over a baby doll, two men looking up vacantly from their game of Chinese checkers. Great-Aunt Marie's room was papered with the prayer cards of saints, their robes and staffs outlined in glitter. Great-Aunt Dora was my first introduction to the idea of spinster. You'd sit in her overheated room in a snowsuit you could not take off, and she would show you pictures cut out from newspapers: women in pompadours beneath hats Dora had made when she was a milliner, now just fine dust in your hands.

 The Boyle Home was only a block or two away from Reid Terrace, the apartment where my maternal grandparents, Lester and Kathryn, lived. Nothing special: just a modest two-story apartment building and inside a modest two-bedroom apartment at the end of a hall. But to me it was the emotional center of town. Here the map of the town's past, the network of family relations and connections, was explained to me. The apartment also offered a vision of escape from that history, a space that seemed decades away from the dark corridors of the Catholic Home just around the corner. Instead, white sofas and glass tables. Liberated of attics and Victorian bric-a-brac, the apartment spoke to me of far-off glamour, the promise of cities I watched on television or read about in books.

For a long time I told people (if they asked) that I'd come to the city because of television, because of screwball comedies and seventies sitcoms, *Saturday Night Live* and *Saturday Night Fever*. From old black-and-white movies, a self began to emerge: The small-town girl, eyes fixed on the spires of the Chrysler Building, arrives in the city to land an apartment all her own. In the kitchenette, she'll listen to jazz and smoke Pall Malls without smearing her lipstick. Once I started watching *Mary Tyler Moore* I gave up on playing house, choosing instead to play apartment: Mary welcoming suitors into her sunken living room—or even better, Rhoda emerging through swinging bead curtains upstairs. Out of paper clips, I fashioned a chain for my bedroom door and practiced peering over it—"Lou, is that you?"

But the other story that had led me to New York was closer to home. In Lester and Kathryn's story (in their apartment) I was introduced to another great American theme—not Thoreau's retreat to the woods or the pioneer's trek westward but desire pointing in the opposite direction; not the turning away from cities but the compulsion, even if just in the imagination, to move toward them. Later, reading Theodore Dreiser or Sherwood Anderson, Sinclair Lewis or Willa Cather, any of those twentieth-century chroniclers of small-town people dreaming of escape, I couldn't help but think of my own Winesburg, my own Main Street. And I couldn't help but see Les and Kathryn—Boppee and Nana to us—hovering somewhere at the margins of the page.

Les and Kathryn visited New York City only once—and by then they were at the far end of middle age. They were not well traveled and never had much money. In every obvious way they were like most of the other middle-class people in our small town. The son of a shoemaker and one of thirteen children, Lester worked at a men's clothing store, T. E. Ahern's, from the time he was a small boy until just months before he died. For sixty years, he sold suits downstairs and overalls for the farmers on the floor above. Kathryn was a math teacher at a Catholic parochial school. She baked a pie nearly every morning, tied her hair up in a scarf on cleaning day, and, like all the other women in the neighborhood, carried in the sag of an apron pocket loose clothespins and a pack of cigarettes.

To me they floated on a glamorous dance floor, a big-city stage. Both were movie star thin, fine boned like birds. When they

Lester Herbert. (author's collection)

danced, the crowd receded to give them the floor. Lester read the *New Yorker* and laughed at the puzzling cartoons. He knew about clothes and wore his hat at a dashing slant—Fred Astaire about to take a spin. Other people said he was the spitting image of Edward, the Prince of Wales, the one who married the divorcée and lost his crown. Kathryn spoke a flapper slang and sped through books, finishing them nearly as fast as she did a pack of Newports or a Hail Mary recited along a string of rosary beads. In his recliner, Lester would explain the funny bits in a W. C. Fields film while Kathryn, her red fingernails drawing circles along my spine, whispered in my ear some story about her romantic past, maybe the one where the boy climbed to her window from a tree branch, maybe the one where on her walk home from her job at a brewery in Milwaukee she caught the attention of one of the Three Stooges in town for a performance. He followed her home. She would never say which Stooge, and she would never say what happened after that.

I suppose the glamour was partly just a matter of contrast. At my paternal grandparents' house, we sat on straight-backed chairs at a table where the water had no ice, the potatoes no salt, and my grandmother Clem's face beneath her snowy braids showed no trace of makeup; "no paint, no drink or cigarettes either," she said, "in all my life." When we visited Lester and Kathryn, they offered us 7UP in a cocktail glass and a plate of hors d'oeuvres, smelly cheese you spread on a cracker with a little ivory-handled knife. The living room of their small apartment—the white sofa, the shelves artfully arranged, books in a stack—made me think of penthouses from the movies, staterooms on ocean liners headed out to sea. They set their martinis on the glass coffee table and rested their cigarettes on the curved edge of an art deco ashtray shaped like a flower uncurling from its bud.

As I grew older, though, the urban glow cast by my grandparents dimmed a little. I began to make out the shadows. In the sigh my mother sometimes released when she spoke about her father, I heard regret, a thwarted dream. To piece the story together, I listened in on conversations, envisioning scenes I knew from books and movies, something out of the Frank Capra movie we watched every Christmas Eve, or something out of one of those Sherwood Anderson stories they made us read in school: Midnight on Main Street and a boy walking up and down planning his escape. Or later the boy grown up, retracing his fantasy on the same sidewalk of the town he never managed to leave.

In obvious ways, Kathryn was the more urbane of the two, the one who seemed most like what I imagined city people to be—quick, competitive, fast talking. She had a flair for satire and for rage. I see, fuzzily, the Watergate trials blasting from a television and then my grandmother, a lifelong Democrat, cursing from the couch before sending a book hurtling at the screen. At the bridge table, she bested all the ladies in town, and when she played Scrabble with her grandchildren, she would not be moved by discrepancies in age or education, giggling gleefully when she dropped her x on the triple letter score.

Years later I read Sinclair Lewis's *Main Street*, a novel I knew Nana had read and liked, and saw the resemblance. Like Carol Kennicott, the frustrated small-town heroine of the novel, Kathryn made no bones about her scorn for the provinciality of some of her neighbors. (I remember her sinking into her chair after a bridge luncheon where a local harpist had been invited to play. "If that's what they play in heaven, I'll take hell.") And she was always much more audibly reverent about the culture out east than my grandfather. A master storyteller—my mother would say "a master at embroidering the truth"—Kathryn had constructed an elaborate fantasy about the towns back in New York State her father and grandparents had come from before moving to Wisconsin. Her maiden name was Kent, and in the name, she colored in blue blood—a heritage that would lead her back to East Coast Yankee gentility, maybe even back to an English upper class. Her favorite book was John Galsworthy's *The Forsythe Saga*; when she talked about the well-heeled Forsythe family, it sometimes sounded as if she were referring to relatives from her own not-too-distant past.

My grandfather was always more at ease (and more honest) about his working-class origins. In his pocket he kept a little notebook with a list of new vocabulary words and once attempted a novel in the spirit of the thirties. When asked about it, he would only reveal that it was "the true story of the working man." And while he too was a good talker, he was not as quick as his wife or as sure of himself. He couldn't bear to see anyone wounded. To us, he proffered a stooped tenderness, a bowed attention. In the fall we'd try on our school clothes for him in the fitting room at Ahern's. Pins in his mouth, a tape measure over one shoulder, he'd kneel like some knight before his queen to assess the quality of a hem. Afterward he'd stand back and watch us in rapt amazement, as if what we were doing with the wooden shoehorn or the stub of tailor's chalk had never been tried before.

It was the gentler, more unassuming Les who had the big-city dreams. In his twenties, he tried a stint at art school in Milwaukee. There was even a photo of him cut from an old Milwaukee newspaper: a young man at his sketchpad in a row of other men at their sketchpads. All you could see was the back of his head. I'd stare and stare but could never make him turn around. He didn't stay in Milwaukee long. An aging mother, the unmarried sisters, all the responsibilities of a dutiful son with a decent-paying job called him home.

Sometime in the forties—by then he was married with three children—he got another chance to leave, a job as a traveling salesman, a good job for a restless man. But Kathryn said no. In the fifties, an even better job came along as window dresser for an upscale department store in Chicago. People told me about my grandfather's windows at Ahern's, how in the crook of a tuxedoed elbow, the cock of a hat, he brought a mannequin to life. Here was a stab at Michigan Avenue, crowds pressed to the window and gaping at what they saw behind the glass. Again, Kathryn said no.

Les and Kathryn's quarrels were legendary, and she loved recalling them: always a little madcap, even a little sexy seeming, like a squabble from a screwball comedy. Irene Dunne throws a vase across the room at Cary Grant, but can't hide the twitch of amusement, the fun underneath. But I knew that the row about the Chicago job had been deadly serious—I knew it from the grim look on my mother's face whenever the subject came up. Kathryn wouldn't back down; Lester worked as a salesman at Ahern's for the rest of his life.

What did my grandfather do with all those unsatisfied longings? My uncle Bud tells me he walked—across town to work every morning, then back for lunch, then back again. My mother tells me that nearly every year, Les would get the itch to move. In the course of their marriage, they changed homes constantly, each one a little bigger, a little better. After their children grew up and got married, Les and Kathryn tried apartment living. Every time a new apartment complex went up, Les excitedly drove over for a tour. I remember one apartment they rented in one of the tallest buildings in town. A skyscraper I thought—but it was only eight or nine stories. The place I knew best was the one on Reid Terrace, but even here the space was always changing. Les liked to rearrange the furniture—every visit, the white couch at a new angle, a picture rehung, or a new vase on the coffee table. Moving from place to place around town, rearranging a room, was the next best thing to getting out.

I was too young to quite know what to make of my grandfather's story. The best I could do was cast him as George Bailey in *It's a Wonderful Life*, which, if I think about it now, wasn't far off. Whatever you have to say about Frank Capra's plummeting angels or his feel-good ending, the portrait of the conflicted small-town man hits an American nerve. When the movie played on television at Christmas, my mother, passing through the living room, would visibly wince when Jimmy Stewart (in the role of Bailey) came on the screen. She knew it all too well: the life spent within the bounds of one town, the boy plastering travel stickers on suitcases that never make it on the train, the wistfulness and vicarious pleasure of watching other people go.

Of the thirteen children in my grandfather's family, there were only four boys. One died young. One raised a large family. My grandfather took on the role of the head of the family, caring for his widowed mother and spinster sister, visiting the nuns, giving up each Sunday afternoon to take them all on a drive out in the country. But one brother, Oscar, did leave. He ran off to Hollywood and started a band. He even wrote a hit song, Margaret Whiting's "The Broken Down Merry Go Round," #2 on the charts in 1950. I remember how happy Boppee was when he spoke of Oscar, how he'd show us the sheet music and hum the tune. Oscar was a real Californian, my uncle Bud says, "always sporting a tan, dressed to the nines," and he was married to a real New Yorker, "a little bitty thing and tough as nails." When Oscar came back to Fond du Lac for a visit, Les could barely contain his delight, introducing him over at the Elks Club, driving him around town to visit all the sisters.

The Capra film gets this right as well—the need for two brothers, one who gets away, one who holds down the fort. George Bailey longs for college; his younger brother goes in his stead. A damaged ear prevents George from going to war with the rest of the young men in town; his brother, an Air Force pilot, shoots down so many enemy planes, he wins the Medal of Honor and meets the president.

Uncle Oscar was no military hero, but he did play in the Air Force band behind the Broadway actress Betty Hutton on her goodwill tour through Europe. Les was deemed too old to fight. He spent the war years just as George Bailey had, as a blackout warden. Walking up and down the dim streets, silent but for crickets and the creak of a screen door, he went out each night in search of a forbidden sliver of light.

Lester was revered in our family as a kind of saint. When he died, we found in his billfold, on the back of a folded-up envelope, a prayer. The envelope was yellowing, torn at the edges. How often had he taken it out to read? I won't share all of the prayer—it seems unfair to rifle too freely in someone else's pockets, repeat for strangers the private entreaties of a man to his God—but I'll share some of it: "Help me to learn better what is right to do, and then do it, no matter what the pain. . . . Help me always to blame myself, and to give without thought of return." At the bottom of the prayer along the envelope's flap, like a seal, a motto, a few words written in large block letters: EGO IN MAN IS STRONG.

In the final scene of *It's a Wonderful Life*, George Bailey realizes that all his sacrifices—his loyalty to family and to his neighbors, his resistance to the town's bully-banker, Mr. Potter, and the battle waged between ego and the desires of others—have made him "the richest man in town." I think we all wanted to believe that my grandfather's ending matched George Bailey's: a final scene of tinkling bells, the tributes of one's neighbors, and a round of "Auld Lang Syne."

But Capra's ending is too simple and too certain. The night my grandfather died—I was in the sixth grade—I listened to my mother and father talking in the living room below. Always an eavesdropper, I left my bedroom and crept to the end of the hall. I could see them together down below on the couch, my father's hand on her shoulder, awkward in the face of such unmitigated grief. There was a word she repeated: *regret*. Later, when I was older, she told me that in the week before he died, it was one of the words her father used to describe his wonderful life.

Nearly all the literature taught to me in high school was American. The usual suspects: Hawthorne's *The Scarlet Letter*, Crane's *The Red Badge of Courage*, Wharton's *Ethan Frome*, Cather's *My Ántonia*, and Sherwood Anderson's *Winesburg, Ohio*. Cather, Wharton, and Anderson became favorites later in life, but at the time I found them unbearably dull. Why *Ethan Frome* is so frequently assigned in high school English classes I'll never understand. Now, when I teach Wharton to college students, I have to set aside ten minutes at the start of class for their complaints and for my long-winded promise that Wharton is more than a broken pickle dish and a sled ride down an icy hill. As for Anderson and Cather, I didn't need reminders of sleepy small towns. I lived in one, could look out the window of the old stone high school (the same school attended by my father and his mother before him), and see it plain. Why not take me somewhere new: Europe, the Orient, New York City?

Still I couldn't help absorbing what I read, and I used those novels and stories of small towns to form my opinions. The towns presented to me in English class were bleak ones: there's Starkfield where Ethan Frome lies sacrificed, paralyzed; or, Black Hawk in *My Ántonia* where Jim Burden takes long late-night rambles up and down the streets, "sleeping houses on either side" and inside them "jealousy and envy and unhappiness"; or Winesburg with all its inarticulate townspeople able to loosen their tongues only with the young newspaper reporter, George Willard, the one person who will get away.

Reading *Winesburg, Ohio* now, it seems just as odd a choice as *Ethan Frome* for a teenage reader. What a grim portrait of adult life to offer us. So much middle-age sexual frustration too. I wonder if we picked up on it. There seemed to be no daylight in Winesburg, just darkness closing in: confessions of life-changing mistakes whispered in the alleyways and back porches of a pitch black night. My tenth grade English teacher loved a clean sentence, and maybe it was Anderson's deceptively simple ones—Faulkner called them "primer-like"—that kept us lingering for so many weeks in Winesburg. But I had theories about that teacher, a man who himself seemed a little dreamy, a little trapped. ("Why do people write books?" he once asked. I raised my hand: "Immortality." It's not an answer I would give now. I remember how he stared, as if stricken, how, for a second, he looked as if he might cry.)

That teacher liked to read aloud. Now when I read a passage from *Winesburg*—say, this one, from the story "Mother"—I hear his voice:

> In the evening when the son sat in the room with his mother, the silence made them both feel awkward. Darkness came on and the evening train came in at the station. In the street below feet tramped up and down upon a board sidewalk. In the station yard, after the evening train had gone, there was a heavy silence.

Perhaps Skinner Leason, the express agent, moved a truck the length of the station platform. Over on Main Street sounded a man's voice, laughing. The door of the express office banged. George Willard arose and crossing the room fumbled at the doorknob. Sometimes he knocked against a chair, making it scrape along the floor. By the window sat the sick woman, perfectly still, listless. Her long white hands, white and bloodless, could be seen drooping over the ends of the arms of the chair. "I think you'd better be out among the boys. You are too much indoors," she said, striving to relieve the embarrassment of the departure. "I thought I would take a walk," replied George Willard, who felt awkward and confused.

Was it just those deceptively simple sentences the teacher wanted us to take away with us, or might he have been silently screaming *Get out, get out before it's too late*? This, of course, is just what George Willard does. Unlike the other George, in *It's a Wonderful Life*, he gets his trunk down from the closet and makes it to the train. So too did the author of *Winesburg, Ohio*. At the age of thirty-six, Anderson left his small Ohio town for the city of Chicago, gave up his business — like my grandfather, he was a salesman, and like Silas Lapham, in the paint trade — and dedicated himself to becoming a writer.

My grandfather never said anything to me about his disappointments. Most of what I have to go on is filtered through my mother's memories. There's no way of knowing with any certainty if I've gotten the dilemma right. A gay friend of mine points to the window dressing and gift for the arrangement of furniture as a sign of a very different regret, a possibility I pretend to consider until I remember the palpable charge Boppee gave off when in the presence of a female, my grandmother especially. And who knows if the city dream would have taken a lasting hold; it may have been merely a young man's fancy, one he would have abandoned on his own if his wife and the obligations of family hadn't forced the issue. Perhaps he was even grateful for the reprieve. In the seventies, when I knew him, he liked to read about the horrors of cities in the *New York Times*—stories about gangs, guns, and the indifference of an entire apartment building to a neighbor's midnight screams. Before she went to nursing school, my mother wanted to join the Peace Corps (newly formed by JFK), or if not that, study drawing at the Chicago Art Institute. Les wouldn't hear of it. Too dangerous; she needed to get a decent job, just as he had needed to get a decent job years before. She remembers, though, that when she moved to Minneapolis to work as a nurse in a hospital, her father loved to come visit the city and to go with her on late night crawls to the jazz clubs. He was the oldest man in the room—a crowd of bebop-lovers snapping their fingers to Coltrane—and she says he fit right in.

And who knows how much of my grandfather's story is colored by my mother's own past. She is the only one still living in Fond du Lac; the rest of us have left. But when she speaks of those two years in Minneapolis before she married my father, I hear the exhalation of "what if." Now, she likes to take the train alone to Chicago to visit the Art Institute, then come home and draw what she's seen.

I can't help but ask too whether Lester would have made it in Chicago or New York. Was he too cautious, too accommodating? How would he get a word in edgewise? Even after twenty-five years in New York City, I still find the simple act of extricating myself from a conversation a challenge; my husband, a far more mild-mannered person than I and a more recent inhabitant of the city, struggles even more with this. All the usual signals that in small midwestern towns work to communicate a desire to exit or change the subject—the jiggling of a door handle, the clearing of your throat—simply don't register. Rules you were brought up on, like "don't interrupt," are reversed. Bluntness is obligatory. I've watched my husband at parties, cornered by the monologuists and the bores, and I imagine my self-abnegating grandfather— "teach me always to blame myself"—faring even worse.

Reid Terrace

But all of this conjecture is beside the point. Les's regret, embellished and enlarged by the books I read and the movies I watched, took hold of me. It felt personal, a family legend I inherited and had no choice but to interpret as an obligation—the completion of someone else's unfulfilled dream.

◇

In the final chapter of Willa Cather's *My Ántonia*, the novel's narrator, Jim Burden, returns to Nebraska to visit his childhood friend Ántonia. Jim hasn't seen her in twenty years. Cowardice has kept him away. Friends tell him that Cuzak, Ántonia's husband, "was not a man of much force" and that "she had had a hard life." Jim fears seeing his early illusions destroyed, the shining figure of his childhood "aged and broken." But once Jim meets Ántonia, it's clear that while she's physically worn, she hasn't changed in the essential things. She is still there, in "the full vigor of her personality, battered but not diminished." Life on the farm has been a struggle, but Ántonia is happy with her husband, her ten children, the orchards she's planted. "I belong on a farm," she tells Jim. "I'm never lonesome here like I used to be in town."

For Cuzak it is a different story. He loves his wife and family but belongs to "theatres and lighted streets and music," the "excitement of the crowd." Somehow Ántonia had managed to hold this city man to a farm "in one of the loneliest countries in the world." Jim pictures Cuzak in the evenings "nursing his pipe and listening to the silence; the wheeze of the pump, the grunting of the pigs," and then he wonders "whether the life that was right for one was ever right for two!"

This line always gives me a pang. My mind drifts to Lester walking an empty street, "listening to the silence," and to Kathryn, who refuses to budge. But sometimes when I read that scene from *My Ántonia*, I wonder what would have happened if it had gone the other way. What if Les had won the argument? What new family legends and unfulfilled fantasies would haunt me? I imagine Ántonia, with her love of her trees ("I love them as if they were people") in Cuzak's lighted streets, lonesome in the crowd. And then I see my grandmother Kathryn, adrift and uprooted.

I never heard them say it outright, but my mother and her siblings must have blamed my grandmother for getting in the way of their father's dreams. My mother was always fiercely loyal to her father and felt he'd been too frequently sacrificed to Nana's migraines and morning moods. On particularly bad days Les would carry a tray of coffee and toast into the bedroom. My mother remembers how she and her sister, Connie, would seethe: "How can you pamper her?" But he just put his finger to his lips. "Don't. You'll wake her. You girls need to be kind. You don't know what she's been through."

Later on, my mother and Connie learned more about what Nana had been through, and although I can't be certain their teenage resentments were ever completely purged, I do know they forgave their mother for refusing to move to Chicago. Before marrying Les, all Kathryn had known was displacement. Her mother died only a few weeks after she was born; she grew up shuttled among relations. Her first husband died during an operation to remove his appendix, leaving her in her late twenties alone with a little boy, my uncle Bud. It was the Depression, and for the next eight years, she moved again, from relation to relation, town to town.

My grandmother and I were close, and by the time I knew her, she'd mellowed, a shift in temperament my mother and aunt ascribed to the aftermath of menopause. Still I could see that she had "nerves," could see that beneath the veneer of confidence were all the insecurities of the orphan and the widow. At church, she'd frighten me with the way she'd clutch the pew in front of her and rock back and forth—not prayer but panic—until finally my mother would reach over, still her with a whisper and a hand on the knee.

Only a short distance separated my junior high school and Reid Terrace, and for a few years I went to Nana's apartment nearly every day after school. She'd sit across from me in her den and tell stories. If I tried to steer her to the years before she married

Les, she'd go blank, skillfully rerouting the conversation away from tragedy to the funny bits: the Three Stooges or those lovesick boys at the window. "Cagey Kate," my grandfather used to call her. After Nana died, I turned to my uncle Bud for answers about the early years. He can't tell me much; for most of Nana's early widowhood, he'd lived apart from her, boarding at a German couple's farm in central Wisconsin, but he does remember the place they lived just after his father died: a hotel owned by Nana's cousin in the little town of Wautoma, Wisconsin. Nana worked there as a waitress. The hotel was directly across the road from the train station, and usually it was filled with traveling salesmen. "Drummers," Nana would have called them. Bud remembers the vastness of the dining room, the snowy tablecloths laundered in the steaming basement below, and the spare little room he and his mother shared at the top of the stairs.

Two years ago I took my uncle Bud back to the hotel in Wautoma. The steps that once led to the front door were gone, the paint peeling. It looked uninhabited, but when we knocked, two hollow-eyed men, aged beyond their years, emerged. "Crystal meth," I decided. They looked distrustfully at Bud's pressed sport coat and opened the door just a crack, just enough to see into what was once the hotel dining room: sleeping bags piled in the corner; a few ragged sofas pulled up to a crate. The room wasn't vast as Bud had described it. Like all places we remember from childhood, it had shrunk to normal size.

As we drove away, Bud told me that when he'd lived there, the walls of the dining room were lined with canary cages, and in the center of the hotel lobby, another cage—"maybe six feet wide by four feet high"—and inside this cage, tree branches and a collection of flying squirrels. Every night, after the guests went to bed, the waitresses would free the squirrels. Bud remembers how they leapt between the tables and landed on his shoulder, and how they tamely returned to their cages when called. I try to picture my grandmother there at the end of her shift, worn out by the ogling salesmen, the cousin's charity. I imagine a summer night at dusk, the sort of night on which a young girl might go out walking with

My grandmother standing in front of her older sister, Grace. They are posing in front of a billboard advertisement for Guinness Beer, Necedah, Wisconsin, about 1925. (author's collection)

her lover. I can't help but wonder what grief looked like in such a place—the squirrels digging their little nails into her shoulder and those cages all around.

After Wautoma, there were other jobs, other towns, and for a while Kathryn worked in a brewery in Milwaukee, where she lived with her older sister, Grace, and Grace's husband in their tiny one-bedroom apartment. As usual, she never talked much about this until one afternoon, almost offhandedly, she told me about the day she left work, got lost, and sat "right down on the steps of an office building and had a nervous breakdown." It sounded like her usual hyperbole, and I made sure to verify this with my mother and with Grace. They told me Nana couldn't remember her name or her address; the stranger who found her crying on the steps had to rifle in her purse to find out who she was.

A writer like Theodore Dreiser would have known just what to make of that lonesome girl swatting at the squirrels and cigar smoke in the hotel dining room. He'd have steered Kathryn out the door, piloted her across the street and up onto a train departing for the city. To that huddled figure on the steps of an indifferent city, he'd have stretched out a hand, led her away from the misery of factories and the fold-out cot in her sister's apartment, and sent her straight into the arms of a bounder. Her fate: crisp ten-dollar bills and department store windows, trains and hotels, theaters and city streets.

But this is not how my grandmother's story goes, and if she had been asked to choose an author to take on her life, Dreiser would not have been her pick. With her Old New York pretensions and admiration for the likes of John Galsworthy, she would have preferred someone a bit grander, Edith Wharton, say—and for a second I see a woman's gloved hand extended to lift Kathryn to her feet. Of course, people like my grandmother were not Wharton's natural subjects; when she took on the small-town American girl, she usually turned her into an object of satire (the social-climbing, hotel-dwelling Undine Spragg in *The Custom of the Country*) or into a creature of crude Darwinian instinct (the sullen Charity Royall in *Summer*). But I can imagine Wharton authoring that scene in Milwaukee; she would have known what to do with that melancholy figure in the darkening Milwaukee night. A writer who excelled at depicting and designing houses, who decried the restlessness and hotel-living ways of Americans, and who never stopped stressing the importance of the home, she would have understood where my grandmother wanted to go, would have recognized that what Kathryn craved in that moment of despair wasn't a glittering object behind plate glass or the lights of Fifth Avenue, but something much simpler and perhaps, to her mind, much harder to get.

At the end of *The House of Mirth*, Lily Bart is alone, ill, penniless, and close to collapse. Wandering back one night to her shabby New York boardinghouse, she recognizes a young woman on the street, a working-class girl named Nettie Struther. Nettie takes Lily home to rest in her flat. In the tiny kitchen, Lily sits before the fire, holds Nettie's baby, and listens to Nettie's history: how she'd been deceived and abandoned by a gentleman, how she'd lost her innocence—working girls "don't always know how to look after themselves"—and how a childhood friend married her despite it all. Nettie's tale is like a reverse mirror turned on Lily's own disappointments. On hearing false rumors about her, Lawrence Selden, the man Lily loves, believed them and turned his back. That night after she returns to her boardinghouse, Lily has a kind of epiphany. No longer is it "material poverty that she turned from with the greatest shrinking" but a "deeper impoverishment . . . the clutch of solitude at her heart, the sense of being swept like a stray uprooted growth down the heedless current of the years." Like my grandmother, Lily had grown up never knowing a real home. Reared in hotels, raised by a mother "blown hither and thither on every wind of fashion," and dependent on the charity of an indifferent aunt, she has spent her life unanchored, a "mere spin-drift of the whirling surface of existence." All her life she had tried to take root, but had been trained to set her sights on a drawing room and on the wealthy husband who might give it to her. For the first time Lily realizes she's gotten it wrong and that in Nettie's kitchen—a fire in the grate, a baby in her lap, a husband's acceptance—she had caught her first glimpse of a home:

> The poor little working-girl who had found strength to gather up the fragments of her life, and build herself a shelter with them, seemed to Lily to have reached the central truth of existence. It was a meagre enough life, on the grim edge of poverty . . . but it had the frail audacious permanence of a bird's nest built on the edge of a cliff—a mere wisp of leaves and straw, yet so put together that the lives entrusted to it may hang safely over the abyss.

After the job at the factory, Kathryn left the city and earned a teaching degree. For the next few years, she moved from one little Wisconsin school to another until she landed at a school in Calumetville, just down the road from where our house on Highway 151 would someday be built. At a dance in town she met my grandfather. By then Les was already in his late thirties and, with his Duke of Windsor good looks and courtly ways, the most eligible bachelor in town. Nana told me that for years she would get dirty looks from strange women at the grocery store, women who'd seen their hopes dashed the night they saw Kathryn and Les on the dance floor for the first time.

Not long after they met, Les and Kathryn drove out to the farm where my uncle Bud had been living. Bud was seven years old. He remembers a shiny 1935 black Buick pulling into the yard and, stepping out of it, a woman he barely remembered (his mother) and a sleek stranger wearing a snap-brim fedora (his new father). In the yard the farmers stood around staring at the car. Bud said good-bye to the dog he loved and to the family he had begun to think of as his own. For him, the day was somber, even frightening, but for my grandmother, it must have seemed like the end of a bad dream. In the back seat, the son she hadn't seen in years. Next to her in the driver's seat, a kind man with a good job, a family who for generations had been rooted in one place, even a religion.

Just before the wedding, she abandoned her Protestant faith and converted to Catholicism.

I like to imagine the drive back to Fond du Lac. The smell of leather and the hair pomade Les always used. Out the window, a horse in a field, sparrows in formation. From the driver's seat, Les leans around to offer a piece of candy to the boy behind him while Kathryn presses her feet to the floor as if she might get home faster that way. I feel the car as it turns onto the road to town, as it turns into the driveway of a little house. The engine ticks to a stop, and in that brief stillness before the car doors swing open, I understand how a car parked in a drive might feel a little like a nest hanging safely over the abyss.

It's no surprise that Nana said no to my grandfather's becoming a traveling salesman—those years at the hotel would have told her something about that kind of life. And it's no surprise that she couldn't embrace his vision of the glamorous metropolis. I see her still, a young girl leaving work on a wintry night. The weight of a gray sky, the "clutch of solitude at her heart."

But this narrative I've constructed—the imposition of a split down the middle, Les with his fantasies of Pullman rides and city streets on one side, Kathryn, with her settled life on the other— is its own kind of fiction. It could not have been so neat an opposition. Because I viewed my grandparents from an idealized distance, I attached to them inviolable characteristics, clear divisions. I could never have done this with my own parents, even though at a glance their marriage appeared to follow a similar pattern: the rooted spirit at odds with a restless one. I think of my mother at the kitchen table under a desk lamp, scrutinizing the account books in hopes of someday paying off the mortgage, and then of my father running, as he was always running, through an airport terminal in some city far away. I remember the old Hertz commercial featuring O. J. Simpson. "I used to run through airports," Simpson says, a garment bag flung over one shoulder. "Now I fly through them."

(There's even a story that once, in the days when this was possible, my father ran out onto an airport tarmac and stood waving his arms in front of a plane until the pilot turned off the propellers and lowered the stairs.) But I know both my parents too well for the lines between them to stay firm. I think of my father prone on the graves of his ancestors; or I see my mother on the train to Chicago, a little case with sharpened drawing pencils on her lap. A girlish seventy-year-old looking excitedly out the window, like Sister Carrie leaving her Wisconsin town for the first time.

One could read Jim Burden's line in *My Ántonia*—"is the life that's right for one ever right for two?"—less as a statement about the divisions in a marriage and more about Jim Burden's own internal struggle. Jim is the country boy who longs for universities and culture, trains and cities. He is the big-city railway executive looking out the window of a speeding Pullman car and thinking back to the one place he called home. One life—one place—sacrificed for the other. Both true to who he is. Or there is Thea Kronborg, the heroine of Cather's novel *The Song of the Lark*, who knows she will leave her small Colorado town for the cities of the East: "She loved the familiar trees, and the people in those little houses, and she loved the unknown world beyond Denver. She felt as if she were being pulled in two, between the desire to go away forever and the desire to stay forever."

Cather never stopped writing about her "incurable passion" for the prairie towns and farms where she started. "When I strike the open plain, something happens," she once wrote. "I'm home." Yet she lived most of her adult life in the cities of the East Coast. She visited Nebraska, but was never able to write about it when she was there. Edith Wharton never stopped stressing the "grave endearing traditions" of home, but was also driven, as Henry James once put it, by a "wild, almost incoherent restlessness"; a "high-flying kite," he called her, "the great and glorious pendulum," "oscillating" from country to country in her motor flights across Europe. I see Wharton drifting through her gardens at the Mount, but just as often I see her behind the wheel of her motor car, a pair of driving goggles in place, a head-scarf trailing.

This is my dilemma too—the call to take root, the call to set forth. In grade school I wrote an essay about my desire to live in a covered wagon on the Oregon Trail, and I remember the trouble I had with it. How to conclude? Should I just keep going, the wheels rolling on forever, or should I pull in the reins, build myself a cabin, sow a field of corn, plant a lilac bush at the gate, and stay long enough to watch it grow? There they were: the contending urges. When I first came to New York I needed a story. I took Lester's—a pining for the city and all that came with it, restlessness and a nomadic hunger for the lights and the crowd, a desire to move the furniture around. But not long after arriving in New York, I discovered that it wasn't just Lester's story I carried with me to New York, but Kathryn's as well.

7

Manhattan

The city began for me in a wood-paneled windowless box, a basement room in a split-level not far from the commuter station in a New York suburb. The house was in Bronxville and belonged to the parents of Ed, a friend of a friend. I didn't know Ed or his parents; I didn't know anyone in the city when I arrived that September. I was twenty-one. My hosts handed over the back pages of the real estate section of a newspaper—a hint I didn't need—and showed me where I'd be sleeping downstairs. After that, they seemed to forget I was there. All night they argued: shrill, then hoarse; drawers opening and slamming shut; high-pitched pronouncements like "don't you dare!" I tried to stay calm. I ironed my taupe interview suit. (Its taupe-ness was somehow significant to me; it said I was my own person. No black or brown or navy blue for me. There were even taupe shoes to match, high heels.)

Encamped on the sofa bed, I kept myself awake for most of the night watching movies. The first film, *Wall Street*, had just come out on video, and Ed, himself a Wall Street trader, had left it on top of the television; the next, *Rosemary's Baby*, was showing on late-night TV. What I saw that night—Michael Douglas barking orders to his driver and Mia Farrow crooning to her monstrous child—offered a grim prospect on both the city I'd moved to and the adult world I was preparing to enter. The conjugal hostilities thundering overhead didn't help. This was not how I'd imagined my first night in the city. I'd pictured the streets of Manhattan and me walking them, wide-eyed, emboldened; instead, I found myself back in the American basement, lit by the flickering of a television set, as cut off from the streets of the city as the trader in his limousine or Rosemary in her Dakota apartment. Leaving the basement the next morning, I half expected to find Ruth Gordon barring the door.

In one way, that suburban house in Bronxville wasn't a bad place to begin my move to the city. It fit a formula. Wasn't wood paneling and the commuter train just where an escape to the city is supposed to start? On my walk to the train that morning I heard Pete Seeger in my head: "Little boxes on the hillside, little boxes made of ticky-tacky . . . there's a green one and a pink one . . . and they all look just the same." Bronxville filled in a gap, gave me, even for just a night or two, the suburban suffocation I'd never actually suffered. I was so homesick that morning (for my mother, for the woods, for our house sold just a few months before) that there was a strange relief in beginning the narrative in the appropriate spot—from a place I could not wait to leave.

Once I arrived at Grand Central, once I made my way onto the street, my mood lifted. Virginia Woolf's Mrs. Dalloway crosses her threshold and steps out into a London morning: "What a lark! What a plunge!" This was my first lesson, my first New York cliché: how the city never stays put, how it can send you from the bleakest basement to the intoxication of a perfect autumn morning, or how it can send you out in a taxi high over the Brooklyn Bridge and deposit you at the end of the night in a deli's dark corner, the blink of the ATM machine reading a balance of less than zero while outside the meter ticks. I'd get used to this: rapture to calamity and back again.

That morning, I had an interview for an editorial assistant job at a backwater publishing company that put out titles on balloon animals and seafood grilling. They gave me the job: $13,000 a year and an office on Fifth Avenue. I called my mother from a pay phone and then walked over to a travel store on Thirty-Sixth Street to buy a map. For the rest of the day, I walked—the ecstatic walk of a first day in a strange city—up to Central Park, then back to Washington Square, feet blistered, hardly able to wobble any farther in those taupe heels, and finally back to Grand Central to catch the train. The next day I found an apartment with a roommate in Queens. A "ticky-tacky" kind of house but with a difference. The landlord who lived downstairs quoted from memory long passages from Joyce's *Ulysses* and liked to sit in the backyard and sing arias in a language I couldn't identify. This, I thought, was more like it. Just a few miles from Bronxville, but what vast territories had been crossed.

I even made my first New York friend that week. Her name was Dee, and it was she (white bob, white pearls) who buzzed me in for my job interview on the first day. She was in her sixties, tiny, scowling, dressed all in black behind the reception desk. It took me only a few weeks to discover the grandness was all a pose, and only a little longer to discover that talking to Dee was all I liked about my job. Her habits had been formed in the office culture of the sixties: at lunch she liked to slip to the ladies room, a pewter flask in her pocket. At the copy machine or at a Hamburger Heaven down the street, she told stories of all the jobs before this one. During the fifties and sixties, she'd worked in publishing houses and ad agencies—the letters B, B, D, and O she'd say so fast I could hardly catch them—and after that, odd jobs all over the city, including a stint as Bette Davis's assistant ("pronounced *Bet*," she'd remind me, "like on the horses").

Those early years in New York belong, in their way, to the cliché. All of it: how the crossing of a street stirred and confused me, the way a season change might have back in Wisconsin; how gazing at a man across the table, I was never sure if the tremor was coming from him or from the street scene glimpsed in the window behind his head. I had trouble making eye contact; place and person got mixed up. I liked the solitude here: the wonder of an afternoon alone in a diner or a museum or a matinee; the exquisite loneliness of a cavernous side street in the East Twenties on a summer night, silent except for the faint clink from someone rummaging through bottles in the garbage. And I liked the feel of friendship here: those fast-moving walks up an avenue in twos or threes, or a dance of shifting pairings, faces coming at you, words in one ear. One night I walked into a bar in the Lower East Side and saw the face of a future lover smiling from a booth. The distance between us an invitation, a call to cross over, like the Brooklyn Bridge in the Joseph Stella print that hung over my bed.

And then there was that almost immediate sense of belonging. On one of my first visits to the Film Forum, the art house theater down in SoHo, I went to see William Inge's *Picnic* with Kim Novak playing the stunning (and stunned) blonde and Susan Strasberg as Millie, the watchful younger sister, dark haired, flat chested, always reading. The scene that got the biggest laugh from the audience was not Novak's sultry dance with bare-chested William Holden, but Millie's cry of liberation. From behind her spectacles and from behind a copy of Carson McCullers's *The Ballad of the Sad Café*, Millie announces that her sister "can stay in this jerkwater town and marry some ornery guy and raise a lot of kids, but I'm going to New York and write novels that'll shock people right out of their senses." When the audience applauded, crowing with campy delight, I felt a release, as if I had been wandering the school cafeteria all my life and here at last was a lunch table where I might want to sit down.

Still, however happy I was in those early months in New York, the shock of my night in Bronxville lingered. Watching Michael Douglas in *Wall Street*, I was reminded of what I'd hoped to forget: I'd arrived in New York in the wrong era—the late eighties. Before landing in the city, I had turned a deaf ear to my mother's warnings of Manhattan bankers living in opulent fourteen-room co-ops, isolated from the poverty below—details she'd gleaned from reading Tom Wolfe's *Bonfire of the Vanities*. Naïve though this might sound, I had planted in my imagination an idea of New York that belonged to my parents' era, or further back to my grandparents'. I envisioned a New York City from the thirties or forties, mostly borrowed from movies. There was Irene Dunne, a small-town girl descending upon New York to assume a voluptuous pen name for her off-color novel in *Theodora Goes Wild* (1939) or Katharine Hepburn checking herself into a boardinghouse in *Stage Door* (1937). Sometimes my New York belonged to the sixties and seventies: John Travolta's girlfriend in *Saturday Night Fever* making her exultant escape from Queens to Manhattan, or the gritty landscape of a city in decline in thrillers like *Klute* or *The French Connection.*

And then there were the literary associations. These I've never been able to completely shake. Almost anything—the weather, a street corner, a voice—can still light up some pocket in my brain where a line from a poem or story is stored. Some associations are seasonal: the first hot day in spring, predictably, gives me Irwin Shaw's "Girls in Their Summer Dresses," and autumn, Alfred Kazin walking through Brooklyn, head down, in the rain. Others are geographic: West Twenty-Third Street calls forth the poet James Schuyler looking out his window of the Chelsea Hotel, while the fountain in Washington Square Park summons a couple holding hands in James Baldwin's *Another Country.*

I'm not the first to carry a library of expectation in my airplane carry-on. Or the first unable to detect the studio back lot in the storefronts and street scenes of my favorite New York films. Others before me had been similarly seduced. Italo Calvino recalls how as a young man he had come to Paris through Baudelaire and the novel cycles—Balzac, Zola, Proust. No, if there is anything unusual about my jumble of preconceived notions it may simply be the length of time I took to let go of them. How determined I was in those early years to make my vision of the city match up. And how disoriented I became when I discovered it wouldn't.

When I first landed in New York I imagined I'd find bohemia—or a simplified romantic version of it. Naïvely, I even confused my bohemias, mixing up cities and their histories. In high school a short-lived but consuming obsession with Ernest Hemingway's memoir of Paris, *A Moveable Feast*, had created a powerful image. Cities meant café intimacies: a crowd at the table, art created in the public room. Almost immediately, though, I realized the city of my imagination wouldn't line up with the one in front of me. Before coming to New York, I spent the mideighties at the University of Notre Dame, a place where ROTC rallies disturbed my principles and football games my Saturday morning sleep. I didn't fit there, and in response, I organized a literary festival that had a defiantly bohemian vibe. The poet Allen Ginsberg came and gave a reading. Just as he broke out in ribald song, the nuns in the front row stood up and, like penguins sensing danger, scuttled single file for the door. Another guest at the literary festival that year was the experimental writer Ronald Sukenick. He read from a novel without punctuation or paragraphs, and afterward we went out to dinner. He gave me a copy of the book he was writing, an account of the New York counterculture imagined as a succession of bars. *Down and In* begins at the San Remo—that "Village-Bohemia-literary-artistic-underground-mafioso-Pinko-revolutionary-subversive-intellectual-existential-anti-bourgeois café"—and moves on to the Cedar Tavern, the Five Spot, the White Horse Tavern, Stanley's, Max's Kansas City, and finally, the Mudd Club and the punk scene of the late seventies and early eighties. I devoured the book and in my first weeks in New York carried it with me everywhere, like some nineteenth-century traveler clutching her Baedeker in a foreign land.

It didn't take me long after arriving to learn that the landmarks detailed in Sukenick's book had disappeared as effectively as the subway graffiti I recalled from *Saturday Night Live*. More tragically, I was to discover that if this was *The Great Gatsby*, I had arrived at the end of the book. The party was over. I had gotten here too late, a fact my older acquaintances who had come in the sixties, seventies, and early eighties never failed to mention. The musicians decried the end of punk, the writers the sad decline of the poetry scene. The artists complained that SoHo had been laid to waste by developers, and everybody knew the East Village was on its way.

Had I read Sukenick's conclusion more carefully, I would have also understood that the underground he was talking about—one that could be located on the map—was gone. The material condition necessary to keep a subterranean culture alive—cheap rent—was a thing of the past. Even by the early nineties, I was hearing the complaints that Williamsburg had fizzled, that artists were moving farther out into Brooklyn and Queens in order to afford a place to work. I pictured them pushed to the edge of the continent, spilling over into the Atlantic where no NEH grant could save them. Finding my people would not be as simple or spontaneous as heading for the nearest bar; it would require long subway rides and wearisome logistics. If I wanted the kind of scene described in *Down and In*—a place with an urban mix of artists, writers, and uptown slummers—one friend suggested I avoid the neighborhood bar altogether. Better to feign a drinking problem and go to an AA meeting.

Sukenick had left Brooklyn's Midwood High School and arrived at the San Remo in 1948. "It was a time when the misunderstood genius starving in the garret was the role model for artists of all kinds," he remembers. "I myself could hardly wait to start going hungry." The problem, of course, was that for my first ten years in New York, there were no garrets in my price range, and if I found one, it meant taking on a word-processing job to pay for it. I seemed always to be looking for a place to live. There would be almost as many apartments as the years I have lived here. To this day, I pass a For Rent sign and my heart races. The apartment with a community of like-minded friends waiting down below—even the room of my own that my mother and Virginia Woolf had told me was required—seemed forever out of reach.

I've read only one good description of a New York apartment search. It takes up several long chapters of *A Hazard of New Fortunes*, William Dean Howells's 1890 novel about the Marches, a middle-aged Boston couple who move to New York. Basil March has been offered a position as editor of a syndicate magazine in New York. To take the job, he and his family will have to rent out their comfortable book-lined home in Boston and move to a flat in New York. Basil's wife, Isabel, from an old Boston family, is horrified by the prospect: "I could never," she says, "have any inner quiet in New York." But for the sake of her husband, she gives in and by the time they arrive in the city, she's even a little excited about the prospect. She imagines the search will take a couple of days and, on the morning of their first day, reminds her husband that "we must not forget what kind of flat we are going to look for," one with "an elevator and steam heat, not above the third floor, to begin with. Then we must each have a room, and you must have your study and I must have my parlor; and the two girls must each have a room. . . . And the rooms must all have outside light. And the rent must not be over eight hundred for the winter."

Not surprisingly, only some of Isabel's requirements will be met, and, not surprisingly, the search takes weeks, not days.

The Marches' New York apartment hunt is set more than a hundred years before the real estate booms I lived through, yet it's remarkably true to my own experience. Isabel March is exacting in her demands, but also tends to forget them. She comes close to taking one apartment before her husband reminds her it is empty and that they are looking for a furnished flat. With her "instinct for domiciliation," Isabel can't help but mentally move in to whatever apartment they visit: "It's the only way I can realize whether it will do for us. I have to dramatize the whole thing." My sister moved to New York seven years after I did, and we talk about this, how it's not simply the looking that wears you down, but the fact that in a day you've actually lived in the ten or twelve apartments you know you can't afford. You've drawn floor plans and measured out the width of a bookshelf and decided upon what you'll have to leave at the Salvation Army to make it all fit.

Isabel even has a classic real estate nightmare: "It was something about the children at first and then it was a hideous thing with two square eyes and a series of sections growing darker and then lighter, till the tail of the monstrous articulate was quite luminous again." Her husband laughs: "Why my dear, it was nothing but a harmless New York flat—seven rooms and a bath." Even the length and pacing of the apartment section (almost a hundred pages) feels accurate. You might say it goes on too long, or that there's no narrative arc. But Howells, the great realist, won't give you a narrative arc because apartment searches don't have them; they are slogs, ups and downs, moments of "yes, this is it," only to discover that heat's not included or there's a crazy tenant in the apartment next door. When the Marches finally do settle on an apartment, they choose one they'd seen on their first day—smaller than they wanted, stuffed with an agglomeration of "gimcracks": China pugs and Japanese fans, dragon candlesticks and Arab scarves. The Marches' search ends anticlimactically. It ends as all my searches in the nineties ended, with the taking of an apartment that had once seemed impossible.

About three weeks after moving into my first apartment in Queens, I moved out of it. The opera-singing, Joyce-quoting landlord turned out to be a perpetually inebriated Irishman down on his luck. He fancied himself a playwright—and he fancied me. At the time, he was reading Joyce's biography and began to call me Nora. One night he opened the door to hand over his prize possession, a bundle of letters from the Irish playwright Sean O'Casey, which I took upstairs to read. Their substance: deftly worded discouragement, unregistered it seemed by the recipient. On another night I awoke to find the landlord standing above my bed; he loved me, would I consider going to an AA meeting with him? There was a scene, ending in more deftly worded discouragement. The next night my roommate found us another apartment on the other side of Queens Boulevard. The landlord refused to give us our security deposit back. By accident, I took with me—and then lost—the O'Casey letters. I still hope they will appear someday stuck inside a book.

And so it began: ten years during which great swaths of time were spent moving in or out of an apartment, lining the cupboards with shelf paper or hooking up a speaker. I became an expert at finding free boxes, at knowing just when to snap forward the wrist when unrolling a duct tape dispenser across the lip of a box, and I had more than once managed to slide a futon over a subway turnstile and then support it against a pole like some life-size rag doll or a drunk unable to stand up.

After the two apartments in Queens, I tried Manhattan. The first apartment was on West Eleventh Street, a room that had once, literally, been a closet. If I peered out the window and craned my neck, I could see a glimpse of the Hudson River. From the fire escape, I heard Audrey Hepburn strumming "Moon River" on a guitar. I shared the apartment with two chic Yale graduates who approved of me only because of the books I absentmindedly removed from my bag at our first meeting but who then complained about my having too many of them.

On East Twenty-Second Street I lived in a studio so small that when I opened the sofa bed, I could touch all four walls and almost, not quite, reach into the kitchenette and lift the teakettle from the stove. The only window faced a brick wall. When my father came to visit, he reacted to the space with visible panic: he sat down, stood up, but there was nowhere to go. He drew a sketch of how I might cover the walls in mirrors, but instead of expanse, the mirrors gave me nothing but an unremitting vision of just me wherever I looked.

On West Fifty-Sixth Street, I shared an apartment above a French restaurant with tin ceilings and aged Broadway actors hunched at the bar. More like a corridor than a room, it offered, at the far end, one touch of beauty, a white-painted security gate, an elaborate filigree of ironwork that reminded me of a window in a Matisse painting. Tangiers or Morocco. Behind the window, a scrawny ailanthus tree whose branches, together with the design of the gate, cast quivering shadows on the walls at night. What my friends remember of that apartment is playing Scrabble with me in the kitchen and the cockroaches scuttling over the tiles. Or they remember the night the restaurant kitchen downstairs went up in smoke.

In Inwood, a neighborhood at the northernmost tip of Manhattan Island, I lived in a prewar studio with casement windows that rattled romantically when it rained. From the futon I could hear the disappointed cries of Columbia University football fans. In the nearby park, I took long walks, the caves and paths reminding me of the ledge back home. This apartment had a Mary Tyler Moore sunken living room, but rarely did I hear a knock on the door. The city fell below me like a sheer drop—an endless A train away.

On Eighth Avenue in the West Fifties, I lived in a sublet with a view—of what was left after Robert Moses came through and what would soon disappear once Donald Trump got started. One of the buildings I faced, a shaft of windowless concrete, seemed always just in the way of the sun as it set. At the top of the building, visible all night, was the BMW logo, a blue neon disc. My mother, when she visited, mistook it for the moon. The apartment was decorated by its owner to look like a stateroom on the *Titanic*. Lying on the velvet sofa, I listened to the keening brakes of faraway buses and envisioned the ship about to sink.

There is no question my adolescent fascination with cities and apartments came partly from a desire to do the opposite of what my parents had done. They had escaped to the country; I would take a different route. Our house was so defining an influence that I needed to create in my imagination a different form of inhabitation, something temporary, like a tent or a hotel room. I had been formed in a room where the bed, the desk, the bookshelves were locked in place. What would it be like to have the freedom to arrange it all, not just the interior but the view outside the window? What would it be like to live fleetingly, lightly in space, to change neighborhoods and selves on a whim? My grandfather's habit of rearranging the furniture is one I've inherited. Three in the morning, all the books off the shelf, and me pushing an armoire on an old towel across the already scraped-up floors.

In the beginning, the apartment moves seemed to fulfill these fantasies, each one a clean start—new neighbors, new habits, a different coffee cart to frequent, a fresh face behind the counter at the laundromat. It didn't take me long, however, to see that I wasn't choosing my nomadic state so much as being forced into it. There were some exceptions: out of a desire to be left alone, I gave up the contemptuous roommates in the West Village and, out of loneliness, the studio in the far reaches of Inwood. But mostly I had no choice. A sublet would end, or the landlord would jack up the rent. For the first fifteen years in New York I lived on limited funds and was driven to find a deal. My jobs—publishing, freelance writing, teaching—could barely pay the rent, and my parents were not the sort to offer much financial support to their children after college; it would spoil us and our chances for a meaningful life. Even if they had been willing, those were the years when my father and my brother were running from bank to bank trying to keep the company afloat. Most of my apartments were above what was, for my friends, the dividing line of coolness: Fourteenth Street. When they visited me, they'd ask why I lived in so unfashionable a region, and then I'd watch their expressions change once I told them how much I paid. Except for the last, none of those Manhattan apartments or shares cost me more than six hundred dollars a month. I am not by nature a braggart, but on this subject I tend to crow.

On my second or third move, I noticed I had become, like so many of my friends, a real estate bore. I spent too much time looking for apartments, talking about apartments, or constructing elaborate fantasies about apartments. I help an elderly woman across the street; she is so grateful she invites me to move in to her classic-six apartment on West End Avenue. Like Isabel March in Howells's novel, I began to have real estate dreams: I break through the back of my closet, and on the other side, a secret room. A fire escape blooms into a garden. Or my favorite: a great real estate bubble that for so long has been pressing down on me finally bursts. During those years I grew envious, like some Little Match Girl, the real estate pages of the *Village Voice* tucked under my arm, peering in the windows of apartments I couldn't afford. The really extravagant—built-in bookcases, a fireplace, the shock of a grand piano—I could overlook. The apartments I longed for were the kind that in any other city would be easy enough to find and afford: a room in a neighborhood close to work or school. My envy was stirred most of all by vacant apartments, unlit windows, the privilege of space unused.

Something was changing—and it frightened me. How I had related to place back in Wisconsin seemed under threat; intimacy with a landscape was in danger of being replaced by the colder enticements of property—acquisition with all its primitive urges. To respond to the threat I began—unconsciously then—to make New York over to fit my childhood. I loved Inwood Park because Inwood Park was familiar, a rocky spine with caves and bluffs left behind when the Wisconsin glacier came through. By retreating to that neighborhood at the end of the A train, I'd re-created another familiar map: the physical separation of country and town, trees and pavement. Even in the apartment in the West Fifties, I noticed myself following a familiar routine on my days off, a round of nature, books, and—I will confess—fast food. I'd start at Coliseum Books near Carnegie Hall, and then take my new purchase to Central Park and read on a rock beneath a tree. After that, I'd head straight for the McDonald's on the corner of Eighth and Fifty-Fifth, buy a coffee and a carton of french fries, and sit in a corner booth. Nobody disturbed me. I could read for hours. Unconsciously I was shaping my days around the pattern of my teenage years—woods, books, and orange Formica under fluorescent lights.

By the end of my tenure in Manhattan, I found myself thinking more and more about that bedroom backed into the ledge: the knotholes in the ceiling, the nicks in the desk, the indentations in the carpet from a bed frame that never moved.

◇

Willa Cather lived in New York for forty years. She wrote about her share of New York spaces, and sometimes on my walks around the city a lit window will summon one: the Waldorf hotel suite in "Paul's Case"; the artist studio in "Coming, Aphrodite!"; or that apartment overlooking Madison Square Park in *My Mortal Enemy*. Outside, a snow-covered square; inside, velvet curtains and a woman singing an aria from *Norma* in the moonlight. But materializing most often in my Manhattan years was a room set far from New York—Thea Kronborg's attic in *The Song of the Lark*, a child's bedroom under the eaves of a simple frame house in Moonstone, Colorado:

> It was the end room of the wing, and was not plastered, but was snugly lined with soft pine. The ceiling was so low that a grown person could reach it with the palm of the hand, and it sloped down on either side. There was only one window, but it was a double one and went to the floor. In October, while the days were still warm, Thea and Tillie papered the room, walls and ceiling in the same paper, small red and brown roses on a yellowish ground. Thea bought a brown cotton carpet, and her big brother, Gus, put it down for her one Sunday. She made white cheesecloth curtains and hung them on a tape. Her mother gave her an old walnut dresser with a broken mirror, and she had her own dumpy walnut single bed, and a blue washbowl and pitcher which she had drawn at a church-fair lottery.

Cather modeled Thea's room on her own attic in Red Cloud, Nebraska. Visit that house today, and you will see for yourself the cheesecloth curtains, the red and brown wallpaper, the double window to the floor. I didn't know this for a fact when I read the passage the first time, but I guessed it to be true. Something in the specificity of the description told me that here was a meticulous recollection, a room so familiar its author knew every corner by heart.

Willa Cather's childhood bedroom, Red Cloud, Nebraska. (courtesy, Willa Cather Foundation, Barb Kudrna, photographer)

The description of Thea's bedroom summoned my own recollections as well. "[How] very quickly," the philosopher Gaston Bachelard writes, "at the very first word, at the very first poetic overture, the reader who is 'reading a room' leaves off reading and starts to think of some place in his own past. . . . The values of intimacy are so absorbing that the reader has ceased to read your room: he sees his own again." You'd find no wallpaper, no walnut furniture, and no attic in the house my parents built in Wisconsin, but I can't read Thea's room, even now, and not see the bedrooms my father designed for us at the back of the house: the one window, the trees brushing up against it, the walls "snugly lined with soft pine" and a sloped ceiling "so low that a grown person could reach it with the palm of the hand."

Just as familiar is the effect of the space on its inhabitant. "In a small room, you will think smarter," my father used to say, which

I assumed then was his excuse for designing such proportionally tiny spaces for us and such an airy room for himself and my mother at the front of the house. We slept in a nook; they slept with a vista. But my father was entirely right about the power of those low-ceilinged spaces. The attic room stands as "one of the most important things that had ever happened" to Thea. From the day she moves to the upstairs wing, she "began to live a double life." In the attic her "mind worked better. She thought things out more clearly. Pleasant plans and ideas occurred to her which had never come before . . . thoughts which were like companions, ideas which were like older and wiser friends." At night in the summer "she used to drag her mattress beside her low window and lie awake for a long while, vibrating with excitement . . . pulsing with ardor and anticipation. It was on such nights that Thea Kronborg learned the thing that old Dumas meant when he told the Romanticists that to make a drama he needed but one passion and four walls."

 The fact that this room took such vivid shape in my early years in New York seems easy enough to explain. You could call it a simple case of homesickness. When Thea leaves her Moonstone bedroom for the final time, she knows she'll never be able to return. Sitting one night on her old bed in the attic, she thinks it "would be her last summer in that room. . . . Its services were over; its time was done." She knows she will "never think anywhere else as well as here. She would never sleep so well or have such dreams in any other bed. . . . When she went away from it for good, she would leave something that she could never recover."

 And Thea never does recover that first room. A few spaces will approximate the feeling of the original home—later she will travel to the Southwest and find in a cave, a "nest in a high cliff, full of sun," some of the feeling of her attic refuge—but by the novel's end, when she is flourishing as an opera star in New York City, rooms no longer matter. She moves beyond them. Cities offer skilled teachers and appreciative audiences, but they don't give her rooms she will love. In New York, she lives impersonally, distractedly. She may have a preference for one restaurant over another, but beyond that, the city seems to be only vaguely discerned—shadows and light seen from a carriage or through curtains absently pulled back from the hotel window. My students, when they read the novel, never fail to comment on the absence of friendship and community in the closing chapters. More jarring to me is that pale New York landscape; except for the opera house and the hotel bathtub into which she sinks at the end of the day, Thea doesn't seem to care where she is at all.

All this may explain why I've never liked the ending of *The Song of the Lark* half as well as I like its beginning. Like Thea I had an intense attachment to the childhood room, but unlike her, I believed I could re-create it. In my first ten years in New York I lived in eight apartments. I painted nearly all of them—the walls, the baseboards, the cupboards, even the interiors of a closet. As if making a commitment to a place offered a guarantee that the landlord would make a commitment to me. As if moving a paint roller across a wall might ensure permanence and bring me back to that original space—not just to the room itself, but to the city I'd first dreamed up inside its four walls. At the time I wouldn't have admitted any of this. Wasn't a certain level of homelessness what I'd wanted—to be someone who moves through the world with her house like a shell on her back, a hotel dweller, a freefloating citizen of nowhere? But I can't now ignore the urgency fueling all those apartment searches, an urgency that couldn't have been just about shelter, just about the rent.

I don't see my Manhattan apartments clearly anymore. With time, they have lost their edges: each year, the distance between a door or a window shifts. Each year, another picture falls from its nail. Only one apartment from those early years do I see vividly, the way I see the rooms of my childhood. This apartment was on Fifteenth Street, and it belonged to someone else—to Dee, the friend I met on my first day in the city.

Nearly as small as that windowless studio on Twenty-Second Street, it fit together like a puzzle. Dee's last name was McAuliffe, and the place could easily have been an Irish cottage or a Dublin bed-sit; you expected a gas heater and a slot where you'd drop your coin. The apartment had two rooms, the first about eight feet by ten. Against one wall a single daybed and behind it three paintings: a yellow bird flying across a purple background, the masts of a ship, a muddy-colored storm. The painter, Dee told me, had lived in the apartment before her. Opposite was an old-fashioned nonworking fireplace, the mantel crowded—porcelain angels, a miniature grandfather clock, a transistor radio. Presiding over the room stood a massive corner cabinet that had been hauled in through the window since it couldn't fit through the door.

On the one window in the room hung lace curtains, perhaps once white, now yellowed like everything else in that apartment from years of cigarette smoke. Built around the casement were shelves crammed with books. A Jungian guide to dreams, a biography of Brendan Behan, a history of Greenwich Village. Propped inside, a painting on cardboard of a face and a gaping mouth in cobalt blue, something like Munch's *Scream*, but I liked Dee's version better. She painted it just after she'd moved to New York. Her blue period, she said.

The one window in the room faced an inner courtyard. To reach the apartment, you had to first walk through the hallway of one red brick building, then through the tiny courtyard to another red brick building at the back. Since the two buildings shared an address, Dee's address read *113 and $^1/_2$ W. 15th Street*, which seemed to fit her and the place where she lived: a bit tilted, cock-eyed. The address made me remember a picture from a children's book where everything in a room has been sliced in half: the chairs, the footstool, the teakettle and cups. The remoteness of the place—an interior inside an interior—accounted for some of the apartment's charm and for the sense I had of having found the Village of my imagination. Eugene O'Neill, Dee told people, had once lived upstairs.

On the back wall was a door leading to the kitchen, a room even smaller than the first. Here sat a rickety café table and two tiny chairs, the ironwork at the back shaped like hearts. The chairs, I assumed, were for effect, since there was hardly enough room to use them. (Only once in twenty years of visiting that apartment do I remember sitting in one of them. This was at the end, when a nurse shunted me into the kitchen.) On one wall, a tiny stove, a counter the size of a checkerboard, and the bulge of an ancient refrigerator. She managed this kitchen expertly. Sometimes I brought friends for dinner. We'd crowd in the doorway to watch: a balancing act of bamboo trays, a practiced negotiation of pots on the stove.

Even the bathroom I liked. It must once have been part of the kitchen; the partition wall was flimsy, the door impossible to shut, and for privacy you needed to yank on a bit of string tied to the handle. Behind the toilet, Dee had papered the wall with a collage of photos: James Dean in a cowboy hat, Bette Davis in the film *Three on a Match*, and whatever children were then in her life. The tub was cracked and yellow—half the size of a regular one, more like a hip bath—with a shower pole above it. I don't remember a shower curtain, but I do remember that if you came over for dinner, this was where she'd hang your coat.

For the first years I lived in New York, I visited that apartment at least one night a week. On special nights, when we had money, we'd go to Marie's Crisis, a piano bar in the Village where Dee would sing her two favorites: "Send in the Clowns" and "Is That All There Is?" She delivered these melancholy standards off-key and with a kind of savage glee. Or we went to a dusty Italian restaurant on Eleventh Street called Gene's—still there—where the elderly waiters in their red jackets paid Dee court. When the smoking ban was enforced in 2003, the waiters looked away when she lit her cigarette under the table and when smoke came out of her nose after she came back up. Most of the time, though, we spent our evenings in her apartment, drinking scotch and eating off those bamboo trays. Our evenings began the same: cocktails and a folding table set up at the couch with olives and cheese. Then the questions. "What are you reading?" followed by "Who have you seen?"

Afterward she told her stories. I stretched out on the rug; she sat on the daybed, knees folded under her, and told of working at the War Resisters League or volunteering at Dorothy Day's *Catholic Worker* or driving a taxi; of her stint as a voluntary policewoman and how they gave her a club to swing; of a kiss in a snowstorm in Washington Square Park and the time she stepped out of a taxi and there, on the curb, huddled in a dirty raincoat, was Greta Garbo. I saw Manhattan in the scenes she described. In the cadence of her speech, I heard a New York dame. After Dee died, Lisa, a close friend, wrote about Dee's "patois of 1940s slang":

> Houses were "lit up like a tickle-park," empty bottles were "dead soldiers," flirts came at you "like a Mack truck, blinking and smiling," an enthusiastic embrace "squashed you like a marshmallow." "Listen Sister," she loved to say, that and "nothing doing!" She was "up against it." It was "a good wrinkle." She put on her "best bib and tucker." This one had "bats in the belfry, was crazy as a bedbug," that one was "four sheets to the wind," the other "sat there like a bump on a log." Things were "hunky dory" till they "came to a sticky end." She would "give you a buzz, mosey along, was raring to go, then all tuckered out."

After a few drinks, certain themes were bound to come up: the severity of nuns she knew, the hypocrisy of priests. I had grown up with this story; my mother was sent to Catholic school and still visibly twitches in the presence of a nun. But my mother had long since brushed off the cobwebs of her Catholicism, left it all behind. Dee had not. Instead, she returned obsessively to her falling out with the church, the wrath of a betrayal, a scab peeled back again and again to ensure it never completely heals. My mother had traded in religion for a matter-of-fact atheism, but Dee still sought out the mysteries. She found them in all sorts of places: books by

Edgar Cayce and tarot cards, Native American totems and angels. Once she even took me to a dark room over a store on Sixth Avenue to meet her psychic group, elderly people so pleased to have lured a potential young member to the group they half-convinced me I had the second sight.

Sometimes, she talked about her childhood. Abandoned at birth by her mother and deposited at the Catholic foundling hospital, she spent the next eighteen years moving all over Queens, from one foster home to the next. None of the people who took her in had much compassion, except the last, a woman she spoke of tenderly and sometimes called "mother." In school she was taught by nuns, and for four or five years when she was in grade school, she lived with two particularly sadistic ones. A friend of Dee's used to say that anybody else with that childhood would have ended up a serial killer. The only effect I could make out was a ferocious independence, a refusal to take any kind of charity. She liked to volunteer at orphanages and hospitals where she would hold the babies until they fell asleep.

My friends and I, then in our twenties, were inclined to dramatize our dysfunctional childhoods. Dee listened to our stories and would shake her head. "Parents. Maybe it's just as well I didn't have them." Whether she believed this or not, I can't say. I do know that when she was in her forties, she tracked down her birth mother and showed up at the door of her house on Long Island. A woman opened the door—her half sister, Dee discovered later—who explained that Dee's mother had died just weeks before.

The years that came after moving to New York were always hard to piece together. She'd give you bits, then change the information; you'd have to go back, check facts, reorganize it all chronologically. Sometimes, you'd get the picture only secondhand: a summer job in Provincetown in the fifties, the Chelsea Hotel lobby, a loft in SoHo, Dee leaning against a grand piano singing a show tune to a crowd of admirers. Later I learned that the woman who'd painted the bird, the ship, and the storm over that daybed had once been in love with her.

◇

Dee's apartment represented an ideal—the dot on the Manhattan map, the pointed arrow spelling out the words You Are Here. This might seem odd. Why, over all the more likely urban spaces—the parks and bars, the museums and street corners— choose an interior cell cut off from the street, a dusty room crammed with Irish teacups and books on the occult?

Like that ancient corner cabinet hauled in through the window, Dee's studio had the appeal of a dollhouse. Or even better, one of those horse-drawn Irish caravans she loved. "If I could live anywhere," she told me, "I'd live like an Irish gypsy in a house on wheels." I liked this image—the portable house. I imagined the wheels in motion, the road beneath us, while inside, nothing changed. Everything knew its place, every space was functional, every hook in the kitchen put to use. Wasn't this my fantasy of the city: a place for travel and change, and at the same time, a room that stays put?

The studio also gave me the city I'd wanted and hadn't found. Here was the elusive café—at the table, a circle of friends: the brassy dame singing show tunes off-pitch next to a woman in white pearls quoting from Cummings and Dorothy Parker; across the table, an astral-traveler stares into her crystal ball. Here was the single girl's kitchenette and the story I'd brought with me from Wisconsin: the classic escape from a provincial backwater, the leaving of working-class Queens for West Village Bohemia. No more church, no more handouts. "I had to get away," Dee told me. "Or I thought I might die."

Like my grandmother Kathryn, Dee had the orphan's craving for a home of her own, but here was a different model of the nest and one I particularly needed at the time. Not the security of a family or a partner, but a refuge formed for friendship and for solitude. I remember the first time my mother met Dee. "What a sweet woman," she said later in the taxi, "but don't you think it's a bit sad, that life?" For some reason I didn't ask my mother what she meant by this. Was she referring to Dee's perpetual smoking or the pleasure she took in her scotch? Or was this the usual middle American shock at the size of a New York apartment, no bigger than a Wisconsin pantry? I tend to think it was Dee's entrenched singleness that worried my mother. She feared I'd spend my days alone in a closet-sized room. I couldn't have explained to her the appeal of this version of a home, nor could I have explained to anyone back in Wisconsin the relief I felt being there.

The apartment also offered me a refuge from all that whirling apartment anxiety; $113^{1}/_{2}$ was rent controlled—even better than rent stabilized. A little boat anchored against the tempests of New York real estate—or, as Edith Wharton might have put it, a "nest hanging safely over the abyss." I spent a lot of time complaining then about my real estate troubles. Dee would nod sympathetically—she'd been there herself—but I wonder now whether she was secretly rolling her eyes at my middle-class panic. Who was I to worry about living on the streets in a cardboard box when I had parents to fall back on? She lived under the shadow of genuine homelessness; I did not. When I visited Fifteenth Street, she often talked of how "piss-elegant" the West Village had become. New York in the nineties and the early two thousands confounded her. She would not have admitted it, but it must have frightened her too. With almost no savings, she'd lived hand-to-mouth for years. Soon after I quit the first publishing job on Thirty-Third Street, the outfit closed down and left Dee without a job. She was in her sixties. After that, she supported herself on her Social Security check, which couldn't have been much, and for a while, she took care of her friend Lisa's two boys. Sometimes when we'd talk about the transformation of the city, I saw her look around the room as if to reassure herself, as if to confirm it was all still there.

Usually when she left town for summer weekends, Dee would call up and offer me her apartment. This was when I was living in Queens. She hadn't lost her old prejudices against the boroughs and felt sorry for me: "A night in town," she'd say, "will perk you up." I took her up on the offer only once, but I remember that weekend clearly: the pleasure of stepping across the courtyard late at night, turning the key, and then lying on the narrow couch and watching the shadows move across the walls. From this position the room took a new shape. I recognized a space from my past—the childhood bedroom. Looking up at the mantel and the bookshelves—the porcelain angels, the clock, the cardboard painting from her blue period—I thought of a little girl in bed at night taking comfort in the outline of familiar objects. It occurred to me that not having had a first place—Thea Kronborg's retreat under the eaves—Dee had been compelled to make one up. The next morning, as I walked out through the garden and down the corridor separating the rear building from the front, I thought of another hallway: that narrow passage leading me out from my dark little room into the vast space of a living room. The same rush of sensation, but this time what swelled before me was not the height of rafters or a descending view but the city's beautiful roar.

A few months before Dee died, we held a meeting at 113½ West Fifteenth Street. There were eight of us: Dee; her doctor; her home health-care aide; her hospice social worker; and her friends Lisa, Michael, Gloria, and me. Dee lay on the daybed. We stood looking down at her. It was so crowded some of us had to lean in from the hallway outside. We were there to tell her that she had to leave that apartment for good. She hardly flinched. "Shit," she said, but kept her face blank. The social worker explained that either she'd have to move into a hospice facility or someone would need to stay with her overnight. He didn't need to point out that this was impossible; the size of the apartment spoke for him. Her only other option: she could move in with one of us.

Lisa had a large apartment on University Place, a duplex with a basement room. Her teenagers could move out. Dee could move in. The home aide could take the day shift, we decided, and the rest of us could take shifts at night. Dee didn't say a word as we worked out the details, but for a second, I saw her face change: the look of a fugitive caught, surrounded. I thought of those early years in the foundling hospital and then the years living as a dependent in other people's houses. She lit a cigarette, but she didn't make us wait long. When she spoke, she kept her answer short. "It'll have to be Lisa's." she said. "And I'm sorry for the trouble." Just before departing, the doctor told her how much he liked the apartment—he'd never seen a room quite like it—and asked if he could take a picture. We all stepped out of the way. I framed that photo in my mind: Dee propped up, head high, half-scowling, half-smiling for the camera, behind her the corner cabinet and, dimly visible through the kitchen doorway, a café table and chairs.

For the next few months I spent every Wednesday evening in a basement room on University Place. It didn't have a window but it did have a steel door at the far end, cracked open so Dee could smoke. Lisa and her husband had worked to make it cheerful—table lamps and an easy chair, a television at the end of the bed—but the move had been hasty and there still hung in the air the odor of teenage socks and, on the walls, little strips of dirty tape from where the boys' posters had been ripped away. She did not complain about any of it or ever say a word about going home. I was surprised one day to find that she had taken to watching soap operas with her aide and could hardly tear herself away from the dramas on television. (I thought of Lillian Hellman visiting Dorothy Parker in an East Side rooming house at the end of Parker's life, and her shock to find the urbane Parker glued to the soaps.)

Then came the night in February. Lisa and her husband, on call all the time, were exhausted and needed a night off. I was alone in the apartment with Dee. She seemed agitated, almost frantic. I called my friend David and his partner Scott, the hospice nurse who had coordinated Dee's care from the time she'd gotten sick. They were in the neighborhood having dinner. When they walked through the door, they smelled of the outside (New York winter, Saturday night). Scott immediately knew what to do, putting everything to right, shaming me by how effortlessly he straightened the sheets and counted out the pills. But Dee was still restless, still frantic, craning forward as if desperate to say something. Scott held her hand and asked, almost matter-of-factly: "Do you want to go back to your apartment now, Dee? Is that what you want?" She looked him in the eye—hard—and gripped his hand. Then, just as deftly as he had arranged the bed, the room, the sheets, Scott arranged the rest. He called the nurse service, and a few hours later an ambulance came and took her home.

As soon as Dee heard Scott's promise, she went still, as if released. Afterward, she stopped trying to talk. We (the team of friends and hospice nurses) spoke on the phone the next morning and all said the same thing. "She was just waiting for the chance to go back to Fifteenth Street," words that had the ring of the platitude, but I'm still sure are true. Dee had lived in her studio for almost sixty years. It was more than a refuge, more than a nest. It was like a second skin. She knew that room in her body—every curve of the cushion beneath her, every thump of the radiator, every smell.

The next morning I went to Fifteenth Street and spent a few hours sitting across from Dee. When I left to go back to work—left her lying under the bird, the ship, the storm—I knew I'd never see her again. Outside, a crisp New York winter afternoon, jackhammers and smoke rising from a manhole. On Sixth Avenue, a rush of taxis and people holding their cell phones in mittened hands. All the incongruities: blue sky and life racing past while inside a dark room, a nurse sits listening to the in and the out of another person's breath. Before descending into the subway at Fourteenth Street, I had a momentary vision. I saw a girl standing on that corner sixty years before. It is her first day in her new apartment and maybe she is on her way to the hardware store to buy nails and a hammer. On her way, she steps into a diner for a coffee. "This will be my diner," she thinks to herself. "This will be my town." She chooses a stool at the window so she can watch us, the crowds of people passing on the other side of the glass.

After Dee died, I talked to the landlord on the phone. He told me he'd known Dee since he was a little boy when his father had owned the building. "Every year," he said, "since I was five, she sent me a birthday card." I caught a tremble in his voice, which might not seem surprising unless you consider he was a New York landlord who now could charge ten times the amount for that apartment. Dee was good with birthday and thank-you notes — dime store cards arriving in the mailbox. Her handwriting, faint and flawless, always made me think of a nun guiding a little girl's hand as she moved a pencil across the page.

After I hung up with the landlord, I had to smile. She'd thought it all through. She'd figured it out. In a city that never stops, she'd found a way to build a refuge, so that all the pleasures of moving, all the changes, could happen where they ought to — out on the street.

8

Lafayette

In 1998, I moved into my last Manhattan apartment. Two years later, just after the ball dropped on the new millennium, I started looking in Queens and Brooklyn. I had arrived in the city with an image of John Travolta and his girl in *Saturday Night Fever* crossing the Brooklyn Bridge into Manhattan, but I spent the first six months of the new century searching in the opposite direction. I went looking all over the outer boroughs of Queens and Brooklyn: Long Island City, Kew Gardens, Sunset Park, Cobble Hill, Boerum Hill, and even Midwood, the neighborhood in Brooklyn Ronald Sukenick had abandoned in the fifties. Finally I found it: a rent-stabilized one-bedroom in Fort Greene, Brooklyn, an old brownstone neighborhood not far from Brooklyn's downtown. In the nineties, the neighborhood was a mecca for African American artists; it attracted me because of the racial mix and the architectural charm—brownstone streets lined with trees, New Orleans–style ironwork, tiny storefronts that half-reminded me of a seventies episode of *Sesame Street*.

The apartment I found was on Lafayette Avenue, on the third floor of a ten-story building constructed in the thirties. It stood where once a line of old brownstones had faced the street and was only a block from the ancient plane trees and oaks of Fort Greene Park, a small jewel of a park designed by Frederick Olmsted in the late 1800s. With its window boxes and tiny gardens, the neighborhood in spring looked like some elaborate trellis overhung with blossoms. In summer, coming home from a day in midtown

Manhattan—blasts of heat rising from the sidewalk, the air conditioners chugging overhead—I'd emerge from the stink of the subway to the shade and perfume of linden trees.

Whoever had designed the building had been a sensible kind of person: no wasted space; deep closets, one not much smaller than the room I'd lived in on West Eleventh Street. The place had the feel of an old rooming house or a single-occupancy hotel. Every apartment in the building was laid out the same: a recessed kitchen as you entered, opening to a box of a living room with one double window. On the left, a tiny bedroom and bathroom. The kitchen cabinets were pale yellow and made of tin, like a toy kitchen I had played with as a child.

Across the hall lived Goodwin, a Nigerian who worked at a nearby bank and who liked to talk to me about public schools and the usual topic, New York real estate. Next door lived Sharon from Trinidad, who had lived in that building for years. Someone in the building told me that in the thirties either a Marx brother or a Stooge was supposed to have rented Sharon's apartment for his girlfriend. I hoped it was a Stooge, only because it drew a line, a link, from Brooklyn all the way back to Milwaukee and my grandmother eighty years before.

I was very social in the apartment on Lafayette, always giving parties. Once I managed to squeeze sixty people inside its six hundred square feet. Dee came and held court in the corner. A sofa still bears a trace of her that night—the scorch of a cigarette burn on the back of a cushion.

But what I remember best about the place is my desk pushed up against the window.

Some writers prefer facing a blank wall, but I liked the moving back and forth, the scene before me filtered through the scenes I was reading and writing about—not a doubling of views so much as an overlay of them, like two transparencies lowered on the screen of an overhead projector. From my chair, I could see the clock tower of the old Williamsburg Savings Bank (now one of the most expensive condo buildings in Brooklyn), a row of brick townhouses—one with boarded up windows and a giant X across the door and another with flower boxes trailing vines—a bodega, a barbershop, and over a hair salon, a roof deck, its railing strung with lights. Out my Brooklyn window, though, I also saw another view—Manhattan fifty years before. The Biltmore clock. The shadow of the Third Avenue el train. The dining rooms of the old Brevoort and Lafayette hotels off Washington Square.

At the time I was finishing a PhD dissertation on mid-twentieth-century women writers and urban spaces. Most of the writers I turned to in those years were American satirists (people like Mary McCarthy and Dawn Powell), but my favorite was Maeve Brennan, an Irishwoman with a more oblique kind of humor, hardly ever barbed. She wrote fiction set mainly in her native Ireland (Dublin, Wexford, and Coolnaboy) and nonfiction mostly about New York, the city she'd adopted as her home at seventeen. From 1949 to the early seventies, she contributed a regular Talk of the Town column to the *New Yorker* and wrote under the byline "The Long-Winded Lady." Nowadays I have trouble finding anyone who has heard of her; her books are always going in and then back out of print. This surprises me since she's so good, one of a handful of writers I turn to when I need to remember how to write a sentence or focus my eye.

It wasn't the writing, though, that first lured me to Brennan, but a series of photographs I discovered while flipping through a magazine. The photographs were taken by the photographer Karl Bissinger in 1948, the year before Brennan began working at the *New Yorker*. All appear to be from one sitting. Brennan sits or stands, a sleek Holly Golightly look-alike in an elegant room. She is dressed in black, the ash of a cigarette dangerously long, her hair pulled back. A fire is in the fireplace, and roses are in the vase; there are stacks of books, a smoky mirror, a cut-glass ashtray to catch the ash. "To be around her was to see style being invented," recalled her friend the *New Yorker* editor William Maxwell. She painted the ceiling of her office at the *New Yorker* a Wedgewood

Maeve Brennan. (courtesy, Estate of Karl Bissinger, Karl Bissinger Papers, University of Delaware Library)

blue, knew the difference between the colors "bone" and "taupe," and early in her career had worked as a copyeditor at *Harper's Bazaar*.

It didn't take me long to learn that this image of midcentury glamour (the fashionable magazine writer in a tasteful Manhattan apartment) wasn't the whole story. For one thing, the photographs turned out to be all smoke and mirrors, taken in the borrowed apartment of a wealthy friend, the Irish American theater critic Thomas Quinn Curtiss; Brennan did not own expensive things and rarely had a long-term address. She often lived in short-lease apartments, usually with no kitchen and usually with a stray cat. More regularly, Brennan lived in hotels. After a brief hiatus in Sneden's Landing in upstate New York—coinciding with an equally brief marriage to the *New Yorker* writer St. Clair McKelway in the midfifties—she lived at the Hotel Earle, the Royalton, the Iroquois, the Prince Edward, the Algonquin, the Westbury, the Lombardy, and the Holley Hotel on Washington Square. Gardner Botsford, a friend and editor at the *New Yorker*, remembers that when Brennan moved, she could, "like the Big Blonde in the Dorothy Parker story," "transport her entire household, all her possessions and her cats" in a taxi.

In the early Talk of the Town pieces, Brennan keeps all this hidden; she pretends to be a suburbanite, just down in the city for lunch. "The Long-Winded Lady," her biographer Angela Bourke explains, was intended to be a "two-dimensional" figure, a woman seemingly "supported by a private income, and venturing forth only to shop." Brennan's daily excursions around New York often record a bounded and familiar terrain, a landscape in which any woman in town from the suburbs might feel right at home: a lunch at Longchamps, a view of a raucous party of sightseers in the Waldorf lobby, an afternoon martini at Le Steak de Paris. But by the early sixties, Brennan seemed to drop the suburban persona altogether, to reveal herself as a "traveler in residence," a flaneur of daily life in midcentury New York. She also began to seem less interested in shopping sprees than in the city under siege.

Read together, Brennan's *New Yorker* pieces take the reader on an extended walking tour. She describes a drugstore on Tenth and Sixth, a crowd gathered outside the Criterion Theatre on Times Square, two lovers walking down Sullivan Street, trucks backed up on Forty-Eighth Street, a tourist riding a bus up Fifth Avenue. She has a reporter's eye for details of the street, and at times her prose meanders, following the contours of a city stroll. Often, her descriptions also have a kind of writing-exercise quality about them: describe a dress from top to bottom, describe a woman from hat to shoes. (In an interview with *Time* in 1974, she explains that "if you are writing about people in the street, you have to describe their clothes, all of them. Clothes tell a lot.") She does the same with public spaces: describe a walk from start to finish, describe a street from end to end. Her renderings of the city are marked by a fixation on the specificity of the landscape as if she is safe in the assumption that her reader knows the city well.

Ḥer map delimits three neighborhoods. She writes about the back-street hotel world of the "Latin Quarter" (today we call it Hell's Kitchen); the hotels and inexpensive restaurants of Greenwich Village, often tracing the same route from the Hotel Earle to the University Restaurant; and the upscale midtown hotels. She wonders whether she should go to the Algonquin, "which is so small and familiar, or to walk a little further, and east, to the Biltmore, which is so large and familiar."

Brennan's strolls have the intensity of a walk through the well-known rooms of your childhood house, and in the later essays and stories, one can't miss the disorientation, the sense that overnight the rooms have been rearranged. In her essay "The Last Days of New York" (1953), she describes a view from the window of her hotel room on Washington Square: Down below is a "narrow gap" in place of the Holley Hotel, the residential hotel she'd inhabited years before. Beneath her window, "brand-new, drearily uniform apartments" take up one corner of the north side of the square, and beneath her feet, the floor of her hotel room is "already shivering under the wrecker's boots." Later in the essay, she describes a demolition viewed from her office on the twentieth floor of a midtown building—presumably the *New Yorker* offices on Forty-Third Street. "In the afternoon, when I went to lunch, I found a whole block of Sixth Avenue gone." She experiences the bewilderment common to anyone who has lived, even if only for a short time, in New York City: the missing of the taken-for-granted, the loss of what you never knew you had. "It is very disconcerting to have a gap suddenly appear in a spot where you can't remember ever having seen a wall."

From the start, so much about Brennan intrigued me: her glamorous persona and beautiful prose, her intimate neighborhoods, and, of course, those Manhattan hotels. Her hotels fulfilled my old fantasies of a free-floating mobility. Here was privacy without the isolation, an affordable room upstairs and down below, an automatic social life. Hotels like the Brevoort on Fifth Avenue and the Lafayette on Ninth Street were also the closest things in the thirties and forties New York had to the Parisian cafés of my imagination. Once again, I had the feeling that I'd come too late, had missed the wits at the Algonquin Round Table, missed the poets and painters down at the Brevoort and Lafayette. I started to imagine the Fort Greene apartment as one of those hotels Brennan describes—a space that by its affordability, its simplicity, had given me the street below—and for a while, I even got a little fetishistic about this. Friends would bring me hotel postcards they'd found at flea markets, and one friend gave me a locket in the shape of a book, the cover embossed with the words *Lafayette Brevoort New York*.

But it was not just the romance of Brennan's transient existence that drew me. There was also her nostalgia for a world she wanted to see stay put. The New York depicted in Brennan's essays from the fifties and sixties is a "capsized" one, its inhabitants clinging "to the island that is their life's predicament." Her essays written in the fifties and sixties tell of the closing of Wanamaker's and Stern Brothers department stores and Schrafft's restaurants. Another essay mourns the Eighth Street bookstores that have moved or closed because of the high rents imposed in the sixties. She laments the "execution of the Hotel Astor" and in one essay describes what was once the grand entrance of a turn-of-the-century hotel, now a darkly lit lobby, a third its original size, with an old orange leatherette sofa and a badly working elevator. Her hotels, if not destroyed, have been eclipsed by the slabs of office buildings and apartment complexes being erected all around.

In the years she was writing her elegies for New York, the city was undergoing a dramatic escalation of office construction. "The Great Manhattan Boom" was what *Time* magazine called the commercial building fever of the 1950s: "Manhattan, written off long ago by city planners as a dying city because of its jammed-in skyscrapers and canyonlike streets, has defied and amazed critics with a phenomenal postwar building boom." All across the city new homes were being built—large-scale, high-density low- and middle-income housing projects—while others were crumbling, cleared away to make way for the new public housing complexes and office buildings, for expressways and civic centers.

At the time I was reading Brennan, I was living through my own great real estate boom and, like her, felt as if I were experiencing the "last days of New York." My husband says I was born elegiac—"Before you even walk in a room, you're remembering it." This is true. I arrived in New York already missing the place, and by the time I'd been in the city ten years, had joined the ranks of those who felt that Times Square had gone to slickness, that overheard cellphone conversations didn't compare to the stimulating street debates of earlier days, that Starbucks was killing the Korean deli. I became another kind of New York bore. A friend of mine has abandoned those he met when he first came to New York and taken up with a younger crowd because, he confesses, he can no longer bear to listen to "back in the day" prefacing every observation.

Certainly some of my "back in the day" carping can be traced to a nostalgic predisposition—or to the simple fact of aging—but not all of it. No one could miss the swift transformation of the city in the years after 9/11. Back in Manhattan, neighborhoods I remembered as sites of surprising turns, of grit and riveting tattoos, were now foreign, pocked by condo boxes and banks on every corner, overrun by fashion boutiques where rail-thin clerks eyed me up and down as if to say, "You are too uncertain," or, later, "You are too old." Coliseum Books, the store I visited nearly every day when I lived in midtown, could no longer afford the rising rents and closed down, replaced in 2003 by a bank and a Daffy's clothing store.

Most stunning was the transformation happening right outside my window in Fort Greene. For the first couple of years, around the time of 9/11, the neighborhood seemed to be in a developmental lull—the same couple of restaurants, the same people on the street. Then almost overnight closed-up storefronts were converted to bars, hip clothing shops opened up. Shafts of glass condominiums loomed above the Brooklyn church spires, and fewer and fewer affordable housing units were going up to keep pace. Familiar neighborhood figures were disappearing—or getting lost in a crowd of faces I didn't recognize.

In those years, I'd stand dazed on the corner, unsure of where I was, Rip Van Winkle stupefaction in the blink of an eye. By the time I moved out of the apartment on Lafayette, the dry cleaners down the street had become a high-end clothing store. I was glad the new owners had kept the sign over the door—in a midcentury cursive flourish, the words "French Cleaners" with a miniature Eiffel Tower above them—and I had to admit that the clothes inside were beautiful, laid out on long farm tables, hung in color-coordinated groups on the racks. But it was all too much for me. The last time I stopped in, I saw on the front table, next to the handbags, copies of Strunk and White's *Elements of Style* artfully arranged in a pile, but in this edition, grammar rules filled only half a page; the rest of the book was devoted to etchings of shoes and sandals. Laid out at the other end of the table, another touch of Brooklyn cool: an expensively produced magazine on sustainable living and organic produce, glossy photos of purple cauliflower and oddly shaped carrots heaped in a basket. Before leaving the store, I tried on a T-shirt and then flipped over the price tag: $300.

It was all a far cry from where I'd been when I first moved to the neighborhood only six years before—and I can't deny that some changes I welcomed. I'd be lying if I said I didn't like some of those new restaurants and bars, the folder of take-out menus thickening in my drawer. Window boxes and tiny brownstone gardens grew even more lush and surprising. The neighborhood was safer too. In the first year of living on Lafayette Avenue, I came home late one night to yellow police tape cordoning off the lobby entrance and a pool of blood on the ground where a man had just been shot. Now I could walk through Fort Greene Park on a summer night and hardly think about who was behind or ahead of me.

But what some people called resurgence, a neighborhood on the rise, I read as an ending. What I'd liked about the neighborhood was the racial mix; over those six years, more and more new people were moving in, and nobody could miss the fact that displacement was occurring along color and class lines. The more upset I got about all this, the more I found myself face to face with my old dilemmas of place and property. The neighborhood as it was when I first moved there—the racial makeup of the streets, the corner with its one or two restaurants, the flower shop and the barbershop, the regulars from the neighborhood walking past— all seemed just right. I froze my ideal neighborhood at the moment of my arrival, just as I had preserved, as if in amber or a little snow-globe you could shake, my ideal Wisconsin landscape inside my memories of the seventies, the years just after our house was built. Once more, I resented the future and ignored the past.

But it was hard to ignore the facts for long: the gentrification of Fort Greene had begun ten years before, some would even say ten years before that. When I looked dismissively down on the parade of twentysomethings taking their leisurely late-night saunters down Lafayette Avenue, when I listened to their regular flip-flop sashay under my window, or when I imagined I could see a $300 price tag hanging from their T-shirts, I had to stop myself and remember, just as I had once had to remember back in Wisconsin, that these people were my own. Wasn't I partly responsible— partly to blame—for what I saw every day out my window? I too had been an interloper. Soon after my arrival at the apartment on

Lafayette Avenue, someone undoubtedly looked down at me and saw the demise of a neighborhood.

And yet what could I do? When I looked at all the newcomers to the neighborhood, I could hear my father's voice: "people have to live somewhere." Most of the new people, like me, had been forced out of a more expensive neighborhood, just as the people leaving were now being forced out of this one.

I liked to talk to my neighbors Sharon and Goodwin about the changes in Fort Greene. Sharon and Goodwin approved of some of the changes: the amenities, the safe streets. They regaled me with stories of the old days—how you couldn't even walk outside at night by yourself. But after a while I sensed uneasiness. Something in the way Sharon's eyes would dart to her door during those conversations—as if to check that the apartment was still hers, check that she was safe—reminded me of the way Dee sometimes looked when talking about the "piss-elegance" of the Village and the rises in rent all around her. Living in a rent-stabilized apartment, Sharon knew she was safe, yet she also knew that many others in the neighborhood were not.

And then, after a new company bought the building, we started wondering whether even rent stabilization could protect us. Each time the management vacated an apartment, they could make improvements and raise the rent for the next tenant, and once the rent crossed a certain line, the apartment was no longer rent stabilized. In that year, the company began a campaign of intimidation, a pattern repeated in the half dozen other rent-stabilized buildings they bought in the neighborhood. If I was a few days late on my rent, which I often was, an evil-looking envelope from an impressive-sounding law firm landed in my box: small print interspersed with bold and underlined sentences about court dates, fines, and imminent eviction. Panicked, I finally called a lawyer friend who read the letters and laughed. He worked for a firm that actually was impressive, and after he called up the management company, I was never harassed again. Only later did I learn I was not the only target; there were lots of scared people in the building that year, some so scared they moved out and left the neighborhood altogether.

By now I've lived in New York City for over twenty years, and I've often wondered about the effect of living in this city—a place where people with middle-class incomes have so much difficulty finding housing. Does it make us more compassionate, more aware of others facing genuine homelessness? I think of all the searches when I seemed to fold into myself, head down, self-interested, almost blind. If I noticed others around me, I saw selectively and enviously. I saw only the people with higher incomes who could afford the places I could not.

Yet some apartment searches have pulled me out of myself, opened me up, and stopped me in my tracks. To me, what's most brilliant about William Dean Howells's apartment search in *A Hazard of New Fortunes* is that it includes that moment of confrontation—and that question: what are my disappointments compared with yours? One day, as they continue their search for a furnished flat with steam heat, an elevator, and bell-pulls at the door, Isabel and Basil March are stopped in their tracks, horrified to come across a well-dressed man stooped over a garbage can and sifting through it for food. Or another day, they walk through the tenement district downtown. Afterward, Basil turns to his wife and asks that age-old question: "Doesn't it make you feel rather small and otherwise unworthy when you see the kind of streets these fellow beings of yours live in, and then think how particular you are about locality and the number of bell-pulls?"

However obviously Maeve Brennan spoke to the concerns of a middle-class audience—readers of the *New Yorker* connecting to her nostalgia for places like Wanamaker's and the Hotel Astor—she also moved beyond those concerns to reflect on the problem of real homelessness. Gentrification was never really her theme, but displacement was. As someone who was perpetually "scurrying out of buildings before the wreckers," Brennan moves beyond her middle-class nostalgia to address a greater threat.

In her short story "I See You, Bianca," the owner of an apartment on Fourth Avenue lives in a "neighborhood with too many buildings half up and half down, and too many temporary sidewalks, and too many doomed houses with big X's on their windows." Nicholas, the owner, builds bookshelves and cabinets and fixes the furnace, hoping to create a "permanent refuge" he knows is bound to fail: "his house is to be torn down." Looking out his window, he observes the sidewalk down below:

> They stand outside their apartment houses on summer nights and during summer holidays. They stand around in groups or they sit together on the front steps of their buildings, taking the air and looking around at the street. Sometimes they carry a chair out, so that an old person can have a little outing. They lean out of their windows, with their elbows on the sills, and look into the faces of their neighbors at their windows on the other side of the street, all of them escaping from the rooms they live in and that they are glad to have but not be closed up in. It should not be a problem to have shelter without being shut away.

In one sense, Nicholas's desire for "shelter without being shut away" speaks to the fear of being forced *into* a home, the threat of being shut away, distanced from the activities of the street, sealed up in one of those brand-new beehive cement blocks high above— or obliged to leave the city for good. Nicholas's view from his window beautifully echoes what the urban historian Jane Jacobs called the "ballet of the city sidewalk." Jacobs's argument in *The Death and Life of Great American Cities* was that most urban planners at the time were, in fact, anti-urban. They wanted to build slum suburbs in the sky, towers that bred crime and isolated people from the street life below. Jacobs wanted a return to the diversity and vibrancy of neighborhood, "the ballet of the city sidewalk." To illustrate her point, she traces a day in her life on

Hudson Street. She observes the children leaving for school, mothers making their way to the corner grocery store, old women on their stoops, shopkeepers sweeping the sidewalk, secretaries heading to work, the myriad sights and views of one street on one particular day.

Brennan's phrase "it should not be a problem to have shelter without being shut away" also speaks to another anxiety: the fear of being forced out of one's home, a plight shared by thousands of New Yorkers at the time. It even, I'd say, describes in perfect terms why so many people in the first half of the twentieth century chose to live in hotels: the safe room and the city just down below.

The year Brennan published "The Last Days of New York," demolition began on the Lafayette and Brevoort hotels to make way for a gigantic fourteen-story apartment house. Two years later, in 1955, the novelist Dawn Powell memorialized the Lafayette in her novel *The Wicked Pavilion*. For Powell, the destruction of the Lafayette and Brevoort marked the end of a social world, the end of her subject: café society in Greenwich Village. Yet the final scene also records the effect of the wrecking ball on the people who reside upstairs. Along with the artists and writers watching the hotel come down there is also a "rouged and dyed old lady elaborately dressed in the fashion of World War One," dabbing at her "mascaraed eyes with a lacy handkerchief." She has come not only to watch what had been her home for over thirty years transformed into rubble, but to guard the welfare of her birds; they had made a nest outside her upstairs window, right above the café. One of the workmen in the demolition team makes his own observation: these women, the "old birds," were being sighted, looking lost and confused, everywhere around the Village. One could see a whole "nest of them" feeding the pigeons in Washington Square Park.

In eulogizing the New York hotel, Brennan and Powell record not only the end of a period of voluntary rootlessness available to middle- and working-class people, but also the beginning of a period of real homelessness for thousands of New Yorkers. The dramatic depletion in the number of residential hotels, SRO (single room occupancy) buildings, and rooming houses in the sixties and seventies would ultimately be a root cause of the homeless crisis of the eighties. Since the end of the nineteenth century, residential hotels had been one of the main housing options for poor single adults and childless couples. In the fifties, when New York began to adopt its policy of "deinstitutionalization," the YMCAs and SROs and cubicle hotels had also been a resource for discharged patients of state psychiatric hospitals. Yet in the sixties, many older residential hotels were being destroyed to make way for office buildings, and by the seventies, those that were left were swiftly being converted into higher-cost housing, especially in areas that were gentrifying, like the Upper West Side. Between 1972 and 1982, a hundred thousand SRO units disappeared. The only option, then, for many of the urban poor, was the street or the shelter.

The desire for shelter without being shut away seems eerily prescient of what would happen to so many New Yorkers in the seventies and eighties—and of what would happen to Brennan herself. By the late seventies she began experiencing psychotic episodes. Gardner Botsford recalls that she began to obsessively listen to Billie Holiday records and called him from Yaddo, the writers' colony, convinced that the people there were engaged in a plot to harm her. At one point, she was found sleeping in the ladies' room at the *New Yorker*. She was institutionalized for a period, then released. For a time, she seemed to be taking her medications, but when she went off them, she stopped speaking to her friends at the *New Yorker*. She disappeared, until in the early eighties she was sighted by one of her colleagues at the magazine stand near Rockefeller Center among a group of homeless people, feeding the pigeons, just like one of the ladies she had described from her window in "The Last Days of New York," and like one of those "old birds" Powell describes adrift in Washington Square. Although no one knew for sure, it was thought that the "traveler in residence"

may have been homeless. A receptionist at the *New Yorker* noticed a bag lady in the waiting room one afternoon but had no idea who the woman was, and only later realized that the woman was once a glamorous staff writer for the magazine. Brennan briefly returned to Dublin to live with relatives, but then with no warning called a taxi and moved into a hotel. She did the same in Illinois, after a brief period living with her brother. Every once in a while, there would still arrive at the *New Yorker* a Talk of the Town piece, with no one sure where it had been written or where she was. Maeve Brennan died in a nursing home in 1993, with no recollection that she had ever lived in New York.

9

Brownstone

If I liked to imagine my place on Lafayette as some residential hotel room, I was not so addled to forget the difference. The affordable hotels dotting the New York landscape in the nineteenth and twentieth centuries offered a double guarantee: a secure nest that could be seasonally reconstructed to present a different view. You might not be able to rearrange the furniture, but you could rearrange yourself, pick up and leave on a whim, check in to another equally affordable hotel across town.

But a rent-stabilized apartment is never easy to leave. It can become a trap. I know people who have forsworn relationships because they can't give up the safety of a cheap room, others who pass up far-flung adventures so their super will see them regularly picking up their mail. They suffer insults. Friends of mine in the East Village inhabit one of the last rent-stabilized apartments in a building overtaken by NYU students paying market rent. They accept like the weather the pounding of the stereo bass, the vomit on the stairs. On Lafayette Avenue, I lived over a bus stop—every ten minutes, a long shriek of brakes, the growl of an engine idling. But I never thought of leaving, and had circumstances not pushed me into it, I probably would never have done so. I saw my future and accepted it: earplugs and a storage locker rented in Queens.

Then in 2004 I fell in love. I'd first met Andre in college and had stayed close to him for twenty years. He never seemed the sort to settle down—years teaching in Southeast Asia and a stint living on a mountaintop in Costa Rica, a job driving Europeans in a tiny tour bus across America and a solo canoe trip down the

Mississippi. Landing in my living room was someone inclined, like Huck Finn, to "light out for the territory" now confined to a room with one window. I couldn't help worrying—or wondering, as Jim Burden wonders in the final pages of *My Ántonia*, "whether the life that was right for one was ever right for two." When Andre walked in the room, he seemed to fill it, to rattle the shelves. For a desk, he resorted to a board balanced across the arms of an easy chair. Other couples might have been able to live together in those tiny rooms, but already we were at a disadvantage: two lifelong bachelors unschooled in the customs of cohabitation.

Living on Lafayette had given me a six-year hiatus from apartment search anxieties, but as soon as we started looking, I recognized the old panic. "This is not a big deal," Andre said, as we marched on our way to the first apartment on our list. He saw my face. "It is the *biggest* deal," I told him.

Unbelievably, we found a place in less than a week—on the second floor of a brownstone on Washington Avenue in Clinton Hill, a landmark neighborhood blocks from where I'd lived in Fort Greene. More unbelievably, it was something out of a fantasy. Priced under market—we could just afford it—the apartment was the kind of place you see on television and roll your eyes. "She's a waitress! She's a teacher! Waitresses and teachers in New York don't live in places like that." The first time I opened the door (wide airy rooms, high ceilings, a fireplace with a marble mantelpiece) I seemed to be stepping into a photograph—Maeve Brennan in a beautiful apartment that belonged to someone else. At the back, blossoming trees and a church covered in ivy; at the front a study with a bay window facing Underwood Park, named after the typewriter tycoon who once had a mansion there. Standing in the fold of the bay awakened in me an intense desire, partly inspired by all those lost typewriters, to sit down to write.

Just after I'd moved to New York, a hairdresser, seasoned in the ways of the city, explained to my reflection in the mirror that everyone in New York gets one great apartment and one great relationship. "Someday, honey," she said, snapping her gum, "you'll get them both."

⟢⟩

Unless they are brand new constructions, most apartments come with a built-in history. Having grown up in a place created from scratch, I found this a great novelty when I first moved to the city. I liked the idea of all those people who had come before me, their history alive in the walls, the dust of their DNA still floating in the air.

The brownstone in Clinton Hill had been built before the Civil War. Families of lawyers and Episcopalian ministers climbed the stairs in the 1870s and 1880s, and there are still alcoves in the hallways for maneuvering the caskets of the genteel boarders who died here at the turn of the century. In old issues of the *Brooklyn Daily Eagle* I can read about the apartment in 1880, how the living room was done in "leather pressed paper, with handsome frieze" and the ceiling "frescoed in flower effect, light and airy, with birds flying." The birds are gone, but the apartment does have transom windows scraped clear of paint and a view of trees in winter that makes me think of a Stieglitz photograph or an Edith Wharton afternoon glimpsed when lace curtains are pulled away.

Every neighborhood has its ghosts, and I have always liked searching them out. When I lived in Manhattan's West Fifties, someone told me the side streets off Eighth Avenue—a neighborhood convenient to the office, close to the commuter train—had been popular with men in the 1940s and 1950s seeking discreet rentals for their mistresses. On walks up the avenue, I conjured the presence of all those kept women, languishing ghosts, wraithlike beauties with poodles tugging at the leash. In Inwood, I ended my hikes in the park at the boulder marking the spot where in 1626 Peter Minuit is said to have purchased Manhattan Island with a few handfuls of beads. Whenever I stopped there, I saw the two hands outstretched.

This interest in neighborhood history only intensified after we moved to Clinton Hill, a landmark neighborhood steeped in the kind of history that encourages walking tours and a frequent thumbing of architectural guidebooks. In the mid-1800s the neighborhood rivaled Brooklyn Heights as the most prominent

Brooklyn suburb for the middle and upper classes. The well-heeled lived, as they so often do, high up—on the Hill, on the Heights. By the late 1800s, captains of industry were drawn to the area, building ornate mansions all along Washington and Clinton Avenues. Many of these houses are still standing. So are the institutions built to accommodate the new arrivals. From my window I look down every day on an imposing red-brick edifice that was once a home for elderly women; when opened in the 1850s, it was called the Graham Home for Aged, Indigent, and Respectable Females, shortened in the 1870s to an even stranger name: the Graham Home for Old Ladies. The place always makes me think of the Boyle Catholic Home in Fond du Lac where my great-aunts Dora and Marie lived out their final days. A few blocks away stands the old Masonic Temple, now rented out on weekends for rock shows. Everywhere, there are churches. A historical guide tells me that in 1900 Clinton Hill boasted a total of eighteen: "four Episcopal, one Reformed Episcopal, three Baptist, two Presbyterian, two Methodist, one Congregationalist, one Reformed, one German Lutheran, one Universalist, and one Quaker." One of these churches stands just behind our apartment, the Baptist Emmanuel Church, so close I can lie in bed on Sunday mornings and listen to the gospel choir.

    The period of great wealth that led to this abundance of churches lasted only a short time; by the twenties, the very wealthy were moving back to Manhattan, and Clinton Hill returned to being a largely middle-class district. During the Depression, brownstones began to be divided up into multiple-family homes and rooming houses, and in the years after World War II, the area began to see a racial shift. Many of the old houses were torn down. Across the park from me, a row of brownstones was torn down to make way for a housing development built for the Brooklyn Navy Yard workers, a block of tall buildings with a park in the middle in the tradition of Le Corbusier. North of Myrtle Avenue stands a low-income housing development built in the forties—Walt Whitman Houses, named in honor of the neighborhood's most famous writer.

The Graham Home. (courtesy, Picture Collection, New York Public Library, Astor, Lenox and Tilden Foundations)

Underwood's mansion was torn down in the fifties, and his widow and daughter bequeathed the land to the city for a park; according to one neighborhood historian, the Underwood women believed the area "was entering a period of physical deterioration and didn't want their home to be part of it." Around the same

Brownstone

time, the Graham Home for Old Ladies closed; the new owners painted the bricks black and opened the place as a brothel—the Bull Shipper's Motor Lodge. The old-timers on the block tell me these years—from the sixties up to the eighties—were the rough ones: high crime, buildings abandoned and falling apart.

By the early eighties, the neighborhood saw a crack epidemic and at the same time the beginning of gentrification, with both white and black middle-class families moving in. Sharon and Jim Barnes, the owners of this brownstone, bought their first house in the neighborhood then and, like the other house lovers moving here, painstakingly and lovingly renovated it, returning it to its former glory. Along with the restorers came the artists: jazz musicians, hip-hop artists, theater directors, actors, spoken-word poets. A local historian, Nelson George, made a film, *Black Boheme*, about the neighborhood artist scene he lived through in the mid-eighties into the nineties, which includes interviews with many of the people who lived here then. Branford Marsalis lived just down the street on Washington. Spike Lee built a film studio in Fort Greene. Rosie Perez still lives around the corner.

I can't help but get romantic about those years: so much beauty unearthed, so much beauty created. In one room, the sound of paint being scraped away from an old mantel; in another, the wail of a trumpet. Once again I arrived at the tail end of yet another bohemia. This time, though, I missed out on it not just because of when I came but also, of course, because of what I am—white. My friends tell me about all the writers who now live in the neighborhood. It may not be bohemia, they say, but still I should join in. I'm never tempted, and this has made me wonder a little about all those old longings for artistic community. Perhaps I've changed. Or perhaps I never really wanted to join in and intentionally kept my ideal community in the elusive past, preferring to remain at the edge of it—looking back, looking in.

As I write this now, in 2012, the neighborhood is seeing prosperity and gentrification on a dramatic scale. Down the street, a weekly upscale flea market (artisanal cheese, distressed mirrors, eighties pumps, and retro turntables) attracts crowds here every

Saturday. The neighborhood is still defined by hipness—but now it all seems too expensive. There are those who say the neighborhood has come full circle: the robber barons have returned, expensive strollers roll beneath my window every morning, brownstones sell for four or five million. Many of the artists have moved out. So have many of the families who lived here for generations. When Branford Marsalis lived on this street in the early eighties, Underwood Park was a home for crackheads. Today the park is a thriving playground. On Saturday mornings, I close my window to muffle the ice-cream cart and the eternally creaking swings. The Bull Shipper's Motor Lodge (née the Graham Home for Old Ladies) is now a high-end condominium.

Like most urban neighborhoods, Clinton Hill offers up multiple and conflicting histories—histories of race and class that come in contact, overlap. My street won't stay put; it won't remain within the limits of any one story. I often think of the years when the brownstone was first built. I look down on Washington Avenue from my study and see in my mind's eye a family on their way to church. A woman, her face hidden beneath a poke bonnet, holds the hand of a child; a man lifts his umbrella to catch the first drops of Sunday rain; at the rear, a servant girl pushes a perambulator.

But I can never keep my eyes focused on this picture postcard for long—or keep it inside its pretty frame. The neighborhood's early history won't be defined by a fixed narrative of upper-class gentility—not by those eighteen Protestant churches, not by any of those architectural features ("neo-French-gothic façades" and "Romanesque-revival stoops," "modillianed cornices" and "eyebrow lintels") that pack the pages in my architectural guidebook. Almost immediately other histories trespass on the scene. Sometimes I'll see a bearded man, his shirt open to the chest: Walt Whitman striding up the hill from where he lives with his mother in a plain clapboard house near the Brooklyn docks a few blocks away. I watch as he moves toward the family on their way to

Brownstone 185

church, watch how the woman stares and how, as he passes, she pulls back her skirts.

Or sometimes the servant girl turns to me, and I recognize her. A few blocks north from where we live is Myrtle Avenue, a commercial street that divides Clinton Hill from the low-lying area near the Brooklyn Navy Yard. Just after we moved here, I came across mention of the street in Harriet Jacobs's *Incidents in the Life of a Slave Girl*. Jacobs tells of fleeing north in the years before the Civil War and of arriving in New York, hopeful that she'll be reunited with her daughter Louisa. (In the narrative, names are changed. Jacobs is Linda Brent, her daughter Ellen Brent.) From Manhattan, Jacobs takes the Fulton Ferry across to Brooklyn, and on her walk up Myrtle Avenue encounters by accident Louisa walking with a friend on the street. It's a joyful reunion, but also a disappointing one. Jacobs had entrusted her daughter to a white family. The family, who live nearby—presumably in Fort Greene or Clinton Hill—had promised to send the girl to school, but Jacobs soon discovers that Louisa can barely read; the family is raising her as a lady's maid. After that, my vision of the imaginary church-going family changed: the girl pushing the perambulator turns in my direction. I see Louisa's face.

The early years of Clinton Hill resist a simplified story, and so too do the years that followed. History is easy to divide up neatly: the rich and the poor, decline and resurgence, white and black. I've thought a lot about the stories I hear about this neighborhood—how terrible it once was, how much better it is now. And I believe this version of history, even remember it for myself. Judith, a friend of mine who moved here after college to study at Pratt, the art school around the corner, was killed by a mugger just down the street in the late eighties. Both of us had been in New York for only a week, and on the day I'd planned to meet up with her for a drink, I woke to see her face on the front page of the *New York Post*.

But this picture of danger and crime is just as partial as the golden age of ruffled prams pushed up Washington Avenue on

Sunday afternoons. Perhaps we highlight this story because we are uneasy about our own role as gentrifiers: "look how much I'm improving it; look how much better it is now." This story won't stay put either. I read too many nostalgic blog posts these days by people reminiscing about their childhoods here in the seventies; they do so with as much affection and regret as expressed by Henry James when writing about his childhood neighborhood off Washington Square Park. These bloggers acknowledge the crime, but also write warmly of stoop parties and street games, of fathers coming home from work, and of Sunday morning in the neighborhood churches. (The Baptist church behind our building, once the house of worship for the industrialist William Pratt and his family, has had a mainly African American congregation for many years.) What one person calls the "bad times," another calls his first place, as dear to him as the house on the ledge is to me. And while the neighborhood's racial makeup changed, this too is complicated. Sharon, our landlady, a font of knowledge about local history, reminds me that many people who bought buildings in the area were upwardly mobile African American families. She tells me too that because of the presence of the two colleges in the neighborhood (Pratt and St. Joseph's), there was more stability and racial diversity during the sixties, seventies, and eighties than people sometimes remember.

There's a long passage in William Maxwell's novel *The Folded Leaf* about the act of travel—about what we must do when we move through foreign landscapes. He writes:

> Seeing clearly is everything . . . You must somehow contrive, if only for a week or only overnight, to live in the houses of people, so that at least you know the elementary things—which doors sometimes bang when a sudden wind springs up; where the telephone book is kept; and how their lungs feel when they waken in the night and reach blindly toward the bed for the extra cover.

You are in duty bound to go through all of their possessions, to feel their curtains and look for the tradename on the bottom of their best dinner plates . . . You should test the sharpness and shape of their scissors . . . and try, with your fingernail, to open the locked door of the liquor cabinet . . . Through all of these things, through the attic and the cellar and the tool shed you must go searching until you find the people who live here or who used to live here but now are in London or Acapulco or Galesburg, Illinois. Or who now are dead.

For me this is a guide on how to live in a city—or live in an apartment where so many others have lived before. One must live inside another's history. Touch the dinner plates. Test the locks. Reach out blindly in the night for all the people who are gone.

When I was younger, I tended to erase the people between me and the distant past. On my walks through our woods in Wisconsin, it was just me and the Menominee Indians. Now I find myself far more interested in the history closer to my own, the people inside the gap between the building of those mansions and my moving to the neighborhood a hundred and fifty years later. Walking around this apartment, it's not those leisured ladies in their poke bonnets I think of most often. To be honest, it isn't the artists blowing their horns from just ten or twenty years back either. The people I imagine in this house are usually a family of working-class or middle-class people living out their lives. Most often they are African American or Caribbean, families who themselves found they were living inside someone else's history.

In 1959 Paule Marshall, a Caribbean American writer, published a semiautobiographical novel, *Brown Girl, Brownstones*, about the Barbadian community living in Brooklyn in the thirties and forties. It opens with Selina Boyce, the novel's heroine, walking through the rooms of the brownstone her family rents in the Brooklyn neighborhood of Bedford-Stuyvesant, and imagining, as I like to do, the people who lived there before her: first, "the Dutch-English and the Scotch-Irish who had built the houses" and after that, the white families that followed, "each generation unraveling in a quiet skein of years behind the green shades." Now it is 1939; the white families are leaving—or dying—and the West Indians are moving in.

For Selina, the house is alive. She sits on the top floor landing, light pouring in from the skylight at the top of the stairs, and listens to the house's "shallow breathing" and to "all the lives that had ever lived here." She sees it: tea in the afternoon and skirts "rustling across the parquet floors." She walks downstairs "full of ponderous furniture and potted ferns which the whites had left," the floor-length mirror still retaining "their faces as the silence did their voices." As she walks from room to room, she sees them gliding "with pale footfalls up the stairs. Their white hands trailed the bannister; their mild voices implored her to give them a little life."

I know those rooms well. I have caught a glimpse of the floor-to-ceiling mirror in the parlor-floor apartment downstairs; upstairs, the oval skylight casts its dim light down the stairs when I head out for work. I even know the neighborhood. The area where the Boyces live—Stuyvesant Heights—is just a few subway stops farther out into Brooklyn, a neighborhood that today is in the midst of gentrification. Lots of people who are now priced out of Clinton Hill—many of them middle- or upper-middle-class families, many of them white—are buying homes there: brownstones that for almost a hundred years have belonged to African Americans and West Indians. I can't help wondering, as the new owners walk through the rooms, whether they imagine their own Selina gliding up the stairs, and whether they've found a way to give her life.

Around the time this brownstone was constructed, Fort Greene and Clinton Hill were in the midst of another great real estate boom. It was the 1850s: The Fulton Ferry had just been built; some of the marshland near the river had been drained, and Manhattan was dirty and overpriced. People were leaving the island in droves, heading for the more peaceful tree-lined streets of Brooklyn.

Lots of developers took advantage of the boom, and I was recently surprised to learn that Walt Whitman was one of them. In "Leaves of Grass and Real Estate," Peter Riley examines Whitman's years in Brooklyn in the 1850s. Whitman, Riley explains, was not just an "unemployed lower middle-class poet-loafer" or a "disaffected artisan poet"; he was also a businessman, forging "a restless marketplace persona." Where before I'd looked out this window and seen a working-class dreamer, I now saw an "urban speculator" as well, a developer who between 1848 and 1855 built and sold four homes, moving his family in quick succession as soon as the last was sold. Whitman was the main breadwinner, and to support his family he needed to make money.

I knew Whitman had built houses nearby—one of them, on Ryerson Street, still stands, a run-down nondescript building close to the expressway—but I'd always viewed him simply as a carpenter. The truth, though, is that Whitman "took a predominantly administrative role in the construction process—hiring builders, sketching designs, writing receipts—rather than contributing manually," a fact he later obscures so as "to align this period with the overly nostalgic artisanal mythologies" his readers expected. Reading this, I couldn't help but think of how my father seemed to prefer the word *builder* to describe himself, a word that called to mind sawdust and calloused hands.

I also recognize in Whitman's Brooklyn years some of the same conflicts I'd seen in my father—and in myself. In 1845 the *American Review* published an article by Whitman called "Tear Down and Build Over Again" in which he complains about the "rabid, feverish itching for change," the American "pull-down-and-build-over-again" spirit. "Good-bye, old houses!" he cries, as he walks past the remains of dwellings once "stout and sound at heart" now razed to the ground. I couldn't help but think of others who shared his view: Henry James bemoaning the spirit of "restless renewal" that had transformed his hometown; Maeve Brennan regretting the "extinction" of her network of old hotels; Jane Jacobs fighting the replacement of older constructions with Corbusier-inspired housing complexes like the one across Underwood Park and the Walt Whitman houses down on Myrtle Avenue.

But I also couldn't help but think of Spencer Brydon, the divided man in James's "The Jolly Corner"—a man who refuses to sell his old house or to divide it up and at the same time a man with a gift for going into figures and walking planks. Riley writes that while Whitman criticizes the "the 'restless' activities of property speculators who were radically transforming the urban geography of Brooklyn," only a few years later he participated in that transformation himself, "jumping from house to house, project to project, becoming complicit in an urban restlessness of which he had previously complained."

In *Brown Girl, Brownstone*, Selina's mother is consumed by her ambition to purchase the home they are renting—or even, like some of her neighbors, buy more than one. She is not alone; the entire community seems obsessed with saving up their "pennies which would 'buy house.'" The institution dominating this community is not the church but the Barbadian Home Owners Association. People "who had never owned anything perhaps but a few acres in a poor land" loved the brownstones "with the same fierce idolatry as they had the land on their obscure islands." But Selina wants nothing to do with owning a house; at the end of the novel, she turns down a scholarship from the Home Owners Association, rejects her mother's plans for her, and returns to Barbados.

Since moving to this neighborhood, I've had to face some facts about myself. Most of my adult life I prided myself on having escaped, as Selina does, the American romance with home ownership. Renting was good enough for me. But something happened to me here in Clinton Hill. In the very facades of those upright brownstones, I could read a look of admonition. Long rows of connected houses frowning down on my lowly renter's status. However much I define myself as living outside the marketplace—an observer looking down from her book-lined study, her ivory tower, onto the activities of the street—I am not immune to the fascinations of real estate speculation. I even seem to be good at it. Too often I have accurately predicted which neighborhoods are on the rise and which buildings will sell and for how much.

When I was growing up, my father sometimes took us out for long drives around Green Lake, the resort town where he'd built his little bachelor's house in the sixties. These drives almost always included a moment when he'd pull over, point to a golf course driving range or a hillside dotted with houses, and sigh: "Back in the seventies I could have bought that land for chump change." To me, all this real estate regret seemed a waste of time, even illogical: "You didn't have the chump change in the seventies," I'd say from the backseat, "so what's there to regret?"

But after I'd lived in this neighborhood for a while, I started hearing my father in my head. I now have my own collection of "if only" stories: brownstones I could have bought—if only I'd had the money—that doubled in value in a single year. When I introduce this topic into conversation, my friends roll their eyes just as I did years before.

Nowadays, the hype over Brownstone Brooklyn has gone a little crazy—websites and blogs that enable their readers to salivate over every sale. Brownstone Brooklyn has become a concept, one that encompasses more than just the old landmarked buildings. On many streets, modern glass condominiums disrupt the clean line of row houses. A few blocks away, people's homes, under the guise of an eminent domain ruling, have been torn down to make way for a new basketball arena. I don't like all this "feverish itching for change," as Whitman put it, but I confess at times I've imagined how—should some chump change come my way—I might profit by it.

From the start, the apartment in Clinton Hill aroused complex emotions. Sitting out on the stoop the first week, I noticed how the kids from Pratt would exit the subway and peer up as they walked past. I knew that look and remembered all my walks around the city coveting other people's lives from below an apartment window. These days, the brownstone stoop seems to be the urban version of a house on a hill, a sign of arrival—and of privilege.

Even the admiration of my friends flustered me. As soon as they crossed the threshold—so far from the garrets I'd craved when we first moved to the city—I found a way to gracelessly mention the below-market rent, the way my mother sometimes will deflect a compliment about her clothes by telling you they came from Target.

The greatest anxiety, though, stemmed from my almost instant attachment to the place. With attachment came insecurity. This was not a stabilized apartment and the rent could—certainly would—rise. Even in the first few months, I was reminding Andre that any day the landlady would be calling to increase the rent or tell us she was selling the building. "Don't get too attached," I kept saying—although we both knew who was getting attached. As soon as we moved in, I felt the old proprietary tugs: the call of "me" and "mine." Sharon and Jim, the owners, were fastidious about the building and included with our lease a list of rules. Instead of hanging our pictures with nails, we were asked to hang them with wire from the picture railings, a sensible idea since my habit of constant rearranging had left a constellation of nail holes on the walls of all my previous apartments. Harder for me was the rule about not painting the place, an act that has always been my ritual for marking an apartment as home. The rules were probably not meant to be punitive or intended to draw attention to our rental status. Signs of the landlords' love for the building were everywhere. Having carefully restored the apartment—far beyond what landlords typically do with a rental property—they wanted to ensure we'd take care of the place. Still, I couldn't help but read those rules as a reminder: this is not yours; you will not be here for long.

We've now lived here for seven years. We've taken over the rooms. They smell like us and are strewn with our disorder—books and papers spilling out of the shelves, faint grooves in the floor from a filing cabinet that hasn't been moved in years. I am no longer startled by the beauty when I walk in the door, but I still sometimes stretch out my arms to test the expanse, still catch my breath when I turn—windows so tall you get a double view: the tops of two gingko trees and above them a whole pane of moving clouds.

Just a few months ago, the tenants downstairs moved out after their rent was raised to the market rate. Even Andre now admits we are probably not here for long. Already the rent is close to the limit we can pay, and our landlady has started talking about how she plans to sell the building. We will be leaving soon. To prepare myself, I study the place, committing rooms to memory, storing them up so that later I can pull up an image: the strips of shuttered light cast by the streetlights at night, a closet door in the dining room that likes to swing open when you pass. I practice missing the apartment, practice looking at us here from the distant future as if we were ghosts.

One thing I've learned living with Andre is that not everyone shares my attachment to places. My walks around the apartment, staring down the furniture and fixing it to the floor—all this memorizing of rooms—seem strange to him. He is just as perplexed by my attachment to objects: dinner plates, old postcards, nearly every article of furniture. There's the bamboo lamp from the Stork Club a friend left me when he moved to France, the yellow easy chair my friend Laura inherited from her neighbor, the 1950s velvet sectional sofa I found at a Salvation Army in Riverdale and have been lugging around New York—heaving it over banisters, upending onto elevators—from apartment to apartment for almost twenty years. The material is of a color hard to describe, burnished red, faded vermilion in the worn spots. When people comment on it—as they often do—I can't help telling them how little I paid for it. After he first moved in with me, Andre noticed how I winced when he threw himself down on that couch at the end of the day, winced at the wheeze in the springs. "This is not a La-Z-Boy," I told him, and since then, the sofa has become his joke: "If you had to choose between us," he says, "I'm not sure you'd choose me."

In the beginning I think he worried about this fixation on the inanimate, worried I might be some kind of frenetic consumer. But he knows now how much I hate shopping. Whatever my failings, I will never ask him to wait outside a dressing room door. The attachment to things has little to do with buying—better if I find the object on the street. What matters is the story, and it's partly this that explains those walks I've been taking lately around our apartment.

There's a short story by William Maxwell that says this all better than I could. It's called "The Thistles in Sweden," and some might not even call it a story, more a lengthy description, an exhaustive accounting of two people's daily life inside two rooms in a floor-through brownstone apartment on West Thirty-Sixth Street in Manhattan. But if "The Thistles in Sweden" doesn't have a plot exactly—"plot shmot," Maxwell once said to John Updike—it does have a conflict, hardly visible but always pulsing under all that description: the wife, Margaret, longs to have a child and can't and would rather move to the country; her husband, the narrator, loves the "modest perfectionism" of their life together just as it is. He is perfectly happy in the apartment: "Since I was a child, no place has been quite so much home to me."

Maxwell was a close friend of Maeve Brennan's, and there's a similar quality to his prose. Brennan describes a dress top to bottom, a Manhattan street end to end. She was also good with rooms, especially in her fiction set in Ireland: one house in Dublin, modeled on her own growing up, is so exactly (and so often) described that later Maxwell himself could recall it—the hall running down the middle of it, the linoleum in the upstairs bedroom, and the gas fireplace in the parlor.

When it comes to rooms, Maxwell is Brennan's equal, and in "The Thistles in Sweden," we are asked to move into them, to look closely, from top to bottom, wall to wall. We get the layout of every closet and door, the history of every object. While the rooms are "underfurnished," the story is crowded, as if Maxwell is compelled to get it all in: The romantic windows, the stairway from the top floor that leads to the sky, the two doors left open onto the landing, the piece of cardboard taped to the banister to keep the cat from running downstairs. There's a kitchen the "size of a handkerchief," a closet painted "a beautiful shade of Chinese red," and a mural hanging over the bed depicting a Persian tower with children playing a kind of lute and flying fish-shaped kites. Each item in the apartment is remarked upon, even the pattern of the "heavy Swedish linen" curtains Margaret has made—"life-sized thistles, printed in light blue and charcoal grey, on a white background."

Woven into the description of the apartment and its objects are the daily events: Here is where Margaret takes up painting, here is where the narrator writes a novel that he'll later lose in the back of a taxicab. We meet the delivery boys Margaret befriends and the woman out the window who picks through the garbage. We sit through smoky parties—the windows cracked—and share in the familiar New York irritations: the blocked-up chimney the narrator dreams of unblocking, the high-rise building cutting off their view that he dreams of demolishing with his bare hands.

By the close of the story, Margaret gets pregnant, and they give notice. As the couple prepares to leave, the apartment, "feeling our inattention, begins to withdraw from us sadly." Often in Maxwell's fiction, inanimate things are given such life they begin to take on human form. They have feelings. They talk back. The marble fireplace, "remembering the eighteen-eighties, when this was a one-family house and our top-floor living room was a nursery," asks, "*What better place can there be to bring up a child in?*" The stairway is bitter, and thinks: "*They seem as much a part of our life as the doors and windows, and then it turns out that they are not a part of our life at all.*"

The story's final paragraph, a long paragraph, is crowded with everything we've just been living inside. The couple has long since moved away, and now the narrator walks past the old brownstone on Thirty-Sixth Street and looks up at those familiar windows. He sees again the "grey-and-blue thistles," hears again the "sound of my typewriter, and of a paintbrush clinking in a glass of cloudy water." He remembers:

> that happy grocery store run by boys, and the horse-drawn flower cart that sometimes waited on the corner, and the sound of footsteps in the night, and the sudden no-sound that meant it was snowing, and I think of the unknown man or woman who found the blue duffel bag with the manuscript of my novel in it and took it to the police station, and the musical instrument . . . played in the dark over our sleeping bodies, while the children flew their kites, and I think if it is true that we are all in the hand of God, what a capacious hand it must be.

I've never been able to read "The Thistles in Sweden"—or that ending, both mournful and celebratory—without turning to Maxwell's own life. I don't think he'd mind, since he himself confessed he couldn't really write fiction without drawing on his own history. The story is set in the fifties, which was when Maxwell and his wife, Emily, were living in a top brownstone apartment on East Thirty-Sixth Street off Lexington Avenue. They were trying to have a baby and couldn't—and then found they could. Maxwell left a manuscript behind in a cab, and the story goes that it was Maeve Brennan who calmly went about contacting the cab company and getting it back. On my desk, right next to me, is *A William Maxwell Portrait*, a collection of recollections by some of the writers Maxwell influenced. The cover shows a photograph of Maxwell's study, and though that photograph has been staring at me for a while now, only recently did I notice the curtains on the window: "life-sized thistles, printed in light blue and charcoal grey."

Knowing Maxwell's history—and having read his other work—affects how I read this story. So much of its power comes for me in that one line: "Since I was a child, no place has been quite so much home to me." In that sentence, you feel the presence of another house, and you remember all the other walks you've taken with him through rooms filled with familiar objects. Another ending hangs over this one.

Maxwell lived in New York for fifty years and was an editor at the *New Yorker* for almost forty, yet the city was never really his subject. Like Willa Cather, he wrote mostly about the landscape of the Midwest. There are the few exceptions—a collection of fairy tales, a four-hundred-page novel set in France called *The Château*, and a handful of New York stories, including "The Thistles in Sweden." But the space that shows up most often is a Victorian house on an elm-shaded street in Draperville, a small Illinois town modeled on Lincoln, Illinois, where Maxwell grew up. Read his work end to end and when you are through, you'll know that old Victorian intimately: the wicker porch furniture, the elms touching to form a canopy over the street, the trumpet vine, the white lilac bush, the mansard roof, the corners for reading. Much of the Draperville fiction circles around the defining tragedy of Maxwell's childhood, the death of his mother from influenza in 1918 when he was eight years old. It's there in *They Came Like Swallows*, *The Folded Leaf*, and *So Long, See You Tomorrow*, as well as his autobiography, *Ancestors*. The house is a return to a paradise lost.

But it's not just the Draperville fiction that brings us back to that early loss. It is present in everything he wrote, present in all the other spaces he describes. In *The Château*, a midwestern couple, Harold and Barbara Rhodes, travel through France after World War II and spend their first month living with a French family in the Loire countryside. The Rhodeses live in the château for only a month—a difficult month of misunderstandings, postwar rations, and no hot water—yet when Harold leaves the room where they've spent their days, he lingers at the door: "'Where will we find another room like this?' he said, and closed the door gently on that freakish collection of books, on the tarnished mirrors, the fireplace that could not be used, the bathtub into which water did not flow, the map of the Ile d'Yeu, the miniatures, the red and black and white wallpaper, the now familiar view, through that always open window, of the bottom of the sea. As he started down, the thought: *We will never come here again* . . ."

Another leave-taking is described through a recording of objects—wallpaper and mirrors. Another door is shut on a space of happiness.

Roger Angell, a friend and an editor of Maxwell's, reads the later work about married life, especially the New York stories like "The Thistles in Sweden," as obviously connected to the traumas of his friend's childhood. The loss of the household as a boy leads to an intense attachment to adult domestic happiness. Maxwell reacts to having a household of his own in an almost "child-like way" says Angell; there's a "sense of wonder," as if "he felt he never would have these things—as if some miracle had come along." These feelings, while they make for great fiction, says Angell, seem "almost embarrassing in their innocence, in their clinging to what is going on." They "feel naïve—the details about marriage, about children, about making a household, about, also, I think, regular objects."

I know what Angell means: there is something naïve—exposed—in the clinging to a place ("Where will we find another room like this? . . . We will never come here again") and something a little embarrassing in this preoccupation with objects. Like a child who keeps a cigar box under the bed and takes it out at night, emptying every item onto the floors—toy soldiers, grubby playing cards tied together with a snapped rubber band. Objects register your presence, love you back. For years, my mother would embarrass me by telling the story about how one Christmas—I was home from college—she caught me late at night sitting with all my old paper dolls spread out on the bed.

But another way to read this animation of the inanimate is as a practice in memory. In an essay on Maxwell, Eric Ormsby observes that Maxwell "moves through the rooms of his childhood house like a recording ghost; there's something at once spooky and poignant in his exactitude. . . . Only by recovering the smallest details of inanimate things could the lives they surrounded be summoned back. For Maxwell—in this, oddly like the old mnemonic theorists of the Renaissance—memory itself could be represented as a house: forgotten corners and neglected nooks, if correctly recalled, might be coaxed into yielding up some eloquent memento."

Just as Maxwell urges the traveler to move into the stranger's house and go through all their possessions—go "through the attic and the cellar and the tool shed" in search of their story—so must he go in search of his own history. In *The Folded Leaf,* the young Lymie Peters lies in bed and tries to remember the house where they'd lived when his mother was alive: "The odd thing was that now, when he went back to the house in his mind, and tried to walk through it, he made mistakes. It was sometimes necessary for him to rearrange the rooms and place furniture exactly before he could remember the house the way it used to be." And then he tries to do it, climbing the stairs, recalling the layout of the top landing, and turning a corner to memorize the placement of beds and tables and chairs.

I know that soon we'll be leaving this apartment—and maybe leaving the neighborhood as well. I lie in bed at night and picture myself packing it up: boxes piled to the ceiling, the cushions of the sofa stacked at the door. I've been here before, and as usual, I worry about where we will go next—maybe farther out into Brooklyn, maybe even out to the neighborhood Paule Marshall describes in her novel about Selina Boyce. Some friends tell me we might be able to afford a one-bedroom in the condominium development across Underwood Park, the one that once housed workers from the Brooklyn Navy Yard in the forties. Ironically, those apartments are about the size of the rent-stabilized place on Lafayette we'd once found too confining. I wonder if now, after seven years adjusting to each other's rhythms, we might be able to squeeze our differences inside two small rooms. I don't know. I only know that wherever we go, I want the moving (and the waiting to move) to stop—if not once and for all, then at least for a very long time.

When I talk with Andre about this I am reminded of how different we are—and I'm glad of it. I have a kind of literary crush on William Maxwell, but I doubt I could live with someone like him, so similarly inclined to map happiness inside the four walls of a room. Andre spent his summers every year at a family cabin in northern Minnesota near the Canadian border, a place that shaped him as much as our house in Wisconsin shaped me. I see how his face changes when needles are underfoot, see the way his shoulders relax when he's near a body of blue water. But he's not in the habit of making up stories of the places where he lives to tell himself in retrospect. He doesn't walk through rooms grieving over imaginary boxes piled to the ceiling or sit at breakfast and lift up a coffee mug to follow the trail it takes him back to the past. He doesn't linger at the door of hotel rooms or look up at the windows of apartments where he lived years ago.

He doesn't really get all those real estate anxieties either. A few weeks back, after a Saturday listening to my woeful predictions about impossible prices and imminent eviction, he took me to a neighborhood meeting in a church basement down the street. We sat in the back of the room listening as people talked of how Clinton Hill was losing affordable and low-income housing, how families were being pushed out of a neighborhood they'd called home for generations. On the way back to our apartment, he reached over and grabbed my hand. He didn't say much—and he didn't say it unkindly—but what he said was a reminder of all those other histories in this neighborhood, all the people who had a longer history and faced a greater loss at the prospect of leaving it. "Other people have something to worry about. We don't."

When we got back to our stoop, we sat on the top step where we always sit and watched the procession below: the art students and the two neighbor ladies with their yappy dog; the couples wandering back from the flea market and the children running ahead to Underwood Park; a musician swinging his horn; a prostitute and a respectable old lady stepping arm in arm from the Graham Home across the street; at the rear, Walt Whitman, sawdust in his hair. I thought of all the people who'd sat on these steps hoping they might stay—"I will never find a room like this one"—all the while knowing that someday, they, like the rest of us, would live on here only as someone else's ghost.

The Return

10

Lake City

In the late nineties, I was struggling—boyfriend and money trouble and, as always, the uncertainties of real estate. I seemed to have lost my grip on geography. From a familiar subway I'd emerge and wander south when I wanted to go west, or stand stunned at a green light as if waiting for a courteous stranger to cup my elbow. Nothing could help, not even the Manhattan grid meant to guide me like a railing guides the blind. One night I stood facing an ATM machine in the lobby of a bank on Fifty-Seventh Street and thought of my grandmother sitting on the steps of that office building in Milwaukee. I didn't forget my name or address, as my grandmother had, but I did forget my PIN. The day before, worn down by my routines, I walked up to the booth in the subway and instead of asking for one subway token, as I did every day, I asked for a coffee black, one sugar, and a pack of Marlboro Lights. The woman behind the plexiglass smiled at me as if she'd seen this kind of thing before. That year, I read by accident and for the first time Joan Didion's essay "Goodbye to All That"—read how she knew in her late twenties that she had to leave New York because she cried in elevators and Chinese laundries and because she hurt the ones she loved.

My friend Carole offered some practical advice: "Go west young lady. That's all you need." My mother, when I called her, agreed: "Don't ever let them tell you that you can't run away from your problems," she said, which I still hold up as sage advice.

Sarah, my brother's girlfriend, offered me for the summer her grandparents' hunting cabin in southern Colorado, a small house in a small town of three hundred people in the San Juan Mountains. I could live there rent free if I would scrape and paint the house.

My father needed a company car moved from Wisconsin to Utah by the end of the summer. After subletting my apartment, I flew out to Wisconsin to pick it up, an old Chevrolet with bad brakes and a platter-sized ashtray that slid out like a tray of hors d'oeuvres. I was in graduate school and supposed to be studying for my orals, so I filled the trunk of the car with boxes of books. I made it from Wisconsin to Colorado in four days.

The house where I landed was yellow with a picket fence. It stood in a valley on the main street of Lake City, an old mining town. A river, defined by a curve of cottonwoods, ran through it. Inside the house was a front room with a fireplace built by Sarah's grandfather in the 1950s—boulders coated in a mustard-colored shellac. Even without a fire, the room gave off a volcanic glow. In the back, there was a bedroom with just enough room for a bed, and a bathroom with a wall of shelves over the tub, an altar arranged by Sarah's mother, who came up sometimes in the summers from Santa Fe—a clutter of candles and bird feathers, crystals in little dusty heaps.

Almost immediately there was relief. Revelation. Air and clouds and birdsongs more varied than the New York sparrow. I didn't hook up the phone right away, and the first few weeks talked to nobody but the man in the general store who smiled at me under his Stetson and spread out on the counter yellow paint chips like they were a ladies' fan. I took hikes and collected armfuls of Indian paintbrush. I climbed one of the mountains nearby, every switchback a collapse, ten years of cigarettes and New York exhaust coughed out on the forest floor. In the afternoon, I worked on painting the house: long meditative hours of moving a brush across a board.

Out of my daily walks, I made rituals—my canyon, my meadow—and it wasn't long before I began to discern the shapes of the inhabitants. Happy and Dennis, a couple in their eighties, invited me over in the afternoon to watch opera videos and drink warm watery beer. I talked to a scrawny boy who lived in a tepee and pounded out little silver lockets with a hammer next to the fire and to the construction guys working on the old Victorian house next door. They could stand for hours just watching their dogs fight in the dirt. At the local bar, I met a straight-backed woman who'd left behind a rodeo star boyfriend back in Texas. Like me, she'd come to Lake City to change her life.

I waited a week before removing the books from the trunk of the car—and another week before I had the courage to open the boxes. In the living room I set up a folding table, and for a while I sat at the table every morning studying for my orals exam and taking dutiful notes on little colored note cards, moving through authors in chronological order. I read all of Edith Wharton, then Dreiser.

When I came to Willa Cather, I found I couldn't read her in the same way. I left the table and moved to the bed—or most often to the bathtub. It was as if the enclosure invited expanse, as if I needed water to breathe her air. Turning the tap on with my foot to heat up the water, I'd lie there while the candle wax dripped on the feathers and crystals on the shelf over my head. Cather, night after night. It took just over a week to finish. I gave up chronology, and I gave up the note cards—too difficult to balance on the slick edge of the tub.

Those nights reading Cather I seemed to be sinking—back into childhood, back into my own history. I recognized places I knew well (the streets of Fond du Lac, the rooms of our old house) but also places I'd never been to: my great-grandmother's root cellar and a kitchen table where a woman folds sheets into a basket; a field cleared of stumps. Once when asked how he could have created such detailed descriptions of his ancestors, ancestors he'd never known, the Israeli writer Amos Oz explained that he'd simply "consulted his genes." It was a little like that—a sudden trust in what I knew in my own body.

Only a week after I arrived in Lake City, I went on my first solo camping trip, driving five hours south and stopping in Gunnison to buy a tent and sleeping bag. I spent one day at Mesa Verde. On a cliff ledge over the canyon, I stood behind a rope and looked down: stairs crumbling to a forgotten basement, narrow ladders carved into the rock and climbing. A flat line of blue. I wanted to be alone there. I wanted to see the place without the tourists, without the guide. It was early June, but already dizzyingly hot; we were sweating so much that by the time the guide gave her closing speech—about the mystery of the Anasazi who had one day vanished, nobody knows where or why—we looked for a second like mourners weeping at a grave.

The two Cather novels that mattered most that summer were *The Song of the Lark* and *The Professor's House*. Cather includes an Anasazi ruin in *The Song of the Lark* and modeled Tom Outland's Blue Mesa in *The Professor's House* on Mesa Verde. The first time I read those mesa scenes I felt a little shock, a click of recognition. Perhaps it was the effect of those crystals and candles in constant view from the bathtub, but I was prone that summer to see in everything a divination.

The Professor's House includes within it two narratives, one embedded inside the other. Tom Outland's experiences on the mesa are framed around Professor Godfrey St. Peter's story. St. Peter is a university professor who struggles to come to terms with the weakening of his marriage, the petty jealousies of his daughters, the materialism of the modern world. The great symbol in the early part of the novel of this acquisitive society is a new house, which St. Peter, despite his wife's irritation, doesn't really want to move into.

In 1938 Willa Cather wrote a letter to Pat Knopf, the son of her editor Alfred Knopf, about *The Professor's House*. She explained: "In my book I tried to make Professor St. Peter's house rather overcrowded and stuffy with new things; American proprieties, clothes, furs, petty ambitions, quivering jealousies—until one got rather stifled. Then I wanted to open the square windows and let in the fresh air that blew off the Blue Mesa, and the fine disregard of trivialities which was in Tom Outland's face and in his behavior."

This is how I thought of my experiment in Colorado: fresh air and a square open window. A disregard of trivialities. Behind me was my own cluttered house, a city that seemed to offer nothing but problems: a boyfriend crisis, a dissertation looming, scant job prospects, and, as always, worries about where I was going to live next. Now I was far from all that. At the end of every day, I took a walk at sunset along the canyon road leading outside of town — the lines of striated rock turning golden and pink in the fading light — and thought of Thea Kronborg's retreat to the canyons of Arizona, where the "personality of which she was so tired seemed to let go of her." In Panther Canyon, lined by ancient cliff-dwellers' homes, Thea lies in a cave under overhanging rock, a shelter akin to the room she left in Moonstone, and feels herself returning "to the earliest sources of gladness she could remember." Tom Outland spends a summer alone at the top of the Blue Mesa, studying Virgil and lying out at night looking up at the stars. That summer, "high and blue," is "a life in itself," his "high tide." For both Thea and Tom, those summers in the canyons are a kind of coming home — to nature and to themselves.

With my own return to nature and to myself, I also found I'd recovered old habits of reading. By this point I'd been in graduate school for a few years and had trained myself to keep a distance, to hide how personally I could inhabit fiction. After a while, I began to worry that graduate school had ruined something. I couldn't get it back, that feeling of being entirely *in* it. The covers pulled over your head, the flashlight crooked under your chin. Or that other feeling I used to get when I really lived inside a book — worlds colliding, the contact of the book and the scene happening at the edge of the page. In those months just before I left New York when I was wandering around the city lost, I remember a moment of envy for an eight- or nine-year-old child sitting across from me on the subway. She was reading *Pippi Longstocking*. I watched her eyes roaming over the page and then lift at a stop to take in the line of people across from her—two worlds fusing, separating, then fusing again. The mind a subway door opening and closing: one world on, another off.

In *The Professor's House*, Tom Outland spends his summer reading. He studies, "methodically" and "intelligently," but he also reads ecstatically and too fast, memorizing long passages from Virgil. Later, remembering that summer, Tom reflects: "When I look into the *Aeneid* now, I can always see two pictures: the one on the page, and another behind that: blue and purple rocks and yellow-green pinons with flat tops, little clustered houses clinging together for protection, a rude tower rising in their midst . . ." I can't read Willa Cather now without seeing a little yellow house and behind it mountains black against a sky filled with stars.

I came to Lake City with a fantasy of retreat, Thoreau-style, but somewhere near the second half of my summer I understood that a change of scenery could offer, as always, only a temporary reprieve. Soon the town and its dramas began to encroach. I detected factions, rifts between the locals and the summer people. The mountain climbers seemed to resent the mass of Texans who came every year to escape the heat; the conservative Christians kept their distance from the pot smokers and whitewater rafters. Like everywhere else, Lake City was a place where nearly every resident saw a holy land being ruined by somebody else. The house where I lived that summer was next door to a large purple Victorian whose owner, a wealthy Los Alamos engineer, came on weekends and waved at me across the lawn. One weekend my brother's girlfriend—now my sister-in-law—came to visit, and I noticed how she kept her back to that Victorian house, how her smile stiffened when the new owner and his wife took their evening walk around the property.

Sarah told me the house had formerly belonged to her grandparents; the cabin where I was living had been a kind of outbuilding, a hideaway where her grandfather could go and play cards with his hunting buddies. When the house was sold, Sarah's grandfather insisted that the furniture stay behind. The next summer, on a walk down Main Street, Sarah came upon the relics of her childhood (old tables and rockers) displayed in the window of an antique shop. "Only now it was too expensive," she told me, "and we didn't have the money to buy any of it back." The weekend of Sarah's visit, the owner, seemingly oblivious to Sarah's connection to the place, insisted we come over to see all his improvements: the new furniture, the walls and the kitchen they'd ripped out, the modern fixtures and granite countertops. He marched us around the property line and pointed to the white fence that now divided the little cabin from the newly renovated Victorian. Almost immediately I absorbed Sarah's nostalgia: after that, whenever he came up for weekends, I too turned my back. I couldn't help but think of *The Professor's House*, a novel all about old houses and new ones, about people like St. Peter and Tom Outland who care about the past and people like St. Peter's wife gripped by a longing for the new.

There were other ways in which I saw my idyll confronted by the reality of modern life. This was my summer "high and blue," my ecstatic return to the American Eden, but it wasn't long before I recognized all the signs of Empire—visible not just in the traces of the town's past (silver mining and the Denver & Rio Grande Railroad) but in the present as well. New monster houses were being built at the edge of town, and at the RV park along the river lived a whole village of Texans who came each summer to drive their jeeps and ATVs up mountain passes. I couldn't ignore the machine in the garden: I met it on nearly every hike, wheels spitting up gravel before I had time to step out of the way.

By the end of July, my habits of reading changed too. I moved back to the table, back to my little colored note cards. I reread Cather—and this time with a critical eye.

Standing in front of Sarah's family cabin, Lake City, Colorado. (author's collection)

A few years back, in a seminar I taught on Cather, I asked my students to read Lisa Marcus's "Willa Cather and the Geography of Jewishness." It begins with a commentary on certain kinds of readers, the ones who want to depoliticize Cather, who prefer to think of her as "the author of slightly more grown-up, highbrow versions of *Little House on the Prairie*." This pricked a little—since it pretty much described how I was reading her in the beginning of that Colorado summer. I noticed my students seemed a bit uneasy too, as if they saw a finger pointing their way. I told them not to be ashamed of this; a grown-up *Little House on the Prairie* still has something to offer. Reading Cather the first time had given me a way back to my family—to the old farm, to my great-grandmother folding her sheets, and to a history I felt in my body, in my genes.

I teach at Yeshiva University—all of my students are Jewish—yet I was surprised at how many of them resisted looking at Cather's representation of Jews in the novel. They felt protective—even defensive—of her; it was a feeling I recognized and remembered. That summer in Lake City when I began to read Cather criticism, I felt a bit as Tom Outland and his friend Blake do when they contemplate all the people who might come to the mesa after them: "We were reluctant to expose those silent and beautiful places to vulgar curiosity." For a few days, those critics seemed like tourists crawling all over the books I loved, all over my "silent and beautiful" places.

This may be why, unlike many academics, I always defend Joan Acocella's book *Willa Cather and the Politics of Criticism*, in which she accuses academics of ignoring the aesthetic and politicizing Cather beyond recognition. As one might imagine, Acocella raises the hackles of pretty much every Cather critic out there. But I liked the book, not because I agreed with her critique of political and multicultural criticism—I don't—but because I recognized in her, as I recognized in my students, a tenderness for Cather, a desire to protect her. I was less interested in her attack than in what I saw she was trying to defend. Underneath the argument I heard something personal. Of Cather and her critics, one of my students said: "This book is special to me, and now they are ruining it."

Reading carefully and critically—as well as reading what others have to say—doesn't have to ruin it, I explained to her. Rather than seeing the act of criticism as a swarming all over the text, a colonizing of it, I prefer to see what we do as a sort of flinging open of new windows, some of which the author had no idea were there. At the end of class, we talked about how we might hold on to our affection, our personal connections to novels, while at the same time remaining attuned to the questions and challenges—like anti-Semitism—that arise when we read them.

I usually tell my students that on a second reading of a book, you go back and notice what you are trying to ignore or resist. Or you identify the places in the text that lull you, the places where you find yourself unthinkingly giving in. The scenes in Cather that drew me the first time while I was living in the cabin in Lake City were those in which the frontier experience matched the fantasy of my summer escape. The moment Tom first comes upon the mesa still makes me shiver a little ("In stopping to take breath, I happened to glance up at the canyon wall. I wish I could tell you what I saw there, just as I saw it, on that first morning, through a veil of lightly falling snow"). But on second reading I can't help but stop there, notice how uncritically I'm drawn in. On second read, I notice that Tom's first encounter with the mesa—the "discovery" of the place—is softened and idealized. No violence, no people, just snow lightly falling. A landscape pure, empty, and uncomplicated.

In her letter to Pat Knopf, Cather explains where she got the idea of the metaphors for the two sections of *The Professor's House*—the crowded room (St. Peter's house) and the open windows (Tom Outland's mesa):

> Just before I began the book I had seen, in Paris, an exhibition of old and modern Dutch paintings. In many of them the scene presented was a living-room warmly furnished, or a

kitchen full of food and coppers. But in most of the interiors, whether drawing-room or kitchen, there was a square window, open, through which one saw the masts of ships, or a stretch of grey. The feeling of the sea that one got through those square windows was remarkable, and gave me a sense of the fleets of Dutch ships that ply quietly on all the waters of the globe—to Java, etc.

Critic Deborah Karush reads that view from the open window (the "fleets of Dutch ships") as another example of how Cather softens and romanticizes empire: the ships "ply quietly" on their journey to the Far East. In a similar way, Karush explains, Cather's *Professor's House* idealizes the American frontier experience, so that we are in danger of forgetting that here too is a story of empire, only this time the fleet moves through a sea of prairie grass; the ships travel on wheels and over steel rails. Tom builds a log cabin, the "chief icon of the nineteenth-century frontier," right on top of that mesa and its history. Yet another American house looking down on someone else's holy land. And then there is Tom's appropriation of Native American culture, his sense that he has taken private possession of the place and its history, which reminds me a little of how I used to feel about our woods in Wisconsin and how on my walks there I sometimes regarded the Menominees as mine.

In so many ways Cather was the ideal author that summer. It was a summer of first and second readings. A summer of changing views. Out one window was Eden, a view I never lost—the long solitary drives through mountain canyons, the blue sky in the morning, and the way it turned pewter in the afternoon just before it rained. Those nights reading in the bathtub. But I also don't forget the fleets of ships—or our American version of them: All those rolling wheels scrambling over the mountains in pursuit of a new frontier. The prospectors and the tourists; the covered wagons and railway cars, the jeeps and ATVs, and behind them my own battered Chevrolet.

◇

Near the end of my summer in Lake City, a friend in New York sent her teenage son out for a visit. I couldn't think how to entertain him, so I bought another tent and we drove south to Mesa Verde. Once we got there, I saw the long lines at the ticket office. It was even hotter than the last time I'd been there. I told Max to go in by himself and waited for him in the parking lot with a book. He gave me a strange look as he walked away. It amazes me now—the mesa just a few feet away, and there I sat inside an air-conditioned car. I still can't quite explain it, but I think it must have been a way to tell myself I was through, that I was going home.

For a while, I considered staying on in Lake City. My friends Happy and Dennis came up with a plan where I'd move in with them and they'd get me some work at the local newspaper. The construction crew working on the Victorian next door offered me a job as crew foreman. All summer they'd been eyeing me over the fence, jealous of how fast I scraped and painted the cabin. I finished the house in about the same time they managed to paint one picket fence. I couldn't decide if they were very meticulous or very stoned.

But I said no to both offers. As much as I loved the landscape of the Southwest, I began to wonder if I could ever live in a small town. People noticed what time I turned out my lights at night. Cars slowed, and strangers craned their necks when I took my walks down Main Street. I missed New York. I was homesick for my friends. I wanted to go to a rock show and stand in line for a Sunday matinee.

Of course I felt torn. The day I left the construction guys drove up to say good-bye, waving from their pickups, their dogs panting out the back. I almost called after them. Happy and Dennis stood out on their back deck, and we all cried. I thought of Thea Kronborg leaving Moonstone the first time: "She felt as if she were being pulled in two, between the desire to go away forever and the desire to stay forever."

This is Cather's constant story—always the longing to go back to the past (to nature, to the small town, to childhood) and always the desire to leave it again. Thea Kronborg returns to her "earliest sources of gladness" in Panther Canyon, but she won't stay; she'll go back to the concert halls of Chicago and later New York. Tom Outland will head east as well, move to a college town in the Midwest. Cather's subject may have been the West, but, as Joseph Urgo points out, "the trajectory of Cather's career, seems, at least in hindsight, to have been characterized by an ambition to return east." She traveled to Nebraska for visits and spent many summers in the Southwest, but she always went back. She told her friend Elizabeth Sergeant that "she got wildly homesick for the West" and would "dash out" to see her family and the wheat harvest, but that she would always flee east again "for fear of dying in a cornfield."

Yet the fantasy of staying out west—and of going back to the state of childhood—is always there. Perhaps my favorite example of this comes in *My Ántonia* at the end of "The Pioneer Woman's Story" when Jim Burden takes an evening walk out in the fields with Ántonia. "I felt the old pull of the earth, the solemn magic that comes out of those fields at nightfall. I wished I could be a little boy again, and that my way could end there." But both Ántonia and Jim know he will never come back. Jim is not a little boy, but an adult who will move to New York, go to law school, and spend his life as a lawyer for the railroads, traveling back and forth across the continent.

After writing *The Professor's House* Cather considered leaving New York for good, but she could never do it. She moved back to her house on Bank Street and lived in the city (with lots of traveling in between) for twenty-two more years until her death in 1947. "She still professed to hate New York and to say that it was becoming ever less attractive as a place to live," her biographer James Woodress writes, "but she couldn't bring herself to leave." An avid museum and concertgoer with a large circle of New York friends, Cather was a New Yorker almost despite herself. She couldn't seem to live anywhere else.

◇

I left Lake City—or at least I thought I did—in a very realistic state of mind. It was time to let go of this childish longing to go home again. I needed to face reality. Someday I would, like Cather, write about the past, but I needed to stop thinking I might actually live in it. I'd face my life: the dissertation, the boyfriend trouble. For much of that summer, I replayed a song in the car whenever I took drives in the mountains. It was by Amy Rigby, a woman I knew vaguely back in New York, a song about going back to a relationship and trying to make it work. "I've been on top of the mountain, and I do believe it's time for me to come down." I played it over and over as I made my way down the mountains and west to Salt Lake City. When I dropped off the car in Salt Lake, I spent a few days with my father. The first morning we had an uncomfortable conversation—one that probably all authors of PhD dissertations can relate to, the one where you're asked "how's it coming?" and you hear yourself offer stumbling explanations, elaborate excuses. My father sat across from me at the kitchen table, his arms crossed in front of him. He didn't say a word, just leaned back in his chair. After I finished, a long silence. Then, without any warning, he lifted his fist and slammed it down on the glass table, the silverware jumping: "This is all crap. It's time to get off your ass," and with that, he walked out of the room. I was angry for a long time, but I can't deny it woke me up from the dreamy state I'd been in all summer, and I'm not sure it wasn't a useful preparation for my reentry to New York City.

11

Ancestors

I

At the end of the 1990s, I spent an hour every week in a brownstone parlor floor in the West Thirties, not far from Port Authority bus terminal. The apartment belonged to Carole, a transplant from Iowa a few years older than my mother. She was a therapist who specialized in alcoholics and creative blocks. I belonged to the second category. After only a few months, it was clear we had broken all the rules, crossed the boundaries of the therapist-client relationship. One day I told her about a weekend spent with my father roaming Connecticut cemeteries. When she heard the name of the gravestone we were looking for, she leapt from her chair—"Stephen Noble!"—returning seconds later with the scroll of a family tree in her hand. She'd recognized the ancestor, and within a few minutes had figured out that we were seventh cousins twice removed. After that we dropped the pretense of therapy. Having found in my father not just a relation but one who shared her genealogical appetites, she grew protective of him and lost all interest in the exhumation of parental dysfunction. If it came up, she changed the subject.

Most of the time we drank coffee and talked about novels, Civil War history, old photographs, and the proper way to hang a curtain. I kept paying her, though—I refused to stop because I liked the guarantee she'd be there every week, a pot of coffee on the trunk in front of the couch. Although she was no good at relationship problems or money trouble or family drama, she had a knack for getting me back to work: "Clear the deck," she'd say. "Paint your cupboards, clean your stove. Start fresh." All familiar advice, very midwestern, the kind of advice my mother would have offered if I had let her.

On other subjects she was equally wise. Once, when I went on too long about my failures—the sluggish days at the desk, the lack of money—she gave me a hard look and said: "But you've lived in this city for more than ten years on little money; you've found places to live and made friends. You've survived here. Isn't *that* success?"

Carole was unapologetically domestic, unapologetically nostalgic. Along with her counseling business, she kept a basement shop where she sold daguerreotypes and old postcards from the nineteenth century. We both liked to talk about the Midwest: her summers living on her grandparents' farm outside of Des Moines, and my own childhood on Lake Winnebago. "The problem with most people," Carole said, "is they don't grow roots." Once she even demonstrated her philosophy. Sliding from her chair, she got down on her knees and pressed her hands into the carpet. "Like this. You need to dig in."

At the same time, she had the American passion for the road, and in the years before she moved to New York with her partner—a mysterious man who sometimes peeked his head through the sliding french doors—they'd moved all over the country in an old RV trailer, driving from town to town, from roadside antique shops to county fairs, buying photographs and cooking their meals out under the stars.

Carole believed in signs and portents. She believed you could change your life. It was Carole who encouraged me to go to Lake City in the first place, and it was she I most wanted to see when I came back. But when we met, she hardly seemed to hear me. She was distracted, excited. She had news she was bursting to tell me. An old friend had written saying her grandparents' farm back in Iowa was for sale. "We bought it. It's ours!" She and her partner would be leaving in a couple weeks. At the end of our hour, she looked up as if remembering I was there. "I guess I can refer you to someone," she said, but we both knew I wasn't really looking for a therapist and that this wasn't what our relationship was ever about.

Still I suppose I felt abandoned. The irony didn't escape me either; I'd come back convinced going home again was impossible. The point was to face the bracing reality of the present. I'd expected to say all this over a cup of coffee and see Carole nod approvingly. Instead, she was doing the impossible, fleeing west—going home again in the most literal way imaginable, back into the actual rooms of her childhood.

For a year afterward, except for the occasional postcard and a phone call at Christmas, we didn't talk. Then one day at work, I got a message from her. Once again, she had news, but this time it wasn't good: cancer. When I called her back, she didn't seem to want to talk about that much; mostly she wanted to tell me about the tulips she'd planted—"maybe I'll be around to see them come up"—and about the renovation of her kitchen. I told her I'd come to visit, but I don't think she believed I would.

Her son Peter called a month or so later to say that things were bad. He and his sister couldn't be there the following week. Would I go and help out? I didn't know Peter, but Carole talked about him all the time. He'd written a successful novel and then a film adaptation: *What's Eating Gilbert Grape*. I hadn't read the novel but knew the movie well: Johnny Depp plays a beleaguered caretaker to his mentally disabled brother, played by Leonardo DiCaprio. Gilbert's mother, so obese she can hardly leave the living room sofa, spends her days camped out in front of the television.

Carole was very proud of Peter and of *Gilbert Grape* and unflinching about the autobiographical elements in the story. "I'm the fat woman," she said. "He didn't want to write me the way I was—a terrible alcoholic. He wanted to disguise me, so he made me fat." But she also told me of how he'd modeled another character in the movie on her as well: a traveler who rides around the country in an RV trailer and who lives in tourist camps. A wise, centered kind of woman. This was the Carole I knew.

I got on a plane to Des Moines, rented a car, and drove a couple hours to the farm. (Before I left I told a psychoanalyst friend where I was going. He went purple in the face: "Ann, do you know how fucked up that is? Do you know how many boundaries you are crossing?" I tried to explain our relationship: We were really just friends. Hey, we were cousins even. But he wasn't convinced by this and pleaded with me not to go.)

Once I got to the farm, it felt familiar to me. Except for the flat terrain, it could have been the Holy Land. A long country road with hardly any cars, a few tractors, and then a white farmhouse, nearly identical to the one where my father had grown up. When I got there, Carole's sister and a hospice nurse were waiting to hand off duties. I looked around for Carole's partner, but they told me he was gone. He'd fled, moved to an apartment over a store in the little farm town nearby. Like Carole he was a devout AA member, the kind who knows the Big Book inside out. Later I heard a rumor that he'd left because Carole had a glass of port after her first treatment for chemo. I never found out if this was true. Still I could never quite forgive AA for that.

Living in the farmhouse with Carole was her younger son. He was someone I recognized, a guy I might have been friends with back in homeroom in high school—someone who maybe once had to take a few anger management classes or got in trouble for racing another car down a country highway in his pickup. But underneath the John Deere hat, you couldn't miss the vulnerability, almost a pleading to be understood.

I found Carole in the downstairs bedroom, a tiny old-fashioned room, the quilt pulled neat around her. She was happy to see me, said I was good for her because for the first time in days she actually felt hungry. At first I wasn't quite sure what to do with myself. I made her a plate of cinnamon toast, but when I came back to the room I was shy. Before I'd left New York, my friend Bernadette, who had lost a lot of friends, told me the worst thing about dying is that people are afraid to touch you. "Just touch her," she reassured me. "That's really all you can do." And so not knowing what to do, this is what I did: picked up some lotion and asked her if she wanted her feet rubbed. Carole's son was standing in the doorway. He watched me for a while awkwardly, and then sat down and took the other foot. I'm not sure I've ever had a stranger reunion.

It was just the three of us alone in that house all week. For long stretches of the morning, she slept, and I waited in the next room for her to wake up. At night, she played a Simon and Garfunkel record to help her fall asleep, "Bridge Over Troubled Water" faintly heard on the baby monitor I took upstairs with me when I went to bed. In the afternoon, we sat together in her room and talked. It might be strange to say it, but we had fun. She asked me to bring up a box of photographs from the basement. (There were boxes of photographs everywhere—storage lockers, rented garages, even some slid under the bed.) We spread the photographs out on the bed, admired the women's pompadours and the expressions on children's faces. One afternoon we managed to get her out of bed. She showed me around her newly renovated kitchen—refurbished with old 1930s cabinets and a deep porcelain sink to look as it had when her grandparents lived here. She even let us carry her upstairs so she could watch TV, something she hadn't done in months. Later that night, Peter called and I told him about our day. He was silent for a while and then said, "It's like you're living in my novel." I didn't know what he meant at first, but the next day remembered the scene in *Gilbert Grape* when Gilbert's obese mother finally gets off the couch and climbs to the second floor, the steps creaking under her weight.

Peter asked me if I'd tape some of Carole's stories while I was there; he sent a tape recorder by overnight mail. After that, we spent our afternoons with the recorder on her lap. I asked questions, and she told stories, mostly about her summers on the farm and about the history of the house. "This was my grandmother's room, just the same as it was"—and then she looked up, surprised, as if it were a happy coincidence: "Do you know, I think it was the room where she died." Her favorite topic was the field visible outside the one window. In the summers, during threshing time, it was her job to carry the water jugs and picnic baskets out to the fields.

She described the kinds of sandwiches they packed, the milk in icy bottles, and the look of the men when they saw her approaching. She told me about running through that field after dinner until it got dark, her grandmother calling from the doorway to come inside for bed.

Threshing time was always a favorite subject of my father's, and the story was the same: the children bearing food out at harvest, the late nights out with the grasshoppers and the rising moon. It occurred to me that Carole and my father were about the same age, two children (cousins even) among thousands, maybe millions, of other children that same summer being called to bed by women waiting in lit doorways.

The night before I left to fly back to New York, I walked into that field myself. It was a remarkable night—a sunset you seem to get only in flat open landscapes. Carole and I had been sitting in her window admiring it when what seemed like thousands of geese, waves of them, appeared, all landing on the fields surrounding the farmhouse. "I've never seen anything like it," she said. Neither had I. They kept coming, flocks in formation against the colored clouds. Carole turned, finally, and asked if I would walk out to the field, so she could watch from her window.

I put on my coat and went out. Each time I looked back, she waved me out a little farther. Some of the geese rose up as I approached, but others seemed too tired to care and just shuffled out of the way. Leaning on a dresser, Carole stood in the lit window. Finally she gestured for me to stop and we faced each other. I could hardly look away from that square of yellow light and inside it, the outline of her body. I understood then that I was standing inside Carole's story—not Peter's version but the story his mother had been whispering into the tape recorder all afternoon.

Whenever I think back on that field in Iowa, I see that scene in *My Ántonia* when Jim Burden and Ántonia are out walking in the fields at sunset: "In that singular light every little tree and shock of wheat, every sunflower stalk and clump of snow-on-the-mountain, drew itself up high and pointed; the very clods and furrows in the fields seemed to stand up sharply. I felt the old pull of the earth, the solemn magic that comes out of these fields at nightfall. I wished I could be a little boy again, and that my way could end there."

◇

After Carole died, the lit window of that farmhouse stayed with me, and I often wondered what would have happened had she lived. She hadn't been back in Iowa long enough to really meet the neighbors or register how the modern world had encroached on the landscape of her childhood. Would her old restlessness have returned? Would disenchantment have set in?

When he was in his fifties, the literary critic and novelist Edmund Wilson inherited an old stone house in Talcottville, a small town in upstate New York. The house had belonged to his family for generations, and Wilson had spent his summers there as a boy. In 1971, not long before he died, he wrote about the house and the area in *Upstate: Records and Recollections of Northern New York*. It's a strange little book—a hodgepodge of local history, family genealogy, and entries culled from diaries—but I loved it almost as soon as I picked it up. There aren't many people who get the chance, as Carole did, to go so literally home again—back into the actual physical space of childhood. Usually, our first places have been sold or torn down. *Upstate* gave me a chance to follow a grown man as he walks through childhood room by room.

After his mother died in 1952, Wilson took possession of the Talcottville property and spent nearly every summer there until his own death twenty years later. You can't miss the pleasure of those summers. Wilson had never had much money, and there are moments when he takes on the persona of a country squire, a house-proud gentleman who has the old silver polished and likes showing you about the place. He liked showing it off to friends as well, many of whom—Louise Bogan, Stephen Spender, Edwin Muir, W. H. Auden, Dorothy Parker, and Vladimir Nabokov— put their mark on the house, etching with a diamond-tipped pen lines of poetry on the house's window panes. In a window over a

A side view of Edmund Wilson's stone house, Talcottville, New York. (courtesy of the photographer, Tara Key)

balcony, the words of Nabokov in Russian: "There are nights when I lie in my bed, and my bed is swimming to Russia."

Wilson marks the house with his own imprint, yet recognizes how much the house and its history—from the religious sects that formed nearby to the genealogical history of his family—have marked him:

> I enjoy "galvanizing" this old house into life, as I feel I have at last been doing, making it express at last my own personality and interests, filling it with my own imagination, yet feeling a continuity with everybody who has lived here, basing myself in some sense on them—the older I grow, the more I appreciate them. Intellectually and geographically I travel further from them, yet also now more fall back on them, probably become more like them; feel more comfortable and myself here probably than anywhere else in the world.

In a review of *Upstate* soon after it came out, V. S. Pritchett notes that no European would write such a book. "In the United States—it seems to my foreign eye—the thrill of not having roots runs together with a nostalgia for them, simply because it is easier than it has ever been in Europe, so far, to lose them entirely." As Pritchett sees it, only an American, for example, would be so stirred by following the intricate web of family relations. (Wilson loved to trace cousinship almost as much as Carole did.) "I know of very few English people who feel a need to 'go back,'" Pritchett claims, "and in this respect Americans often seem to me 'older' than we are." Just typing Pritchett's words, I feel the bookshelves behind me tremble a little: Joyce and Woolf and Proust looking down from their perches in indignation. But I think I know what Pritchett means. There's a certain zeal to the backward glance here that comes of not having the taken-for-granted sense of tradition. It's there in the passion for genealogy, in the lines of people in Atlanta or Phoenix carrying their attic junk to *Antiques Roadshow* in hopes that a family treasure will be unearthed.

Of course Wilson knew, as Thomas Wolfe knew, that he couldn't entirely "go back." Always the present intrudes. He takes his children to the swimming holes and picnic spots he'd haunted as a boy, but finds his children don't much like summers in Talcottville: "the croquet set which I had hoped would occupy them—we always used to play croquet—is still standing by the front door, with nobody ready to set them up." He describes the "enchantment" of the wild landscape—the flowers and fields of his childhood—an enchantment he'll always associate with "the first moments of being conscious that I was capable of imaginative activity and some sort of literary vocation." The literary critic remembers a country drive outside of Talcottville with his parents: "I said suddenly to myself 'I am a poet,' then after a moment corrected myself with, 'No, I am not quite a poet, but I am something of the kind.'"

Elena Wilson, his wife, has no childhood memories to temper the harsh upstate landscape. She prefers Wellfleet on Cape Cod where the Wilsons spend the rest of the year; the sea and air remind her of her own childhood back in Russia. Nothing about the old stone house enchants her—not the musty rooms or the mosquitoes in July or the ghosts she sometimes sees walking about the house at night. Later, she'll write her own recollection of Talcottville,

"My View from the Other Window," a critique of her husband's romance with what she called "the kingdom of asbestos shingle."

The note of mournfulness that runs all through *Upstate* comes not just from Wilson's awareness that his family can't join in his rambles through the past. At times the place is alien even to him. A new four-lane highway is being built just under his window. The town, which in his youth had been "a clean and trim little settlement," is now, like so many upstate towns, dwindling in population and economically depressed—"tumbledown squalid houses" whose inhabitants can "hardly get along" on their factory jobs or unemployment checks. Wilson, the left-leaning intellectual, is horrified to find his town plastered with Birch Society posters. The beautiful elms he remembers are blighted by Dutch elm disease. Of his mother's gardens only clumps of peonies remain.

I can't help but wonder what some of the other writers I include in this book would make of Wilson's moving back into the childhood home. They'd understand it certainly, but should the opportunity come their way, I don't see any of them doing it. Like Wilson, William Maxwell was fascinated by the history of his family and town, a history recorded extensively—with multiple twists of cousinship recorded—in his autobiography, *Ancestors*. His fiction rebuilds that first house over and over again. But it can be reconstructed only through words, found only inside the pages of a book. Cather may have included in *My Ántonia* a fantasy of return—Jim Burden feels the pull of the earth, the desire to end here—but there's no illusion that such a fantasy should ever be fulfilled. At the end of the novel, Jim will get back on the train, head back to his job and unsympathetic wife, move toward his present and away from the past.

As for Henry James, there was no childhood home to go back to. All he has is a fantasy of return: Spencer Brydon walking through an empty house. Colm Tóibín, the author of *The Master*, a fictionalized portrait of James, made a similar point in a lecture I attended a few years back. After presenting a long (and only partial) list of James's complaints against his hometown—from all those ugly buildings to all those ugly crowds—Tóibín concludes with an incongruity. Why would a writer who so loathed the city have chosen for the title of his collected and revised body of work *The New York Edition*? For Tóibín it has everything to do with the fact that the first place, the first house, remains the site where the impressions begin. James had lived in New York during the most impressionable years of a writer's life—between five and twelve. "Union Square, Washington Square, Fifth Avenue, Sixth Avenue remained for him—the most homeless of people—a sort of home," a kind of sacred landscape. The house on Fourteenth Street, James once wrote, was "for ever so long afterwards, a sort of anchorage of spirit," and when his grandmother's house was torn down on Washington Square, he felt as if he'd been "amputated of half his history." It was not the actual New York that leads him to that title for his body of work, but the recollected one: the space of childhood dreams.

Listening to Tóibín from my seat in the audience that day, I thought of the metaphor James applied to his theory of literature—"the house of fiction"—and I saw for a second an image of the New York Edition, all those stories and novels and plays written over a lifetime: bricks piled on top of one another, forming together the walls and stairs of a house built to replace the one that had, like vapor, disappeared.

In the preface to *Upstate*, Edmund Wilson seems to have recognized some of this himself. The "memories of the past, the still lingering presences of the family, which so haunted me when I first came back here, have mostly evaporated. . . . the air seems to be thinner. . . . all the old ghosts are gone." The book he is writing offers him what the house cannot; it will "fill the vacuum," give life to all those ghosts.

Though they might never have gone back to the actual spaces of their childhoods, Cather, Maxwell, and James did make homes for themselves as adults where they must have sought out a corner, a window, a view evoking, if only hazily, the first place. Words are not always enough. There's that apartment on West Thirty-Sixth Street in Maxwell's "The Thistles in Sweden": "Since I was a child, no place has been quite so much a home to me." Or there's Lamb House, Henry James's house in Sussex, England. When he was fifty-five he took a twenty-one-year lease on the Georgian house—the first and only home the adult James ever committed to. James "had been a foot-loose American in Europe," his biographer Leon Edel writes. "The lodging house, the foreign pension, the hotel, had been his way of life for the greater part of a quarter of a century." Now he was settling down, a "reversal of all he'd done in the past."

Initially, the leasing of Lamb House induced terrible anxiety—"the possibilities of Lamb House were a 'blow in the stomach'"; James worried about the money and about becoming an "anchorite, a lonely prisoner beyond London's suburbs." But the anxiety didn't last. He hung his pictures and painted the walls, hired a cook and invited friends over for dinner. He even planted a beautiful garden: wisteria, lupines, and a trumpet creeper; espaliers of figs, plums, apples, and apricots; a mulberry tree, a walnut tree, and a row of Lombardy poplars to protect him from the wind. James lived at Lamb House from 1897 until his death in 1916, and in those rooms, looking out on that garden, he wrote some of his greatest work: *What Maisie Knew*, *The Awkward Age*, *The Wings of the Dove*, *The Ambassadors*, *The Golden Bowl*, *The Turn of the Screw*, "The Beast in the Jungle," "The Jolly Corner"—and the list goes on.

In *The Master* Colm Tóibín imagines what Lamb House might have meant to James:

> He knew that it was merely a house; others bought and sold houses and moved their belongings with ease and nonchalance. It struck him as he traveled towards Rye that no one, save himself, understood the meaning of this. For so many years now he had had no country, no family, no establishment of his own, merely a flat in London where he worked. He did not have the

necessary shell, and his exposure over the years had left him nervous and exhausted and fearful. It was as though he lacked a facade, a stretch of frontage to protect him from the world.

Compared to James, Willa Cather was perhaps even more the rootless wanderer. She was always moving. "Those who wish to see where Willa Cather lived," Joseph Urgo points out, "or to answer the question 'Where was Willa Cather's home?' must do some traveling": Winchester, Virginia; Red Cloud, Nebraska; Pittsburgh; Washington Square, Bank Street, and Park Avenue in New York City. And then there were the "regular summer destinations in Jaffrey, New Hampshire, Grand Manan Island in New Brunswick (where she built a small house), and Northeast Harbor on Mount Desert Island in Maine," as well as all the places she liked traveling to: "Walnut Canyon, Arizona; Santa Fe, New Mexico; Boston Garden; Manchester, Massachusetts; Cos Cob, Connecticut; Quebec City; and of course, she went to Nebraska, often. She told a friend once, referring to her travel schedule, that she kept her suitcases under her bed."

Still, there's no question that the desire for a "stretch of frontage" applies to Willa Cather as well. Cather lived for forty years in New York, fifteen of them in an apartment at 5 Bank Street with Edith Lewis. She "did her happiest writing" there, Lewis remembered. It was where "she completed *O Pioneers!* and worked at all her other books through *Death Comes for the Archbishop*. Although she wrote parts of them in other places, they all came back to 5 Bank Street." When Cather lost the Bank Street home—it would be torn down to make way for an apartment building—her friend Elizabeth Sergeant recalled that Cather "felt like a turtle that was losing its shell. The psychic pain of stripping off this protective integument was unbearable; she was exposed and miserable."

The house I think of most often when I think of Cather's adulthood isn't in New York—or even in the Southwest. It's the little house on Grand Manan Island, the only house she ever bought for herself. Between 1922 and 1940, she and Lewis lived on the island every summer. In 1928 they built a cottage there, a place, as Lewis recalls, that offered "solitude without loneliness and autonomy without guilt, a sort of summer camp where she could come and go at will." It was a "rough little place," Lewis remembers, "with many inconveniences; but it came to have not only comfort but great charm. Above the living room was a large attic from which one could look out over the cliffs and the sea, and this Willa Cather chose for her study. There was nothing in it except a few trunks, and her chair and table." Cather wrote much of "The Tom Outland Story" in that house, and I can't help but think this attic room, the fresh air blowing off the Atlantic, led her back—back to a sea of prairie grass, and back to that mesa, "high and blue."

I used to fantasize about buying our old house. Later this changed to the more practical idea of finding a place nearby—on the lake or on the ledge. I remember coming home one Christmas from New York, standing in a tavern parking lot not far from my father's farm, listening as an old friend, very drunk, berated me from the tavern door: "Five, six generations here. You've got to come back. You can't let it end." At the time I thought she was right.

For years my sister, Susan, and I talked about buying a place together. We sat up one night in my apartment on Lafayette Avenue with a bottle of wine to sketch it out: a cottage—something like the one my father built on Green Lake—but this time on Lake Winnebago. Years later Susan actually did it, bought a vacation place on the lake just down the road from where my mother lives. A tiny one-and-a-half-story cabin, Susan's place is bordered on either side by the kinds of houses people now build on Winnebago: year-round, suburban-sized, and pushed to the edge of their lots. When you walk the road and come upon Susan's cabin, there's a jolt—a cobwebby screened-in porch, towels flapping on the line. Squeezed between the present, a shadow flash of another time, like a movie in color that for a frame turns to black and white.

By the time I had the money to buy a place in 2008, I was married and had a full-time job in New York. My sense of what was practical changed. Andre didn't have the same image of "back home." Where he came from—that cabin in northern Minnesota—the lakes were colder, the houses set farther apart. Even the trees were different. It didn't seem fair to drag him back into my past, where I imagined him, like Elena Wilson up in Talcottville, sullenly trailing me on my sentimental hikes along the ledge and comparing Winnebago and its stinky water to the spring-fed lake on which he'd grown up. Already, by moving to New York City, a city that is not his natural fit, he'd made a compromise. This time we needed a place that could be a return for both of us. And so I settled, as Cather and James and Maxwell settled, for the approximation.

12

Jefferson

I

After my father died in 2005, he left us each some money. Any sensible person, especially one who for twenty years had been consumed by worries about finding an affordable place in the city, would have used that money to buy a New York apartment. It couldn't have bought us much—a studio maybe or a one-bedroom farther out into Brooklyn—but it would have stopped, once and for all, the cycle of real estate anxiety.

I always knew I'd do the impractical thing, though—knew if my father did leave me any money, I'd use it to buy a house in the country. Stronger than the demands of my New York life was a longing for land—"acreage," as my Wisconsin friends call it. Stronger than the reality of daily life was the fantasy of going back. At the time, I told myself that buying an apartment would have been a kind of betrayal. My father didn't really like New York and found real estate here an unfathomable rip-off. But the truth is my decision wasn't really a matter of honoring some unspoken wish beyond the grave. I would have done it anyway.

The idea of a house in the country came loaded with meaning from the start. I didn't miss the symmetry, the story coming full circle. The man who had created the great defining space of my life was now giving me a chance to purchase a house of my own, a home that would, I hoped, give me those trees and those rooms I remembered. I didn't miss the irony either. What afforded my return to the land was money made in commercial real estate.

Parking lots had paid for my escape, just as they had paid for the house on the ledge thirty-five years before.

Instead of the Midwest, Andre and I decided to look for a cabin or a house in upstate New York. Both teachers, we could spend our summers there, and if it was close enough, even go up for weekends. We spent over a year looking—long weekends driving around the Catskills in the back of a real estate broker's van. The broker, who had only just started in the job, didn't seem to care much about houses. Mostly he sold hunting land to middle-aged men from New Jersey. He didn't understand what we were looking for—didn't understand us. We'd ask for a natural landscape, and he'd drive up to a house without the stick of a tree, just a row of plastic gnomes leading to the door. We'd ask to see simple cabins and he'd show us a spotless ranch house, the simulation of a crackling fire on the television screen. What was so disheartening wasn't that these houses didn't match our taste; the problem was that they didn't match our memories. I can't really blame the broker's confusion: "Last time you said you just wanted a one-room cabin and now you say you want a fixer-upper farmhouse." If we were vague, it was because our desire couldn't be explained by any of the words used by real estate brokers. We were looking for the tracings of another time and place.

Too often on that house-hunt we seemed to be walking into the disappointing endings of somebody else's fantasy. This was rural America, and like much of rural America, a place of great natural beauty and few jobs. We toured farms that had gone bust—in one, a woman in her hospital bed was wheeled out of sight just as we stepped in the door. She could no longer go upstairs, and I stood for a long time in the doorway of the second-floor sewing room surveying a mountain of half-finished quilts, scraps of material stuffed into grocery bags. At another farm, we met an ex-advertising man whose back-to-the-land fantasies had fallen apart, saw naked babies scrambling over the woodpile, and felt a palpable coldness when the wife entered the room. That was the worst day—the hospital bed, the disillusioned wife—and afterward,

I thought I'd had enough. I didn't see how, even if I liked the house, I could forget that smell of disappointment, the heaviness that seemed to hang in those rooms, or the look in the wife's face when she turned to us, a look that said: "Go back to the city. This will happen to you, too."

I'd nearly given up when Andre found something online—a house on six acres in the foothills of the western Catskills. Four hours from the city, it was, in all practical ways, wrong. I resisted, kept resisting, even after we stepped through the front door. But after about fifteen minutes, it seemed familiar, as if I'd been there before: A dark brown farmhouse nestled, almost held, in the crook of a hill, with ancient maples on all sides. At the back, a tamarack tree over sixty feet tall with horizontal branches that seemed to extend over us in benediction. Below the house was a creek that ran down through hemlocks, and above the stream, a ridge about the height of the ledge. The back meadow was open and reminded me of a Wisconsin field; the woods reminded Andre of Minnesota. Behind the house were perennial gardens and two octagonal wooden structures, weathered gray, that had once been brooding coops for chickens. They reminded me of something an elf would live in—or a hobbit. At the far end of the property, a row of Lombardy poplars, planted to block the wind; these reminded me of Henry James's garden at Lamb House, but later when the poppies came out, they reminded me even more of Monet's Givenchy.

The house inside was all nooks and odd turns. A steep staircase and old beams hanging low over the living room. Upstairs were three attic bedrooms, one with sloping ceilings etched with knotholes, another with skylights that faced the sunrise, another like the little lofts and landings where we played as children. Some of the rooms had brightly painted floors and all through the place were doors that surprised you as you opened them because they led you back into a room where you'd already been, but this time you approached from a new angle.

After we bought the house, I realized what made the house so exciting was that, while it stood in symmetry to the house on the

One of the old chicken brooding coops at the edge of the woods, Jefferson, New York. (author's collection)

ledge, it was also entirely different. There is nothing modern about it. Behind a wall, the previous owners had found old newspapers used for insulation dating to the 1860s. The ceilings are low and I can touch the old beams if I stretch up my arms. Our house in Wisconsin insisted on its privacy, but this place is built close to the road with a neighbor directly across. The focus (the view of the lawn and garden out back) is to the north, and yet I grew up looking west. After four years, I am still surprised to see the sun setting in the wrong direction. We don't look down on the view but up at it. It is as if someone had lifted up our old house and spun it around.

Still, it brings me back: the nooks and overhangs, the tamarack out back like the one my mother planted in front of our house after we moved to the country, those bedrooms with their sloping ceilings, and the ridge along the creek, so like the ledge. It seems to evoke for everyone an image from a storybook. "You can almost see Gandalf rising up over that hill on a white horse," my sister said the first time she saw it, which is almost as perfect as the name the neighbor kids years back had given the ravine: Devil's Gulch. The name we've given the house isn't so fanciful; our friends started referring to the place by the name of the town at the bottom of the hill—Jefferson—and the name has stuck.

Living here, I sometimes feel as if I've moved back in time. The cellphone never works; the telephone wires sag over the road. We wheel out an old television on a rolling stand. In a way, this makes Jefferson feel almost more familiar than Fond du Lac does when I go back now. The house even smells like the seventies to me. Yet once again, the familiar has been tilted, spun around. There are few lakes around here. Most people swim in ponds they've dug themselves. Instead of hills, we have mountains. I feel the incongruities at the grocery store and on hikes and whenever I talk to the neighbors. From the start, Andre and I were struck by how the people up here seemed more wary, more reticent than our neighbors back in the Midwest. Perhaps this is a regional difference, the reserve of mountain people, of Yankees. Or maybe this isn't Yankee diffidence at all, but simply the automatic reaction of upstaters to anyone from New York City, especially summer people. I remember my mother's response to a certain kind of demanding customer at the bookstore: "Chicago people," she'd say, and usually she was right. To defend against being identified with the city, I find myself emphasizing—and exaggerating—my rural roots and my farming grandparents, just as I used to do on the bus when trying to fit in with the Holy Landers. In this way being an outsider is actually a kind of return. I am used to being an interloper. I grew up as one.

The house in Jefferson came with a vast perennial garden and raised beds for vegetables. I always admired my mother's garden, but I never paid attention to how she created it. I saw her out there on her knees and turned away. I hated those hot July afternoons weeding my father's ambitious rows of strawberries and tomatoes, a task that seemed to have no end. So much excitement at the beginning. By August, vegetables rotting on the vine.

But immediately the gardens upstate called to me. Maybe it was the farmer in my blood, or maybe it was the memory of my parents' early happiness as they walked around the property and talked about the trees they were going to plant, the beds they'd dig up next year. Andre and I took a subscription to *Mother Earth News*, just as my parents had done, and now, every winter, we sit up in bed circling seeds in the catalogs. We bought the house in the fall, so I didn't really know what to expect that first spring. I'll never have a spring like that again, the giddiness of waking every morning to a new miracle. I didn't yet know how to differentiate between a weed and a peony. Everything delighted me. Now, after five seasons here, I've lost some of the feeling I had that first spring. Now, my eye registers the unwanted: the dandelions, a wild geranium that seems to be taking over every corner of the garden. It occurs to me that this may be what farming has always been about, less about a love for plants than a perpetual battle against them.

I have no illusions, though, that Andre and I are some kind of back-to-the-land farmers. We haven't loaded up our effects, given up the city. And I recognize what a privilege it is to have both these lives, especially for someone like me who is always swinging between desires. I can enact, over and over again, the return to the land and the escape to the city, sometimes in just the space of a weekend.

We have a few friends who are now taking a stab at the back-to-the-land experiment. They are reading the Nearings and studying the art of composting. This excites me—the passion for nature and sustainable living. But I also get a little nervous about back-to-the-land fantasies, since I know how often they can disappoint. Kitty-corner from us is an old farm with three huge barns and a white farmhouse that sits up close to the road. It was vacant when we moved here, but just a few months ago Vinny and Masha, a young Brooklyn couple with a baby, bought it. Unlike us, they gave up the city for good. Their plan is to start an organic farm. Already they have two goats and a barn full of chickens. I don't really know them, but feel a little protective anyway. A well-traveled snowmobile path runs along their property. Remembering the conflicts over our old snowmobile trail in the woods and the community outrage when my mother erected a line of barbed wire fence across it, I suggested to Vinny that he begin peaceful negotiations soon. He looked at me as if I were a little crazy—or as if he thought this was none of my business.

Last summer, at a neighborhood barbecue, one man cornered Vinny and gave him a lecture on how hard farming was up here and all the other reasons their fantasies might not work out. I think he was trying to be helpful, recognizing—as all of us sitting around the barbecue did that day—the enormity of their task. "They're so young. They don't know what they are getting into," one neighbor said later, and I thought to myself that probably none of us, if we knew what we were getting into, would do anything at all.

◇

Jefferson is the first place either Andre or I ever owned, and from the start I wondered how ownership might change my ideas about property. Just after our offer was accepted on the house, I had a little panic attack. Yes, I was ecstatic—but I also felt, as Henry James had felt on first leasing Lamb House, a "blow to the stomach." Nobody ever tells you about this—how uncomfortable the prospect of home ownership can be. I imagined trees falling and termites burrowing. I wondered if yard work would now replace travel, and if by purchasing a place in upstate New York, I was severing my relationship to Wisconsin.

But, like James, I got over it, and one thing that helped was our decision, almost from the first day, to share the house as much as possible. We had a big party at Thanksgiving and handed out sets of keys. We didn't want Jefferson to be just ours—there were too many bedrooms, and we had too many friends, many of them artists or writers, who could use the place. Amazingly, it has worked out, and our friends are now almost as familiar with Jefferson as we are.

Of course I can't deny that sometimes I feel those old attachments—the pull of "me" and "mine"—rearing up. Last summer, I heard voices in the woods and went down to investigate. Three boys, about thirteen years old, scrambling down the ridge. For a second, I was overtaken by a sense of violation. I tried to be friendly as I pointed to the No Trespassing sign and to the stone walls at the edge of the property. I'd grown up the daughter of a trespasser, had spent summers crawling all over the farmer's woods down the road. I have never really believed good fences make good neighbors. My reaction surprised—and embarrassed—me. Later, I wondered if this reaction came from all those years living in the city, wondered if this wasn't so much possessiveness—"This is mine, get off it!"—as a desire to no longer have to negotiate personal boundaries. I think of Henry James's relief at finding "a stretch of frontage to protect him from the world." I loved those stone walls for their beauty, for their reminder of hundreds of years of painstaking labor, but I also loved them because they offered enclosure, a sanctuary, a bounded space where nobody, unless they were invited, could come in.

On the first day Andre and I stepped onto the Jefferson property, I was aware that the difference between this place and so many of the other houses we'd looked at was not just a matter of aesthetic sensibility. I registered instantly that the people who lived here had been happy. Later, I met the owners—like us, people from the city who used the house in summers and on weekends. One of them, Cynthia, came up just after we'd moved in to pick up some furniture she'd left behind. As she was pulling out of the drive, she said: "It might be strange to say this but I can't really think of one day up here when I was really unhappy."

Cynthia is an artist—a painter—and the person who first bought the house twenty years before. Later, her friend Bill, also an artist, and his partner, Vivian, bought in on it, and then Cynthia married Bob. So there were four of them. I liked the fact that they too had seen Jefferson as a place that needed to be shared, but I did wonder about the logistics. I imagined rifts, territorial conflicts, and assumed this was why they were selling it, but Cynthia and Bill told me they'd lived together all those years peaceably. They were selling it because they were getting older—the icy roads over the mountains are treacherous in winter—and wanted to be closer to a train line.

I had a lot of trouble imagining how they could sell the place, especially because in a sense, they had built it. It had been a twenty-year art project, a remarkable effort of patience and love. Cynthia gave us a book of photographs taken of the house and property when she'd first bought it. A tiny run-down white farmhouse, almost unrecognizable—no garden and no poplars. The tops of the brooding coops and apple trees were hardly visible in the field of weeds. I looked at those photographs of the dilapidated house and could almost see a pioneer family posed in front of it with their mules and plows, their spinning wheels and quilts thrown over the back of a chair. Now it was something else: they'd enlarged the house, adding on a study over the creek and a screened-in back porch; they'd put in new windows, replaced the siding and the roof, and ripped out all the little warren rooms downstairs; they'd put in a Franklin stove, jacked up one of the brooding coops, trimmed the apple trees, laid down a stone patio off the porch, painted the upstairs floors a beautiful orange. They'd planted all those gardens, and even built an artist's studio down in the woods, which I now use for a place to write.

The first winter, one of my architect friends came up for a visit. In the early stages of building his own house and daunted by the prospect, he needed a retreat. Right off, he loved Jefferson—as all my artist friends do—but I could tell it was hard to walk into a seemingly finished house just as he was starting from scratch. When I showed him those old photographs of what it had looked like before, he almost seemed angry: "Do you know how much work they put into this house? Do you have any idea what it took to do this?" I felt guilty—and maybe I still feel guilty. Yes, we'd paid for the house, but we hadn't made it.

When I was a kid, I had a fascination with the novels of Gene Stratton Porter, a nineteenth-century regionalist writer from

Indiana. My favorite was *A Girl of the Limberlost*—a romantic tale of a nature girl who collects butterflies to pay her school tuition. But the one I read almost as avidly was her novel *The Harvester*, the story of a man who sees a vision of a beautiful woman in a dream and then builds a home for her. He does everything himself, cuts down every tree, digs up the pond, plants beds of perennials, all for a woman he's seen only in a dream. When he meets his vision finally, he brings her home to the perfect house.

The Harvester is a terrible book—sentimental, sloppy, overwrought. Even as a child I knew this. The plot was so improbable and the characters so flatly drawn—the romance so "icky," as I'd have put it then—I felt almost as if I had to read it secretly in the bathroom. But I kept going back to it—not to the icky romance, but to that perfect house. The great pleasure came from watching the house come into being. I knew those gardens by heart. Even now, I can recall every stick of furniture, every quilt on the bed. But the moment the flesh-and-blood girl showed up in the story, I put the novel down. It bothered me—her moving into a perfect house that somebody else had made.

After moving to Jefferson, I thought a lot about what it means to purchase someone else's creation, what it means to move into a place so marked by the personalities of other people. It's a strange kind of intimacy. You don't know the people at all, yet you know them very well; it is as if you are walking through their minds. For a long time I was almost too intimidated to change anything. My tendency now to look out on the garden and see what's wrong with it may come from some belief that it needs to look just as it did when we first moved here. The previous owners had left behind some furniture, not ancestral furniture like my sister-in-law's rockers back in that old Victorian in Lake City, but furniture that seemed somehow to belong to the house. And for a long time, I felt it would be an insult to the house to get rid of any of it.

Before they left, both Cynthia and Bill seemed sensitive to my problem. Bill turned to us on the day we closed on the house and said gruffly, "We've made a lot of changes here. If I come back someday I hope I find you've made even more." Cynthia returned one weekend to give us a tour of the garden. She reminded me to empty the bluebird feeders and told me that should I ever want to dig up the poppies, I should be warned that this was the spot where she'd buried her cats. She worried about the rose-breasted grosbeak who'd been coming to their feeder for many years. "He'll expect a feeder at the window and another hanging on the tamarack." I noticed that Cynthia, like my mother, who is known to compulsively deadhead flowers wherever she goes, couldn't help occasionally pulling up a weed as we walked. "This garden is a lot of work," she said finally. "And you shouldn't feel bad if you let it all go."

After she moved, Cynthia introduced us to some of her friends who live up here. Many of them are artists from the city who bought old farms back in the seventies and eighties when land was cheap. I've met a few of them, and they tell me about all the work that went into their own dilapidated houses when they first bought them. They are all very kind but also, I think, a little suspicious of us. At a dinner, I overheard one woman talking about a young "house-proud" couple from the city who had bought another friend's farmhouse. "They talk of it as if they've discovered it, as if they had no idea what went into making the place." I thought of that Victorian back in Lake City and the house-proud couple taking their nightly walks around the property, oblivious to my sister-in-law's history there. I wanted to rush over to the woman: "But I promise, we're not like that!" When I'm introduced to someone in Cynthia's circle, he or she will invariably say, "Oh, you live in Cynthia's house," and then they will catch themselves and apologize. But I don't mind it, since of course they are right.

One of the first people who came to mind after we bought Jefferson was Ann Hanson, the landscape designer who lived on the other side of the apple orchard. Ann's opinions always mattered to me, and it was in matters of place where Ann's opinions counted most. My sister, Susan, and I agreed that the homes we made for ourselves later in life were modeled as much on the Hansons' farmhouse as on the house where we grew up. When Susan bought her summer cottage on the lake, she painted it a brownish red like Ann and Fred's, and added an L-shaped screened porch that wrapped around two sides of the cottage, a miniature version of the one Ann and Fred had built over their garage. At the lake's edge, Susan spent months hollowing out from the steep side of the bank a stone circle for a fire pit and then drove Ann over to see it since, when it came to the placement of stones, Ann was the expert. I'd watched her help my mother design a border around her fishpond. Too frail to move the rocks herself, she leaned forward from her lawn chair, tapping her cane on the rock. I could sense the frustration of a once-powerful body no longer obedient to the eye's instruction. "No! Flip it over, a little over there, turn it. No! Not so far." Five days of incremental adjustments. My mother said that most people would have laid those stones in an afternoon.

After Andre and I bought the house in Jefferson, I went back to Wisconsin for a visit. Ann and I pored over photographs of the perennial gardens, her magnifying glass held in one slightly trembling hand. She liked what the previous owners had done—"it's good to know there are still people like that out there"—but still she had her opinions: "That potato vine is going to strangle your Beauty Bush. You'll want to rip that out." I hadn't registered the potato vine's existence. Or, on alighting on a bright blue delphinium: "Not a natural color, that blue. Hothouse blue." Finally, she lowered the glass to a small tree at the edge of a photo. "Too bad. An eastern red cedar. Such an unpleasant spiny texture, don't you think? Terrible on the hands." It hadn't occurred to me that the feel of a tree was important, and I didn't have the courage to confess that the eastern red cedar was the first tree we'd planted ourselves. Now, whenever I pass it on my way to the mailbox, I reach out a hand and feel between my fingers Ann's prickly objections.

But I didn't just want to model our property after Ann's; I wanted to model the relationship she had with property. For many years I thought of her and her house as permanent, the one place in the Holy Land that would never change. At the end of every visit, I'd think to myself: this may be the last time. The fact that this dread went unmet again and again—when she turned eighty, when she turned ninety, when she turned ninety-five—half convinced me that here was someone immune to the vagaries of time. If I left thinking I'd never see her again, I always arrived certain that she would be there and just the same. Even in the final years when her world had contracted, shrinking to a view from the window, to the bird on the branch, I was right. The same strong opinions, the same straight back and beautiful handmade clothes. (Fashion was one art where exotic colors were sanctioned—crimsons and unnatural hothouse blues.) The table always a litter of seed catalogs, Kleenex boxes, and marked-up copies of the *New York Times*. The shelves framing the window still holding the botanical and bird guides, the art school portfolios, and the volume I loved to take down when I was little, a first edition of *A Girl of the Limberlost*, the illustrations a revelation, a wisp of transparent paper and underneath a color plate of a woman, her finger extended to a butterfly, wings outspread.

Ann was an example of sustained inhabitation, that once common, now rare phenomenon called "staying put." Seventy years in one place. Ninety-seven years on the planet. After we bought our house, I worried that we had taken on too much for two people with jobs in the city. Andre tried to calm me down: "This isn't a lifelong commitment," he said. "If it gets too overwhelming, we can always sell it." But he didn't understand; a lifelong commitment was the whole point. I wanted what Ann had and what my parents' house, in the hands of one family for less than twenty years, couldn't give me: Extended intimacy, a model of a place that might hold a life. The towering tree you'd mulched and watered in its infancy. The view from a window you knew so deeply it had attached to the eye, like a film on the retina coloring your view of everything else.

But as much as Ann's house was a model of sustained attachment, it was also an example of how to loosen the hold of "me and mine"—how to let go, how to lighten up. She related to the land as a steward, not an owner. Her connection, however rooted, was

Ann Hanson standing near her barn. To the left, a stone shed she and Fred designed and built. (courtesy of the photographer, Susan Peters)

never tight, never clenching. It seemed not just free of the urge for possession, but also of the weight of nostalgia I've struggled with so much in my life. I wondered if, for some people, nostalgia actually diminishes as they get older. Maybe this is the key to staying young. Walking around her property, Ann would tell me of how she planted a tree, curious about how it would look in forty years, long after she'd be gone. When she talked about the future of her house, she seemed almost indifferent. She was passing it on to one of her daughters, but what happened after that was none of her business.

Last summer, I went home to Wisconsin to give a reading from an essay that became a section of this book—the chapter on the Holy Land. Betty Schneider was there and so was Gracie, the woman who bought our house after my parents' divorce. I was relieved they both liked what I had to say. Betty blushed when she heard her name. Gracie and her new partner, Othello, invited me over for lunch the next day. Othello had turned our garage into an artist's studio, so we started there and walked up into the living room from the basement below, an approach I'd almost forgotten about, but it had the same effect: the dark narrow passageway leading up into light and space.

Gracie had been coming to the house much more often since she'd met Othello, and it looked amazing—maybe better than before. I noticed the changes, of course—different light fixtures, new floors, a white Franklin stove instead of the charcoal gray one I remembered. The walls seemed to have straightened themselves, and Othello told me that they'd had work done to fix the problem of the foundation. It was a perfect summer day, and we sat at the kitchen table looking down on the living room and through the trees to the field. I felt myself responding to the house as I always did—as if someone had wrenched a kink out of my back I hadn't known was there. After a while, though, I noticed how the house wasn't responding to me. It was indifferent, maybe even a little cold. I'd been released and forgotten long ago, and as I was leaving, it hit me that Gracie had lived in this house longer than I had.

The next day I flew back to Albany and drove to our house in Jefferson. It was the Fourth of July weekend and we were having a big party with friends from the city. Trixie, the four-year-old daughter of a friend of mine, was trailing me with a watering can when a car slowed in front of the house, inching along from the far end of the property toward the house. When I saw that it was Cynthia and her husband, two of the previous owners of the house, I ran to the car, Trixie behind me, as if it were a game. Cynthia and Bob didn't look as if they wanted to be recognized and got out of the car reluctantly. We walked around for a while, Trixie looking up at me, confused by how nervous I seemed. Cynthia and Bob couldn't get over how tall the trees they'd planted had grown. When she'd planted the tamarack, now sixty feet high,

Cynthia told me she thought she was planting a bush. I was embarrassed about the gardens, the weeds, and apologized for digging up some plants in one bed. "Everyone has her own taste," she said shrugging. It was another gesture of permission, a reminder that I was free to make the place mine.

They didn't want to stay, I could see that, and I told them to come back a weekend in August when we were going to be out of town. I know how it's easier to go back when nobody is there to watch. When they left, I thought of all the things I wished I'd told them: two hemlocks had come down over the creek, the bluebirds had left last year but this year had come back, and because we hadn't been around enough that spring, the rose-breasted grosbeak had given up on us, transferring its affection to our neighbor Freda's feeder across the road.

My father would have liked this house, although I sometimes think of how he might have wanted to rip out one of those attic rooms to lift up the ceiling and let in more light. One wall in the living room blocks the view to the garden, and whenever I look at it, I can hear him: "First thing I'd do is take down this wall." We've been here nearly five years now and still haven't done it. I tell Andre that we need to do it soon, not just to get the view, but because I don't like thinking of my father in terms of an obstruction.

I sometimes have a dream about his coming to visit us here. I see him lumbering toward me up a long dirt road. He's gained weight and seems sluggish, also a little irritated, as if I've woken him from a long sleep. I run toward him, grab his hand, but when he finally gets to the door, the house has changed into something else, a long windowless room unfamiliar to me and filled with unfamiliar objects: old furniture and clothes, ugly mirrors and tables. The back room of the Salvation Army or a hoarder's apartment—so crowded you can hardly move. At the far end of the room is the door to the real house, and I'm desperate for him to walk through it. But every time, the same thing happens. He won't budge, just stands there looking irritated until finally without speaking he walks out. It's a painful dream—as if he, like the house on the ledge, had released and forgotten me. But the last two times I had the dream, something changed. The same old junk, but this time one object of beauty: a fresco covering one wall, something from the early Renaissance. In the foreground, the courtyard of a house, and in the far distance, the hills and towers of Tuscany. Everything painted in deep shades of blue. The tiles of the courtyard belong to a memory of an art class, a lesson on drawing perspective. As my father walks toward the fresco, so close he's almost pressing his face into the wall, I see that it is really a jigsaw puzzle glued to the wall. Reaching up, he pries one of the pieces away, and then, once more without speaking, walks out of the room.

My friend David tells me I am a very literal dreamer; the meaning is always obvious. But I'm not sure how to interpret this one. I know it has nothing do with the house in Jefferson. I suppose it is about the book I've written. I suppose it is about my fear that my father would think I've crammed too much furniture into it. Or maybe I've only managed to pull away one small piece from what looks to him like a vast and intricate pattern, a landscape reaching on toward infinity in deepening shades of blue.

I have to say I think much more about my mother here in Jefferson than I do my father. I'm always sensing her presence, wondering what she will think. I drop the gloves or rake in the middle of a project to run to the house and call her: Do I move the bush now or wait until fall? Do I paint the wall or leave it? How much sugar does the hummingbird need?

When she first visited Jefferson, it was spring, and we pulled up in the car at dusk. We went inside, and she clapped her hands. I wouldn't let her sit down until she'd seen it all. Carrying a wine bottle and two glasses out into the back meadow, we walked the entire property, the poppies glowing—and then closing—in the last bit of light. By the time we finished, the poplars were vague shadows, the stars were bright. I needed to run back for a flashlight. For every tree, she had a name and a story; for every plant in the garden, its designation in common terms and in Latin, all memorized from a book she'd bought in 1971 when we'd moved to the country. She understood Jefferson from the first, and moved through the rooms and along its paths as if she had lived there all her life.

This powerful sense of my mother here reminds me of all that's left out of my story. More and more I see—especially since we bought the place in Jefferson—how much our old house on the ledge was really her creation. My father was a builder of houses, but he wasn't, if I think about it, ever very good at living in them. For long periods during my early years, he was absent—traveling, or at the office until late into the night. I don't remember him touching the house much, but my mother's hands were on it all the time, and in handling it, she brought it back to life. She knew the house the way only a person who cleans and arranges it can know a house: the cracks in the floor where dust settles, the texture of tiles and walls, the way the light hits a chair or a table. In *The Poetics of Space*, Bachelard writes about this: "And when a poet rubs a piece of furniture—even vicariously—when he puts a little fragrant wax on his table with the woolen cloth that lends warmth to everything it touches, he creates a new object . . . The housewife awakens furniture that was asleep."

Yet I don't think of my mother as a housewife so much as an artist. She is always squinting at walls and gardens as if they were paintings. She was always more visual than my father. When my dad first moved to Salt Lake, I never could come to terms with the places he chose to inhabit—so predictable, so empty and unlived in, so different from our place in Wisconsin. I saw, as I hadn't before, that it had been my mother who had filled and lit that first place. I remember Frank Lloyd Wright's message to my father: you are no artist, but you are a great builder. How much of the artistry of our first house came from my mother? I look back to one of my earliest memories—my parents sitting together, night after night, planning out the house—and it is impossible now not to see her directing his pencil. My siblings and I sometimes wonder if we should ascribe certain challenges in our characters to having been born of an unlikely match. But I never forget that from the merging of these two incompatible minds came a strange and beautiful house.

When my parents divorced, my father left the house to her in the settlement. A few years later she sold it when she married my stepfather. How could she ask her new husband to live in a house built by another man? It would have been like living in someone else's mind and in the shadow of another time—the first hopeful flush of a marriage, the ghosts of two heads leaning together over a kitchen table and drawing out a life.

At the time, I understood all this, but I can't lie; I still resented her selling the place. I resented how rarely she talked about it or seemed to visibly mourn its loss afterward. But this is my mother's way. A perpetual student, the kind who memorizes the Latin names for flowers and begins to write poetry at sixty and to paint in oils at seventy, she is simply too curious to find nostalgia interesting. Unlike me—and unlike my father—my mother has always worked hard to live in the healthy present. During my dreamy adolescent phase, I remember a walk on a beach in Florida and how she turned to me, gripped my arm, pointed to a sandpiper, pointed to the surf, and said: "Look around. *Be here now.*"

But I was wrong to think she didn't care—or that she never looked back. I'm almost the same age now as she was when she and my father were divorced, and I understand her better than I used to. If at the time she didn't show it—the loss of that place—now I see how hard it must have been. So much of that house was hers alone. My father planted those long rows in the garden, but she was the one at dusk harvesting them. My father abandoned the rural fantasy, but my mother is still planting trees, still down on her knees, her hands in the dirt. The other day she reminded me—a bit slyly—that our copy of the Nearings' *The Good Life* was much more often on her side of the bed than my father's. I think of all the mornings, before the rest of us were up, when she sat in the kitchen and listened to the silence and the birds. Now, when I'm back in Wisconsin and we are in the car together, I catch her sometimes averting her eyes when we pass the old driveway on Highway 151.

Last Christmas I gave my mother a book on the artist Richard Diebenkorn. As is her way, she didn't just look at each painting, but read every dense word of the text, underlining passages and sticking Post-its all the way through. A few months later, she reciprocated with a painting she'd made inspired by Diebenkorn, a very beautiful abstract in whites and deep purples. She said it reminded her of a hillside near our house in Jefferson. I hung it in an attic bedroom upstairs, and one morning, in that half-dream awareness that comes just after waking, I saw it for what it was. It wasn't Diebenkorn. It wasn't the fields of Jefferson either. It was our old view from the ledge, the horizontal bands of field, lake, and sky.

Acknowledgments

First and most of all, I thank Andre Theisen, who has lived inside this book almost from the day we got married. I remember his sitting me down on our honeymoon and pleading with me to start: "Write for an hour, and then we'll go to the beach." I remember the long middle stretch when he'd come home from work and read another draft of a chapter he'd already commented on multiple times. (I still can't believe my luck: a brilliant editor to boot!) And I will never forget his remarkable patience when I was struggling at the end—the food magically appearing next to the computer, the late-night notes reminding me to "finish strong." In so many ways, this book exists because of him.

Thanks to my amazing problem-solving sister, Susan Peters, and to Tim Harris and Tara Key, inspiring creators in their own right and a crack editorial team. They contributed so much: proofreading, research, photos, even help with a jacket design. For reading this manuscript so carefully and for supporting me at every stage, I am forever grateful to Rachel Brownstein, David Haproff, Natalie Reitano, Tim Seggerman, and Mary Wehner. Thanks to Joy Ladin for encouraging me early on, to Paul Kelley and Richard Reitz Smith for taking time to read and think about the manuscript at the end of the process, and to Kent Herbert and David Peters for checking facts and filling in some of the gaps.

I wish also to convey my warm appreciation to Linda Shires, chair of the Stern College English Department; Willard Spiegelman, editor of *Southwest Review*; and Raphael Kadushin, Matthew Cosby, Sheila McMahon, Logan Middleton and the rest of the staff at the University of Wisconsin Press.

Others who have helped along the way: Sharon Barnes, Vincent Colapietro, Jim Cricchi, Philip Dray, Tom Falvey, David Fechheimer, Sue Garner, Kevin Greutert, Jack Lynch, Michael Massing, Patrick McCabe, Rebecca Johnson Melvin, Matt Miller, Honor Moore, Nora Nachumi, Adam Zachary Newton, Peter Ohlin, Alissa Quart, Nelly Reifler, Richard Rhorer, Jana Richman, Peter Ross, Robert Sietsema, Carole Silver, Scott Stewart, and Tracy Tucker.

Grateful acknowledgment is made to the writer Lisa Martineau for the use of her unpublished eulogy for Dee McAuliffe. The photograph of Maeve Brennan has been reproduced with the kind permission of the Karl Bissinger Estate and the Karl Bissinger Papers at the University of Delaware Library. I thank the Willa Cather Foundation and Barb Kudrna for use of the photograph of Willa Cather's bedroom and the New York Public Library's Astor, Lenox and Tilden Foundations for the reproduction of the 1870 drawing of the Graham Home for Old Ladies. Thanks also to Susan Peters for the Ann Hanson photo and Tara Key for the Edmund Wilson photo. The rest of the photographs belong to my own collection.

Portions of chapters 1, 2, and 3 were originally published in *Southwest Review* 97, no. 1 (2012). Chapter 8 includes an excerpt of an article that originally appeared in the *Gender and Culture in the 1950s* issue of *WSQ: Women's Studies Quarterly* 33, nos. 3 and 4 (Fall/Winter 2005), published by the Feminist Press at the City University of New York.

Notes

Chapter 1. The House on the Ledge

- 17 "a clearing in the woods": Grese, *Jens Jensen*, 137.
- 21 "extended apologia": Gill, *Many Masks*, 27.
- 22 "honest Bucksaw" and "persuasive hammer": Wright, *Frank Lloyd Wright*, 46.
- — "muscles hard": Ibid., 48.
- — "white birches gleaming," "milkweed blossoming": Ibid., 26.
- — "not on the hill but of the hill": Gill, *Many Masks*, 217.
- 27 "Wright put on and discarded many masks": Ibid., 50.
- 28 "it's all pulling tits": Ibid., 48.
- — "inspired to sing of pastoral joys": Ibid.
- 29 "old post hole in the midst of paradise": Thoreau, "Walking," 80.

Chapter 2. The Architect

- 36 "smartened up with a coat": Howells, *Rise of Silas Lapham*, 9.
- — "risen Americans are all pathetically alike": Ibid., 5.
- — "Worked in the fields": Ibid., 3.
- 37 "won't make fun of": Ibid., 29–30.
- — "deep in the heart of the virgin forests": Ibid., 25.
- — "one of nature's noblemen": Ibid., 26.
- 38 "the regulation thing": Ibid., 3.
- — "I ain't a-going to brag up my paint": Ibid., 13.
- — "It's the best paint in God's universe": Ibid., 105.
- — "great hairy paws": Ibid., 116.

38 "saffron-tinted": Ibid., 264.
— "canvased hams": Ibid.
39 "leather-cushioned swivel-chair": Ibid., 2.
43 "curled her chin up": Ibid., 70.
— "Your mother wasn't ashamed": Ibid.
— "Yes, we've heard that story": Ibid.
47 "own the things money can't buy": Roth, *American Pastoral*, 307.
— "of every polite taste and feeling": Howells, *Rise of Silas Lapham*, 377.
— "absurd to paint portraits for pay": Ibid., 96.
48 "see in his averted face the struggle": Ibid., 203–4.
49 "true and only artistic creators": Ibid.
50 "It seemed that he had discovered the fellow": Ibid., 58.
— "crude taste in architecture": Ibid.

Chapter 3. The Second House

54 "triumphant payers of dividends": James, *American Scene*, 60.
55 "tall mass of flats": James, "The Jolly Corner," 605.
— "two bristling blocks": Ibid.
— "mere feel. . . . in the air": Ibid., 610–11.
— "vast ledger-page . . . criss-crossed lines and figures": Ibid., 606.
— "swagger things": Ibid., 604.
56 "proportions and values were upside down": Ibid.
— "walk[ing] planks . . . go[ing] into figures": Ibid., 605.
— "rage of curiosity": Ibid., 613.
— "mere number in its long row": Ibid., 605.
57 "beastly rent values . . . consecrated spot": Ibid., 610.
— "In short, you're to make so good a thing": Ibid.
69 "Things have happened to him": Ibid., 641.

Chapter 4. The Holy Land

74 "narrow fellow in the grass . . . unbraiding in the sun": Dickinson, "A narrow fellow in the grass," 443.
76 "perpetually provisional": James, *American Scene*, 200.
— "ruthlessly suppressed birth house": Ibid., 70.
77 "gross aliens": Ibid., 172.
— "seen a ghost in his supposedly safe old house": Ibid., 66.
— "Which is *not* the alien": Ibid., 95.

77 "without nostalgia, without a disabling elegiacism": Cavell, *Philosophy*, 217–18.
79 "everybody to enjoy the house": Kincaid, *Lucy*, 36.
— "what seemed the destruction": Ibid., 71.
— "vanishing things": Ibid., 72.
— "Many houses had been built": Ibid., 71–72.
89 "Hudson Bay plug tobacco, sumac leaves": Federal Writers' Project, *WPA Guide*, 369.
92 "admired it, just as the wise men from the East": Puchner, "Recollections of the Forties," 69.
— "the majestic calmness . . . glimmering waves . . . gay-colored dots": Ibid., 69.
93 "shy and timid": De Haas, *North America*, 40.
— "a civilized people, Christians": Ibid.

CHAPTER 6. REID TERRACE

123 "sleeping houses on either side": Cather, *My Ántonia*, 140.
— "primer-like": Faulkner, "A Note on Sherwood Anderson," 5.
— "In the evening": Anderson, *Winesburg, Ohio*, 17–18.
126 "was not a man of much force. . . . she had had a hard life. . . . aged and broken": Cather, *My Ántonia*, 211.
— "the full vigor of her personality": Ibid., 214.
— "I belong on a farm": Ibid., 221.
— "theatres and lighted streets. . . . in one of the loneliest countries": Ibid., 235.
— "nursing his pipe . . . whether the life that was right for one": Ibid.
— "I love them as if they were people": Ibid., 219.
131 "don't always know how to": Wharton, *House of Mirth*, 509.
— "material poverty that she turned from": Ibid., 515.
— "blown hither and thither": Ibid., 153
— "mere spin-drift of the whirling": Ibid., 515.
132 "The poor little working-girl": Ibid., 517.
134 "She loved the familiar trees": Cather, *Song of the Lark*, 127.
— "When I strike": quoted in O'Brien, *Willa Cather*, 68.
— "grave endearing traditions": Wharton, *House of Mirth*, 516.
— "wild, almost incoherent restlessness. . . . high-flying kite": quoted in Lee, *Edith Wharton*, 394.
— "the great and glorious pendulum": Ibid., 227.

CHAPTER 7. MANHATTAN

139 "can stay in this jerkwater town": Inge, *Four Plays*, 146.
141 "Village-Bohemia-literary": Sukenick, *Down and In*, 19.
142 "It was a time when": Ibid., 49.
143 "I could never": Howells, *Hazard*, 29.
— "We must not forget": Ibid., 53.
— "instinct for domiciliation . . . It's the only way I can realize": Ibid., 70.
— "It was something about the children": Ibid., 77.
144 "Why my dear, it was nothing": Ibid., 78.
149 "It was the end room of the wing": Cather, *Song of the Lark*, 51.
150 "[How] very quickly": Bachelard, *Poetics of Space*, 14.
151 "one of the most important things": Cather, *Song of the Lark*, 52.
— "began to live a double life": Ibid., 53.
— "mind worked better": Ibid., 52.
— "she used to drag her mattress": Ibid., 127.
— "would be her last summer in that room . . . never think anywhere else": Ibid., 215–16.
— "nest in a high cliff": Ibid., 268.
155 "Houses were 'lit up like a tickle-park'": Martineau, unpublished eulogy for Dee McAuliffe.

CHAPTER 8. LAFAYETTE

165 "To be around her was to see style": Bourke, *Maeve Brennan*, ix.
167 "transport her entire household": Botsford, *Life of Privilege*, 220.
— "two-dimensional": Bourke, *Maeve Brennan*, 191.
— "traveler in residence": Brennan, *Long-Winded Lady*, 2.
168 "if you are writing about people": Brennan, interview, *Time*, July 1, 1974.
— "has never felt the urge": Brennan, *Long-Winded Lady*, 6.
— "which is so small and familiar": Ibid., 8.
— "narrow gap": Ibid., 87.
— "brand-new, drearily uniform apartments. . . . already shivering": Ibid.
— "In the afternoon, when I went to lunch": Ibid., 218.
169 "It is very disconcerting": Ibid.
— "capsized . . . to the island": Ibid., 1.
— "execution of the Hotel Astor": Ibid., 67.
170 "The Great Manhattan Boom . . . Manhattan, written off long ago": Wallock, *New York*, 89.

174 "Doesn't it make you feel rather small": Howells, *Hazard*, 82.
175 "scurrying out of buildings": Brennan, *Long-Winded*, 219.
— "neighborhood with too many buildings": Brennan, *Rose Garden*, 250.
— "permanent refuge . . . his house is to be torn down": Ibid., 256.
— "They stand outside their apartment": Ibid.
— "ballet of the city sidewalk": Jacobs, *Death and Life*, 50.
176 "rouged and dyed . . . mascaraed eyes": Powell, *Wicked Pavilion*, 320.
— "nest of them": Ibid., 145.
177 a hundred thousand SRO units disappeared: Blackburn, *Single-Room Occupancy*, 1–8.

CHAPTER 9. BROWNSTONE

180 "light out for the territory": Twain, *Huckleberry Finn*, 438.
— "whether the life that was right for one": Cather, *My Ántonia*, 235.
181 "leather pressed paper . . . frescoed in flower effect": "Brooklyn People," 5.
182 "four Episcopal, one Reformed Episcopal": *Clinton Hill Historic District*, 5.
183 "was entering a period of physical deterioration": Morrone, "Underwood Park."
187 "Seeing clearly is everything": Maxwell, *Folded Leaf*, 402.
188 "the Dutch-English and the Scotch-Irish . . . each generation unraveling": Marshall, *Brown Girl*, 4.
189 "shallow breathing. . . . all the lives": Ibid., 4–5.
— "rustling across the parquet floors": Ibid., 4.
— "full of ponderous furniture . . . their faces as the silence": Ibid., 5.
— "with pale footfalls": Ibid., 5.
190 "unemployed lower middle-class": Riley, "Leaves of Grass," 166.
— "a restless marketplace persona": Ibid., 164.
— "urban speculator": Ibid., 165.
— "took a predominantly administrative role": Ibid., 171.
— "to align this period": Ibid., 175.
— "rabid, feverish itching": Whitman, "Tear Down," 97.
— "pull-down-and-build-over-again": Ibid., 92.
— "Good-bye, old houses! . . . stout and sound": Ibid., 93.
191 "the 'restless' activities": Riley, "Leaves of Grass," 167.
— "jumping from house to house": Ibid., 170.
— "pennies which would 'buy house'": Marshall, *Brown Girl*, 11.
— "who had never owned anything . . . with the same fierce": Ibid., 4.
195 "plot shmot": Updike, "Imperishable Maxwell."

195 "Since I was a child": Maxwell, "Thistles in Sweden," 488.
196 "underfurnished": Ibid., 489.
— "size of a handkerchief": Ibid., 494.
— "a beautiful shade of Chinese red": Ibid., 491.
— "life-sized thistles": Ibid., 487.
— "feeling our inattention . . . remembering the eighteen-eighties . . . *What better place . . . They seem as much*": Ibid., 504.
197 "grey-and-blue thistles. . . . sound of my typewriters . . . that happy grocery store": Ibid., 505.
198 "Where will we find": Maxwell, *Château*, 200.
199 "child-like way . . . sense of wonder . . . he felt he never . . . almost embarrassing . . . feel naïve": Quoted in Burkhardt, *William Maxwell*, 223.
— "moves through the rooms": Ormsby, "House in His Mind," 136.
200 "The odd thing was that now": Maxwell, *Folded Leaf*, 371.

CHAPTER 10. LAKE CITY

207 "consulted his genes": Oz, Reading from *Scenes from Village Life*.
208 "In my book I tried": Cather, *On Writing*, 31–32.
209 "personality of which . . . to the earliest sources": Cather, *Song of the Lark*, 266.
— "high and blue . . . a life in itself": Cather, *Professor's House*, 228.
— "high tide": Ibid., 227.
210 "methodically . . . intelligently": Ibid.
— "When I look into": Ibid., 228.
213 "the author of a slightly more grown-up": Marcus, "Willa Cather and the Geography," 66.
— "We were reluctant": Cather, *Professor's House*, 183.
214 "In stopping to take breath": Cather, *Professor's House*, 179.
— "Just before I began": Cather, *On Writing*, 31–32.
215 "chief icon of the nineteenth-century frontier": White, "Frederick Jackson Turner," quoted in Karush, "Bringing Outland Inland."
216 "She felt as if she were being pulled": Cather, *Song of the Lark*, 127.
217 "the trajectory of Cather's career": Urgo, "The Cather Thesis," 36.
— "she got wildly . . . dash out . . . for fear of dying": Sergeant, *Willa Cather*, 49.
— "I felt the old pull": Cather, *My Ántonia*, 207.
— "She still professed": Woodress, *Willa Cather*, 446.

Chapter 11. Ancestors

- 224 "In that singular light": Cather, *My Ántonia*, 207.
- 226 "There are nights when I lie": Dabney, *Edmund Wilson*, 478.
- — "I enjoy 'galvanizing'": Wilson, *Upstate*, 115–16.
- — "In the United States": Pritchett, "Old Stone House."
- 227 "I know of very few": Ibid.
- — "the croquet set": Wilson, *Upstate*, 3.
- — "enchantment . . . the first moments": Ibid., 4.
- — "I said suddenly to myself": Ibid.
- 228 "the kingdom of asbestos": Dabney, *Edmund Wilson*, 367.
- — "a clean and trim . . . tumbledown . . . hardly get along": Wilson, *Upstate*, 4.
- 229 "Union Square, Washington Square": Tóibín, "New York Stories."
- — "for ever so long": James, *Small Boy*, 82.
- — "amputated of half": James, *American Scene*, 71.
- — "memories of the past": Wilson, *Upstate*, 6, 8.
- — "fill the vacuum": Ibid., 7.
- 230 "had been a foot-loose American": Edel, *Henry James*, 463.
- — "the possibilities of Lamb House . . . anchorite, a lonely prisoner": Ibid.
- — espaliers of figs: Reavell, "Lamb House Garden," 222.
- — "He knew that it was merely a house": Tóibín, *The Master*, 123.
- 231 "Those who wish . . . under her bed": Urgo, "Cather Thesis," 37.
- — "did her happiest writing . . . she completed": Lewis, *Willa Cather Living*, 148.
- — "felt like a turtle": Sergeant, *Willa Cather*, 226–27.
- 232 "solitude without loneliness . . . rough little place . . . with many inconveniences": Lewis, *Willa Cather Living*, 129–30.
- — "high and blue": Cather, *Professor's House*, 228.

Chapter 12. Jefferson

- 241 "a stretch of frontage": Tóibín, *The Master*, 123.
- 251 "And when a poet": Bachelard, *Poetics of Space*, 230.

Bibliography

Acocella, Joan. *Willa Cather and the Politics of Criticism*. New York: Vintage, 2000.
Anderson, Sherwood. *Winesburg, Ohio: A Norton Critical Edition*. New York: Norton, 1996.
Bachelard, Gaston. *The Poetics of Space*. Translated by Maria Jolas. Boston: Beacon, 1969.
Blackburn, Anthony J. *Single Room Occupancy in New York City*. New York: Department of Housing Preservation and Development, 1986.
Botsford, Gardner. *A Life of Privilege, Mostly*. New York: St. Martin's, 2003.
Bourke, Angela. *Maeve Brennan: Homesick at "The New Yorker."* New York: Counterpoint, 2004.
Bowles, Jane. *Two Serious Ladies*. In *My Sister's Hand in Mine: An Expanded Edition of the Collected Works of Jane Bowles*. New York: Ecco Press, 1978.
Brennan, Maeve. Interview. *Time*, July 1, 1974.
———. *The Long-Winded Lady: Notes from "The New Yorker."* 1969. Boston: Houghton Mifflin, 1998.
———. *The Rose Garden: Short Stories*. Washington, D.C.: Counterpoint, 2000.
"Brooklyn People Setting Their Houses in Order." *Brooklyn Daily Eagle*, September 25, 1888.
Burkhardt, Barbara. *William Maxwell: A Literary Life*. Urbana: University of Illinois Press, 2005.
Calvino, Italo. *Invisible Cities*. New York: Harcourt Brace Jovanovich, 1974.
Cather, Willa. *My Ántonia*. 1918. Boston: Mariner Houghton Mifflin, 1995.
———. *On Writing: Critical Studies on Writing as an Art*. New York: Knopf, 1949.
———. *The Professor's House*. 1925. New York: Vintage Books, 1990.
———. *The Song of the Lark*. 1915. Boston: Houghton Mifflin, 1988.

Cavell, Stanley. *Philosophy the Day after Tomorrow*. Cambridge, MA: Belknap Press of Harvard University Press, 2005.

Clinton Hill Historic District Designation Report. New York: New York City's Landmarks Preservation Commission, 1981.

Dabney, Lewis M. *Edmund Wilson: A Life in Literature*. New York: Farrar, Straus & Giroux, 2005.

De Haas, Carl. *North America, Wisconsin: Hints for Emigrants*. Translated from *Nordamerika, Wisconsin, Calumet: Winke für Auswanderer*. Elberfeld and Iserlohn: Julius Bäedeker, 1848–49. Online version of print edition. Fond du Lac, WI: s.n., 1943. http://www.wisconsinhistory.org.

Dickinson, Emily. "A narrow fellow in the grass." In *The Poems of Emily Dickinson*, edited by R. W. Franklin, 443. Cambridge, MA: Belknap Press of Harvard University Press, 2005.

Didion, Joan. "Goodbye to All That." In *Slouching Toward Bethlehem*. New York: Farrar, Straus & Giroux, 1968.

Edel, Leon. *Henry James: A Life*. New York: Harper & Row, 1985.

Faulkner, William. "A Note on Sherwood Anderson, 1953." In *Essays, Speeches, and Public Letters*. Edited by James B. Meriwether. New York: Modern Library, 2004.

Federal Writers' Project of the Works Progress Administration. *The WPA Guide to Wisconsin*. 1941. St. Paul: Minnesota Historical Society Press, 2006.

Freeman, Lance. *"There Goes the Hood": Views of Gentrification from the Ground Up*. Philadelphia: Temple University Press, 2006.

Fryer, Judith. *Felicitous Space: The Imaginative Structures of Edith Wharton and Willa Cather*. Chapel Hill: University of North Carolina Press, 1986.

Gill, Brendan. *Many Masks: A Life of Frank Lloyd Wright*. New York: Da Capo Press, 1998.

Grese, Robert E. *Jens Jensen: Maker of Natural Parks and Gardens*. Baltimore: Johns Hopkins University Press, 1992.

Groth, Paul Erling. *Living Downtown: The History of Residential Hotels in the United States*. Berkeley: University of California Press, 1994.

Hedges, Peter. *What's Eating Gilbert Grape?* New York: Poseidon, 1991.

Howells, William Dean. *A Hazard of New Fortunes*. New York: Harper, 1891.

———. *The Rise of Silas Lapham*. 1885. Boston: Houghton, 1922.

Inge, William. *Four Plays*. New York: Grove Press, 1958.

Jacobs, Jane. *The Death and Life of Great American Cities*. 1961. New York: Vintage Books, 1992.

James, Henry. *The American Scene*. 1907. New York: Penguin Books, 1994.

——— . "The Jolly Corner." In *The Short Stories of Henry James*. New York: Modern Library, 1948.

——— . *A Small Boy and Others*. 1913. Charlottesville: University of Virginia Press, 2011.

Karush, Deborah. "Bringing Outland Inland in *The Professor's House*: Willa Cather's Domestication of Empire." *Cather Studies* 4 (1999). Accessed March 3, 2012. http://cather.unl.edu/cs004_karush.html.

Kincaid, Jamaica. *Lucy*. New York: Farrar, Straus & Giroux, 1990.

Kisseloff, Jeff. *You Must Remember This: An Oral History of Manhattan from the 1890's to World War II*. New York: Schocken, 1989.

Lee, Hermione. *Edith Wharton*. New York: Vintage Books, 2007.

Lewis, Edith. *Willa Cather Living*. New York: Knopf, 1953.

Marcus, Lisa. "Willa Cather and the Geography of Jewishness." In *The Cambridge Companion to Willa Cather*. Edited by Marilee Lindemann. Cambridge, UK: Cambridge University Press, 2005.

Marrone, Francis. "Underwood Park: Typewriters and Crack." Oral History Interview. Fort Greene/Clinton Hill Audio Tour hosted by Nelson George. Brooklyn Historical Society Blog. http://brooklynhistory.org/blog/2011/01/13/fort-greene-clinton-hill-audio-tour/.

Marshall, Paule. *Brown Girl, Brownstones*. 1959. Old Westbury, NY: Feminist Press, 1981.

Martineau, Lisa. Unpublished eulogy for Dee McAuliffe.

Maxwell, William. *The Château*. 1961. New York: Library of America, 2008.

——— . *The Folded Leaf*. In *Early Novels and Stories*. New York: Library of America, 2008.

——— . Introduction to *The Springs of Affection: Stories of Dublin*, by Maeve Brennan. Boston: Houghton Mifflin, 1997.

——— . "The Thistles in Sweden." In *Later Novels and Stories*. New York: Library of America, 2008.

Mendelsohn, Edward. "The Perils of His Magic Circle." *New York Review of Books*, April 29, 2010. Accessed November 7, 2012. http://www.nybooks.com/articles/archives/2010/apr/29/the-perils-of-his-magic-circle.

O'Brien, Sharon. *Willa Cather: The Emerging Voice*. New York: Fawcett Columbine, 1987.

O'Flaherty, Brendan. *Making Room: The Economics of Homelessness*. Cambridge, MA: Harvard University Press, 1996.

Ormsby, Eric. "The House in His Mind." In *Fine Incisions: Essays on Poetry and Place*. Erin, ON: Porcupine's Quill, 2011.

Oz, Amos. Reading from *Scenes from Village Life*. Presentation at the 92nd Street Y with Ruth Franklin, New York, October 26, 2011.

Porter, Gene Stratton. *A Girl of the Limberlost*. New York: Doubleday, 1909.

———. *The Harvester*. 1911. Bloomington: Indiana University Press, 1987.

Powell, Dawn. *The Wicked Pavilion*. 1954. South Royalton, VT: Steerforth Press, 1996.

Pritchett, V. S. "The Old Stone House." *New York Review of Books*, October 7, 1971. Accessed February 28, 2012. http://www.nybooks.com /articles /archives/ 1971/oct/07/the-old-stone-house.

Puchner, Rudolf. "Recollections of the Forties." In part 2 of *North America, Wisconsin: Hints for Emigrants*. Translated from *Nordamerika, Wisconsin, Calumet: Winke für Auswanderer*. Elberfeld and Iserlohn: Julius Bäedeker, 1848–49. Online version of print edition. Fond du Lac, WI: s.n., 1943. http://content.wisconsinhistory.org/u?/tp,65502.

Reavell, Cynthia. "Lamb House Garden." *Henry James Review* 16, no. 2 (1995): 222–26.

Riley, Peter J. L. "Leaves of Grass and Real Estate." *Walt Whitman Quarterly Review* 28 (2011): 163–87.

Roth, Philip. *American Pastoral*. New York: Vintage, 1997.

Sergeant, Elizabeth Shepley. *Willa Cather: A Memoir*. 1953. Lincoln: University of Nebraska Press, 1963.

Stern, Robert A. M., Thomas Mellins, and David Fishman. *New York 1960: Architecture and Urbanism between the Second World War and the Bicentennial*. New York: Monacelli Press, 1995.

Sukenick, Ronald. *Down and In: Life in the Underground*. New York: Collier Books, 1988.

"Ten-Story Apartment House of Unusual Type Being Built on Lafayette Avenue, Brooklyn." *New York Times*, May 17, 1936.

Thoreau, Henry David. "Walking." In Ralph Waldo Emerson and Henry David Thoreau, *Nature and Walking*. Boston: Beacon Press, 2012.

Tóibín, Colm. *The Master*. New York: Scribner, 2004.

———. "New York Stories." Pen World Voices Series Panel. New York, April 29, 2010.

Twain, Mark. *The Adventures of Huckleberry Finn*. London: Chatto & Windus, 1884.

Updike, John. "Imperishable Maxwell." *New Yorker*, September 8, 2008. Accessed March 1, 2012. http://www.newyorker.com/arts/critics/atlarge/2008 /09/08/080908crat_atlarge_updike.

Urgo, Joseph R. "The Cather Thesis." In *The Cambridge Companion to Willa Cather*. Edited by Marilee Lindemann. Cambridge, UK: Cambridge University Press, 2005.

Wallock, Leonard, ed. *New York: Culture Capital of the World, 1940–1965*. New York: Rizzoli, 1988.

Wharton, Edith. *The House of Mirth*. New York: Scribner, 1905.

White, Richard. "Frederick Jackson Turner and Buffalo Bill." In *The Frontier in American Culture*. Ed. James R. Grossman. Chicago: Newberry Library; Berkeley: University of California Press, 1994.

Whitman, Walt. "Tear Down and Build Over Again." In *The Uncollected Poetry and Prose of Walt Whitman*, vol. 1. Edited by Emory Holloway. New York: Doubleday, 1921.

Wilson, Edmund. *Upstate: Records and Recollections of Northern New York*. 1971. Syracuse, NY: Syracuse University Press, 1990.

Woodress, James. *Willa Cather: A Literary Life*. Lincoln: University of Nebraska Press, 1987.

Wright, Frank Lloyd. *Frank Lloyd Wright: An Autobiography*. 1943. Petaluma, CA: Pomegranate, 2005.

Index

Acocella, Joan, *Willa Cather and the Politics of Criticism*, 213-14
Alcott, Louisa May, 42
Alger, Horatio, 35, 37
Algonquin Round Table, 169
Anasazi, 208
Anderson, Sherwood, 115, 118, 122-24; *Winesburg, Ohio*, 122-24
Angell, Roger, 199
Ann Arbor, Michigan, 32, 66
Auden, W. H., 225

Bachelard, Gaston, *Poetics of Space*, 150, 251
Baldwin, James, *Another Country*, 140
Bissinger, Karl, 165
Bogan, Louise, 225
Botsford, Gardner, 167, 177
Bourke, Angela, 167
Brennan, Maeve, 165-70, 174-78, 180, 190-91, 195-97; "I See You, Bianca," 175-76; "The Last Days of New York," 168-69, 176-77
"The Broken Down Merry Go Round" (song), 121
Bronxville, New York, 136-37
Brooklyn, New York, 78, 139-40, 142, 163-65, 170-74, 179-94, 200-202; Baptist Emmanuel Church, 182, 187; Bedford-Stuyvesant (neighborhood), 188-89; Brooklyn Bridge, 137, 139, 163; Clinton Hill (neighborhood), 180-91, 192-94, 200-202; Fort Greene (neighborhood), 163-65, 170-74, 184, 186, 189; Fort Greene Park, 163, 172; Graham Home, 182-85, 202; Lafayette Avenue, 65, 163-65, 172-73, 179-80; Myrtle Avenue, 182, 186, 191; Pratt Institute, 186-87, 193; Ryerson Street, 190; St. Joseph's College, 187; Underwood Park, 180, 183, 185, 191, 200-201; Walt Whitman Houses, 182, 191; Washington Avenue, 180, 182-87; Williamsburg (neighborhood), 142; Williamsburg Savings Bank, 165
Brothertown (tribe), 89-90, 93
Brothertown, Wisconsin, 89

Calumet, Wisconsin. *See* Calumetville
Calumetville, Wisconsin, 89, 91, 93, 132
Calvino, Italo, 140
Camp Shaganapi, 88
Capote, Truman, *In Cold Blood*, 42
Capra, Frank, *It's a Wonderful Life*, 118, 120-22, 124
Carnegie, Dale, *How to Win Friends and Influence People*, 32

Cather, Willa, 115, 134, 149–50, 198, 207–10, 211–18, 228–29, 231–33; "Coming, Aphrodite!," 149; *Death Comes for the Archbishop*, 231; *My Antonia*, 122–23, 126, 134, 180, 217, 224–25, 228; *My Mortal Enemy*, 149; *O Pioneers!*, 231; "Paul's Case," 149; *The Professor's House*, 208–14, 217, 232; *The Song of the Lark*, 134, 149–52, 208–9, 216–17
Catskills, The, 4, 235–44
Cavell, Stanley, 77
Chicago, Illinois, 16–17, 119–20, 124–25, 134, 217
Chief Little Wave, 89, 91
Chief Oshkosh, 88
Clearing, The, 16–18
Cooper, James Fenimore, *The Last of the Mohicans*, 90
Curtis, Thomas Quinn, 166

De Haas, Dr. Carl, *Nordamerika, Wisconsin, Calumet*, 91–93
Didion, Joan, "Goodbye to All That," 205
Dinesen, Isak, 88
Door County, Wisconsin, 5, 16–18, 89
Dreiser, Theodore, 31, 115, 207; *Sister Carrie*, 31, 130, 134
Dubrovnik, Croatia, 62

Edel, Leon, 230
Eden, Wisconsin, 70, 72
Ellison Bay, Wisconsin, 16–18
Empire, Wisconsin, 70, 108
Esherick, Joseph, 19

Fallingwater, 69
Fitzgerald, F. Scott, *The Great Gatsby*, 45, 47, 99, 141
Fond du Lac, Wisconsin, 3–16, 18–20, 25–33, 44–45, 53–54, 58–61, 70–72, 74–75, 80–97, 99–101, 104, 107–8, 113–21, 125, 127, 132–33; Artesian Road, 24, 85–86; Boyle Catholic Home, 113–14; Cherry Lane, 32, 61; Division Street, 113; Gilles (restaurant), 113; Highway 151, 4, 45, 76–76, 93–95, 253; the Holy Land, 70–75, 80–84, 87–97; "the ledge" (Niagara Escarpment), 5, 11, 18, 20, 30, 74–75, 82–83, 89, 94, 103–4, 108, 233, 253; Main Street, 33, 75, 113; Meadowbrook Lane, 32, 61; Reid Terrace, 114–17, 120, 127; Rienzi Cemetery, 107–8; Roger Peters Construction, 31, 44; Sheboygan Street, 113; T. E. Aherns, 115, 119
Franklin, Benjamin, 24, 33
Franklin, Miles, *My Brilliant Career*, 101
French Connection, The, 140
Frost, Robert, *The Collected Poetry of Robert Frost*, 16
Fuller, Buckminster, 8

Galsworthy, John, *The Forsythe Saga*, 118, 130
George, Nelson, *Black Boheme*, 184
Gill, Brendan, *Many Masks*, 21, 27–28
Ginsberg, Allen, 141
Grand Manan Island, New Brunswick, 231–32
Green Bay, Wisconsin, 4, 89, 91–92
Green Lake, Wisconsin, 45, 107, 192

Hardee's, 33, 58–61
Hellman, Lillian, 160
Hemingway, Ernest, *A Moveable Feast*, 140–41
Hitchcock, Alfred, 3
Ho-Chunk, 89
hotels: The Algonquin, 167–69; The Brevoort, 165, 169, 176; The Chelsea Hotel, 140, 156; The Holley Hotel, 167–68; The Hotel Astor, 169, 174; The Hotel Earle, 167–68; The Iroquois, 167; The Lafayette, 165, 167, 169, 176; The Lombardy, 167; The Prince Edward, 167; The Royalton, 167;

The Waldorf, 149, 167; The Westbury, 167
Howells, William Dean: *A Hazard of New Fortunes*, 142–144, 147, 174; *The Rise of Silas Lapham*, 35–41, 44, 47–51, 56

Inge, William, *Picnic*, 139
Ipswich, Massachusetts, 25

Jacobs, Harriet, *Incidents in the Life of a Slave Girl*, 186
Jacobs, Jane, *The Death and Life of Great American Cities*, 175–78, 191
James, Henry, 54, 190, 228–29, 233, 236, 240; *The Ambassadors*, 230; *The American Scene*, 54–55, 76–77; *The Awkward Age*, 230; "The Beast in the Jungle," 230; *The Golden Bowl*, 230; "The Jolly Corner," 55–57, 63, 65, 69, 191, 230; Lamb House, 229–31, 236, 240; *The New York Edition*, 229; *The Turn of the Screw*, 230; *What Maisie Knew*, 230; *The Wings of the Dove*, 230
Jefferson, New York, 236–45, 248–53
Jensen, Jens, 16–18, 94
Johnsburg, Wisconsin, 79, 81

Karush, Deborah, 215
Kazin, Alfred, 140
Kincaid, Jamaica, *Lucy*, 78–79
Klute (film), 140
Kroc, Ray, 16, 63

Lake City, Colorado, 206–12, 215–16, 218
Lake Michigan, 5, 17, 90
Lake Winnebago, 5, 29–30, 70, 82, 89–90, 92, 107–8, 232–33
Lamb House. *See under* James, Henry
Lee, Spike, 184
Lewis, Edith, 231
Lewis, Sinclair, 115; *Babbitt*, 31; *Main Street*, 118
Lyndon, Donlyn, 19

Manhattan, 54–57, 76–77, 136–62, 163–65, 167–71, 181, 186, 190, 195–98, 205; Bank Street (Cather home), 217, 231; Biltmore Clock, 165; Coliseum Books, 148, 171; Criterion Theatre, 167; Fifth Avenue, 55, 57, 76, 137, 167, 169, 229; The Film Forum, 139; Gene's (restaurant), 154; Greenwich Village (neighborhood), 141, 153–55, 157–61, 168, 176; Guggenheim Museum, 22; Hell's Kitchen (neighborhood), 168; Inwood (neighborhood), 146–48, 181; Longchamps (restaurant), 167; Marie's Crisis Cafe, 154; Schrafft's (restaurant), 169; Stern Brothers Department Store, 169; Wanamaker's Department Store, 169, 174; Washington Square, 55, 138, 140, 155, 165–68, 176–77, 229, 231
Marcus, Lisa, "Willa Cather and the Geography of Jewishness," 213
Marsalis, Branford, 184–85
Marshall, Paule, *Brown Girl, Brownstones*, 188–89, 191, 200
Marytown, Wisconsin, 89
Mary Tyler Moore Show, The, 115
Maxwell, William, 165, 195–200, 228, 230, 233; *Ancestors*, 228; *The Chateau*, 198–99; *The Folded Leaf*, 187–88, 198, 200; *So Long, See You Tomorrow*, 198; *They Came Like Swallows*, 198; "The Thistles in Sweden," 195–99, 230
McCarthy, Mary, 165
McKelway, St. Clair, 167
Mead, Margaret, 8, 63
Menominee, 88–93, 97, 188, 215
Mesa Verde, 208–9, 214–16
Milwaukee, Wisconsin, 75, 93, 100, 117, 119, 130–31, 164
Mitchell, Joni, 15
Modern Jazz Quartet, 15
Mohegan, The, 89–90
Mohican, 89–90
Montauk, The, 89

Index   273

Montgomery, L. M., *Anne of Green Gables*, 72, 74
Moore, Charles, 19
Mother Earth News, 239
Mt. Calvary, Wisconsin, 70
Mount Desert Island, Maine, 231
Muir, Edwin, 225
My Brilliant Career (film), 101–2

Nabokov, Vladimir, 225
Narragansett, 89
Native American tribes: Brothertown, 89–90, 93; Ho-Chunk, 89; Menominee, 88–93, 97, 188, 215; Mohegan, The, 89–90; Mohican, 89–90; Montauk, 89; Narragansett, 89; Oneida Nation, The, 89; Pequot, 89; Stockbridge (Mohican), 89–91; Winnebago (Ho-Chunk), 89
Nearing, Scott and Helen, 10; *The Good Life*, 10, 16, 63, 239, 252
New Yorker, 165, 167–68, 174, 177–78, 198

Olmsted, Frederick Law, 16, 163
Oneida Nation, The, 89
Ormsby, Eric, 199–200
Oshkosh, Wisconsin, 88
Oz, Amos, 207

Parker, Dorothy, 157, 160, 167, 225
Peale, Norman Vincent, *The Power of Positive Thinking*, 16
Pequot, 89
Perez, Rosie, 184
Pipe, Wisconsin, 89
Pittsburgh, Pennsylvania, 65–66, 231
Porter, Gene Stratton, 242–43; *A Girl of the Limberlost*, 243; *The Harvester*, 243
Powell, Dawn, 165, 176–77; *The Wicked Pavilion*, 176–77
Prairie School (of architecture), 16–17, 20
Pratt, William, 187

Pritchett, V. S., 226–27
Puchner, Rudolf, 92–93

Queens, New York, 138, 140, 142, 144, 156, 157, 163

Rachmaninoff, 15
Red Cloud, Nebraska, 149–50, 231
Rigby, Amy, 218
Riley, Peter, "Leaves of Grass and Real Estate," 190–91
Robbys restaurants, 32–34, 42–43, 61
Rochester, Minnesota, 33–34
Rosemary's Baby (film), 136–37
Roth, Philip, *American Pastoral*, 47, 50, 99

St. Anna, Wisconsin, 89
St. Cloud, Wisconsin, 89
St. Peter, Wisconsin, 70, 81, 89
Salt Lake City, Utah, 58, 62–64, 105, 107, 109
Saturday Night Fever, 140
Sea Ranch, 19
Sergeant, Elizabeth, 217, 231
Seventeen, 102
Shaw, Irwin, "Girls in Their Summer Dresses," 140
Simon and Garfunkel, 16, 223
Sneden's Landing, New York, 167
Spender, Stephen, 225
Spring Green, Wisconsin, 21–22
Stage Door (film), 140
Stevens, Cat, 15
Stevens, Wallace, "Sunday Morning," 42
Stockbridge (Mohican), 89–91
Stockbridge, Massachusetts, 89
Sukenick, Ronald, 141; *Down and In*, 141–42

Talcottville, New York, 225–28
Taliesen, 19–20, 22–23, 27–28
Theodora Goes Wild (film), 140

Thoreau, Henry David, 16, 28, 29, 77, 115, 210
Three Stooges, The, 117, 128, 164
Toffler, Alvin, *Future Shock*, 16
Tóibín, Colm, 228–29; *The Master*, 230–31

University of Michigan, 32, 51–52
University of Notre Dame, 141
Urgo, Joseph, *The Cather Thesis*, 217, 231

Van der Rohe, Mies, 28

Wall Street (film), 136, 139
Wautoma, Wisconsin, 128–30
Wharton, Edith, 130–31, 134, 158, 181, 207; *The Custom of the Country*, 130–31; *Ethan Frome*, 122; *House of Mirth*, 99, 131–32; *Summer*, 131
What's Eating Gilbert Grape (film), 221, 223
Whitman, Walt, 185, 190–92, 202

Whole Earth Catalog, 8, 26
Wilder, Laura Ingalls, *Little House on the Prairie*, 213
Wilson, Edmund, 225–29; *Upstate: Records and Recollections of Northern New York*, 225–29
Wilson, Elena, 227–28, 233; "My View from the Other Window," 228
Winchester, Virginia, 231
Winnebago (Ho-Chunk), 89
Wolfe, Tom, 253; *Bonfire of the Vanities*, 139
Woodress, James, 217
Woolf, Virginia, 8, 63, 142, 227; *Mrs. Dalloway*, 137; *A Room of One's Own*, 34
Wright, Frank Lloyd, 16–17, 19–23, 26–28, 51–52, 65, 69, 104, 251; *Frank Lloyd Wright: An Autobiography*, 51–52

Yeshiva University, 213
Young, Neil, "Helpless," 82